MANSON,

SINATRA AND ME

A Hollywood Party Girl's Memoir and How She Helped Vincent Bugliosi with the Helter Skelter Case

by
Virginia Graham

As Told to Hal Jacques

CCB Publishing
British Columbia, Canada

Manson, Sinatra and Me:
A Hollywood Party Girl's Memoir and How She Helped
Vincent Bugliosi with the Helter Skelter Case

Copyright ©2015 by Virginia Graham
ISBN-13   978-1-77143-205-4
First Edition

Library and Archives Canada Cataloguing in Publication
Graham, Virginia, 1932-, author
Manson, Sinatra, and me : a Hollywood party girl's memoir and how she helped Vincent Bugliosi
with the helter skelter case / by Virginia Graham ; as told to Hal Jacques. -- First edition.
Issued in print and electronic editions.
ISBN 978-1-77143-205-4 (pbk.).--ISBN 978-1-77143-206-1 (pdf)
1. Graham, Virginia, 1932-. 2. Women prisoners--United States--Biography.
3. Witnesses--United States--Biography. 4. Manson, Charles, 1934-. 5. Trials (Murder)--California.
6. Murder--California. I. Jacques, Hal, 1916-2007, author II. Title.
HV9468.G73A3 2015   365'.43092   C2015-900682-1, C2015-900683-X

Cover artwork: Illustration of Virginia Graham is derived from a 1995 painting by Dean Hansford. Photographs of Charles Manson and Frank Sinatra are both in the public domain and are used without malice.

Photo of Elizabeth Taylor and Nurse Shannon Gordon is © Shannon Gordon, and is reproduced herein with her express permission. All other photos contained herein are © Virginia Graham.

Notice: Significant portions of text contained herein first appeared in "The Joy of Hooking" by Virginia Graham as published by Zebra Publications, Inc., under the imprint Zebra Books, in 1974, the rights to which were reverted back to Virginia Graham by Bernard Geis.

Disclaimer: This is an autobiographical work, with some names contained herein having been changed in the interest of privacy.

Extreme care has been taken by the author to ensure that all information presented in this book is accurate and up to date at the time of publishing. Neither the author nor the publisher can be held responsible for any errors or omissions. Additionally, neither is any liability assumed for damages resulting from use of the information contained herein.

Publisher:
CCB Publishing
British Columbia, Canada
www.ccbpublishing.com

To My Mother

and

To Vincent Bugliosi:

Forty-five years ago in August 1969 in Benedict Canyon, California some grotesque murders were committed of Hollywood celebrities. Beverly Hills was in a panic. A few months later an informant came forward and helped break the murder case. Vincent Bugliosi, a young, courageous District Attorney from Los Angeles was assigned to the case. Through his diligence and persistence he brought the case to trial and won a conviction against a group called the Manson Family. He also saved many celebrities' lives who had been targeted for murder on a hit list.

I am writing this with the deepest gratitude and respect for Vincent Bugliosi as I, Virginia Graham, am that informant.

Acknowledgements

I acknowledge with thanks such true friends as:
Maureen Cotter
Elsa Ritchie
Mike and Pat Cerney
and Jean Salutz

…and with deep gratitude, special thanks to Ellen Harris

Also, with admiration and respect, Gloria Steinem,
who I've always greatly admired.

Praise received for *Manson, Sinatra and Me*

"Virginia Graham had a heck of a run in her life as a party girl, and has told of her rollicking story very well in this poignant and sometimes very funny memoir of hers. She also happened to be a star witness of mine in helping me bring the Manson Family killers to justice, something for which I will always be very grateful to her."
- Vincent Bugliosi, bestselling author of
  Helter Skelter: The True Story of the Manson Murders

"Virginia Graham's personal tell-all as a party girl is a page-turner from beginning to end. Her writing, breezy, humorously and sometimes harrowingly candid, proves her to be an honest chronicler of her own life and times... and what times these were! Her landing in jail, which brings us to what was then the Crime of the Century, comes as a wallop. This book is a winner."
- Jack Engelhard, bestselling novelist of
  Indecent Proposal and *The Bathsheba Deadline*

"A riveting read from cover-to-cover, with the best sex tales you've never heard about classic Hollywood celebrities like Frank Sinatra and notorious gangsters like Mickey Cohen. Virginia Graham's fateful meeting with Susan Atkins turned her into a national hero for breaking the case against the Manson Family. This book is an important work of true crime and a thrilling peek into Hollywood behind closed doors."
- Dr. Gloria Brame, sex therapist, blogger and bestselling author of
  Different Loving and *The Truth About Sex*

"Whether Virginia Graham writes of her time behind bars or of living the high life as a party girl, every word reads as the truth. I admire this writer because every word, every phase is an education in pushing through any difficulties in life. She is a survivor. This is a memoir that stays with the reader, and is by far one of the best memoirs I have read in a very long time."
- Jasmine Kinnear, author of *Every Cat Has A Story*

Chapter One

I remember reading a book some years back in which the main character was a powerful Italian construction worker who was so sexually potent that every time he put his hand on the doorknob of his wife's bedroom door she became pregnant.

That was me. I was pregnant five times between sixteen and twenty-one and sometimes even by my own husband. My family's advice not to have sex was like telling the fire-horse not to start running every time the bell rang. And some of those guys I went with sure knew how to ring my bell.

I knew nothing about birth control. I went to a doctor and got a diaphragm but for me it didn't work. I didn't find out 'til years later that you were supposed to insert it before and not after.

A Catholic girlfriend even tried to sell me on the rhythm method which didn't make any sense at all and the only thing I could think to say was, "Rhythm method? Now where the hell am I supposed to get an orchestra at three o'clock in the morning?"

My mother somehow never found the time to tell me about "the birds and the bees," but the night before I got married she gave me a book on marital sex. I thanked her and remember thinking that for it to do me any good I'd have to be a helluva quick study.

I was an only child, born Virginia Browne in Philadelphia on December 10th, 1932 into a dysfunctional family and during my very early years we lived with my dad's aunt, my great-aunt Virginia.

My mother was beautiful, and I've been told that I was beautiful, but in her heyday mother would have made me look like one of Cinderella's ugly stepsisters. Mother won her first beauty contest at the age of fifteen at a county fair in New Jersey. With her clear blue-green eyes, her Ava Gardner coloring and beautiful brown hair it must have been no contest.

She was a friendly, quiet woman who had been the last of ten children and never got over the feeling that she was an unwanted child. She

1

never developed a sense of self-esteem and rarely exercised her rights as a person, and if she had any opinions she never voiced them. Her persona was the sum and total of an insecure childhood and growing up at a time when women weren't quite as liberated as they are today.

She was sixteen when she left home and went to live with an elderly aunt in Camden, New Jersey where she became a factory worker for RCA. It was the start of a lifetime of hard work. I loved my mother dearly and if mothers are supposed to be role models for their daughters, I was in trouble early on.

I never saw too much of her during the day. After all, she had to help support the family working as a saleswoman at Gimbel's and other department stores, or as an office receptionist.

Then there was my dad, William Archibald Browne, who wasn't upper middle class or lower middle class but plain middle class, with the mistaken idea that he was high class. Always impeccably groomed, he was a charismatic communicator.

He was very handsome, looked like a Don Juan and behaved like one, knocking himself out trying to latch onto celebrities and near celebrities. A name dropper from way back when, he thought nothing of blowing his entire salary standing his so-called buddies for drinks.

Thanks to my mother's job and Aunt Virginia's income we still lived comfortably. We lived in Cobb's Creek Parkway in Southwest Philadelphia which wasn't bad then, but is pretty much of a slum area now.

For a short while my father was an insurance bonding agent after which he went into hotel management, and before his passing in 1981 was the public relations director for the very posh Walnut Park Plaza Hotel in West Philadelphia.

When I was born he was in public relations and I don't know what sort of salary he earned but it was far from enough to suit his grandiose needs. Mother kept everything from me at the time, but years later she told me how he would stop in at Gimbel's when he was broke and hit her up for money.

Hell, he didn't just ask her for money - he'd threaten to commit suicide if she didn't come across. "Naomi," he'd plead, "the bill collectors are hounding me. If I don't pay they'll kill me!" With everybody in the area staring at this little tableau, my mother would empty her purse just to get rid of him.

She told me that she came home from work one day and found Dad with his head in the oven. There was no doubt in her mind that this was just another one of his money grubbing acts, that he waited until he heard her footsteps and then dashed to the oven.

Somehow I knew that plenty was wrong. Children can feel those vibrations in the air and as much as my mother tried to shield me from all this, I knew that she wasn't crying all the time for nothing.

Until I was eight my father was my English teacher, I must give him credit for that. He was constantly correcting my speech. He never let up and it paid off well because while I never got past the tenth grade in school, I was able to pass myself off as having completed three years in college without anyone ever being the wiser.

I was able to hold my own in conversations with former Presidents, Senators, Congressmen, foreign dignitaries - you name it. Years later I was able to put together some pretty big business deals involving huge sums of money and I also acquired two real estate licenses.

And then the time came when we saw less and less of him. It turned out that he was one helluva skirt chaser with an amazing track record. Whenever this tall, handsome charmer chased the girls they never ran very fast. He had more hash marks than an old army sergeant with twenty years of service behind him.

He just kept floating in and out of our lives. He'd be living at home one day and gone the next. And while he was traipsing around from time to time, there were plenty of men eager to pinch-hit for him with my mother but she was so damn faithful to that worthless father of mine it was a shame. She was so straight, I can't even imagine that it entered her mind to be anything else.

She went out of her way to protect Dad's image. He was my at-home father - when he wasn't moonlighting - only up to the time I was eight years old. World War II was on then and that's when he joined the army and was sent to France with the infantry. He didn't return to Philadelphia until I was twelve.

My mom went to work in a shipyard and with Dad in the service, filed for her allotment. Now she had known for years that he was playing around with other women and I can only imagine the terrible hurt she felt when she'd find receipts for women's lingerie, jewelry and perfume that she never received - knowing that he had bought them with her money. But, for whatever reasons, she chose to ignore the situation.

She chose to ignore it until that day when she received the War Department's reply to her request for an army wife's allotment. It was short and to the heart-breaking point.

According to the army's records a "Mrs. William Archibald Browne" was already receiving an allotment and it was up to my mother to prove that she was my dad's real wife. It was a crushing blow and one that she couldn't ignore.

She took her cause to the military and months later it was straightened out to her satisfaction. She had proved beyond a doubt that she was the real Mrs. William Archibald Browne and received her allotment checks as long as he was in the service.

How the army punished my dad I don't know, but I do know he narrowly averted a court martial. And not too long after he returned to Philadelphia, Mom filed for and was awarded a divorce on grounds of adultery.

From the very outset of that unhappy affair my mother and aunt made the decision to keep me from finding out about it. They kept their secret well. I only learned about it years later.

I was eight and had accepted the fact that my dad was no longer going to be living with us, but I was made to understand that even though my parents were separated he would be with me on Sundays. But even that was too much to expect from someone who was so footloose and fancy free.

Mother usually arranged to bring me to a movie theater where father was to pick me up. It was a rare Sunday, though, when he actually showed up. Usually we'd wait for an hour and then my mother would say, "Well, I guess Daddy had something terribly important to do at the last minute. Let's go on home. I'm sure you'll see him next week."

It was not too long after that that I had to accept the fact that where my father and I were concerned there wasn't going to be any "next week" - ever.

Many times with the passing years while gasping for breath in between beds and gouging men who thought they loved me, I've thought that my life was simply one long hassle in a frantic search to find the sort of sentimental love that I sorely needed, and to settle the score with my father who I felt had deserted me.

With my father out of the picture, my mother did the only thing she was able to do - she kept working - and the dominant person in my life was my great-aunt Virginia, who somehow could never express any warmth but spoiled me with material things.

Aunt Virginia was a colorful southern lady who was terribly hung up on our family's heritage. I was never allowed to forget that on my father's side I was related to the Randolphs of Virginia. My great-great-great-grandfather was General William Rose of the Revolutionary War. I also have many famous historical ancestors including Julia Ward Howe who wrote the Battle Hymn of the Republic, and she and her husband opened the first school for the blind, Perkins School for the Blind.

She was going to raise me in true Southern fashion and make a lady of me. Time and again I was told that I was special, I was pretty and a cut above the kids I went to school with.

For example, the kitchen was completely off-limits to me. Learning to cook or clean or have anything remotely concerned with kitchen chores was better left for the help. Fine, well-bred young ladies did not indulge in such things.

As a result, to this very day, I don't do any cooking and even hate the idea of it. My four husbands were apprised of this early on. My favorite line was, "By the way, I don't cook - now or ever."

Aunt Virginia always drilled into me, "Go after the security and prestige," and then I would have to listen to all the stories about the money our family used to have.

I not only went to church every Sunday but also to Sunday school. I sang in the church choir and starred in all the little morality plays, and took summer ballet classes and piano lessons until I was fifteen.

I was the original Miss Goody Two Shoes. Any hint of sexuality was out. I was the only girl in school who had to wear long skirts. I had short hair with a big Betty Boop bow and brown shoes with steel tips.

My aunt beat into me, "You must sit like a lady, you must talk like a lady." She also told me that kissing a boy made you pregnant. That caused a few anxious moments.

Aunt Virginia always did her best even though she was a mine of misinformation and a bundle of prejudices, and with my mother away all day and my father a will-o-the-wisp, I guess she came closer to being my parent than anyone else.

She was a spinster up to the age of forty-three and after she married Uncle Horace, she was still a spinster because he was the little man who wasn't there. Oh, he went to work in the morning and returned home at night, but that was about it.

Uncle Horace would have dinner with us, then listen to the radio for a while and then go to bed. Sometimes he'd swing a bit. "Dear," he would say, "I think I would like a smoke." And since Aunt Virginia had trained him so well, he knew exactly what to do. He'd get up, go down to the cellar and quietly smoke his cigar.

And then, about once a month, something spectacular would happen. No drinking was permitted in the house but on rare occasions Uncle Horace would say, "Dear, may I have a drink?" And if Aunt Virginia was in a good mood, she would go to the bedroom where she kept a bottle of port in a trunk and hand it to Uncle Horace. He would take it gratefully, pick up a glass and go down to the cellar for his very special treat.

But with me she remained the martinet. No skirt I ever put on was ever long enough for her. She wouldn't even let me dash from the bedroom to the bathroom unless I was fully dressed. If I sneaked out of my room in my slip, I was in for a real tongue lashing.

And I don't think those childhood inhibitions ever really leave you. I've always had terrible guilt about undressing in front of a man. I always try to leave something on, usually a lacy bra or a flimsy whatnot. The rationalization being that it's what a man can't see that excites him.

Aunt Virginia drummed it into my head that God was watching every naughty little thing that I did, so there's another legacy from her. I can't make love in the light. Don't ask me why God can't see what I do in the dark, simply because logic has nothing to do with it.

I first became aware of sex at the age of twelve when I engaged in a session of necking in the back row of a movie theater. It felt real good and I felt real guilty but that only increased the enjoyment. The boy later became a priest, so I guess I didn't corrupt him too badly.

And in the speak-no-evil household where I was raised, my first menstrual period came as a complete shock. I was absolutely certain it was God's punishment for having kissed a boy. It was my mother who finally came to my rescue and told me the minimum facts of having been born female.

It all adds up to the fact that all through my childhood I was a real nerd - a yo-yo with no roots either geographically or emotionally.

Let's face the facts. Instead of getting mad at my aunt for being so strict, and instead of letting my father have it for neglecting me and chasing around with a lot of broads, I was Little Miss Muffet all during my most formative years. All that repressed anger came out later on in my life in an indirect and self-destructive way. It was a stupid way to "punish" my father for not protecting and loving and guiding me through my early years!

I attended five different high schools in Philadelphia and California and made my mark at none of them. I would have graduated, though, if I hadn't married Joe in my senior year.

Oh, yes. I was also terrific on the basketball court.

I was about twelve when I discovered motion pictures, which almost became an obsession. I think I saw Lana Turner in *The Postman Always Rings Twice* five or six times and *The Merry Widow* with Fernando Lamas six or seven times. Many years later I would meet Lamas under very unusual circumstances.

I was thirteen when my mother married Robert Graham, her boss at the shipyard, and we moved to La Puente, a suburb of Los Angeles. Mr. Graham was as unlike my father in every possible way: looks, appearance, intellect and demeanor. Almost at once he criticized everything I did supposedly for my own good. His ranting and ravings were really something.

Every time the phone rang I'd shake with fear thinking that some boy at school had gotten my number and was calling me. I was forbidden to go to parties, dances or any athletic events because in his opinion, "Only harlots go to such places!" As a result I had very few close friends, and even they weren't allowed to come to the house to visit me.

My mother rationalized his actions as his way of "trying to protect you." My experiences told me differently. The man was always making sexual advances toward me whenever we were alone in the house. He was trying to save me alright - for himself.

And when I threatened to tell my mother, he said that he would deny that anything improper had taken place and that I was making those accusations because I didn't like him. I did tell my mother and he did exactly what he said he would do - he denied it. And when she believed him - I was shaken down to my very roots. I was trapped.

I was only fourteen and at a time when other teenagers like myself were having fun at dances and parties and football games, I had to stay at home and fight off my stepfather. For this teenager, life was empty and joyless and I prayed for help - for someone or something to come along and rescue me.

Chapter Two

My life took another turn one afternoon when I was sitting on the front porch swing and heard the sound of approaching footsteps on the sidewalk. It was in 1946.

I turned my head and found myself looking into the bluest of blue eyes that belonged to a tall, sandy-haired Adonis who was just a few feet away, walking past our house.

He nodded and smiled, and I swear, I felt as though my heart was going to pound its way out of my chest. For me it was love at first sight and I couldn't take my eyes off him as he entered a house a half dozen doors away.

I knew then and there that I had to meet him, and since I walked to school with the girl who was my age and lived in that house, it wouldn't be too difficult. That young man was a friend of my neighbor's brother.

And meet we did. His name was Leo J. Valez, Jr., but his nickname was Bill. He was nineteen and had been married for a short time and then divorced. I was fourteen but I lied and told him I was sixteen. I told him how strict my stepfather was and so to avoid making any waves we used to meet blocks away and go for walks and take boat rides in nearby Echo Park.

Bill and I hit it off immediately. We liked each other and would hold hands and kiss, nothing more than that.

Bill was honest and sensitive and it bothered him that we had to sneak around. He was determined that he would meet my stepfather and have a talk with him.

Then one day he showed up at the house, introduced himself to my mother and stepfather as a friend of their neighbor's. He said he was interested in me and wanted their permission to take me to see a movie now and then.

Surprisingly enough my stepfather offered no objections, only that we could attend an afternoon matinee and not be away for more than three hours. A month or so later, Bill told my mother and stepfather that he planned on marrying me when I reached my eighteenth birthday.

Those three or four months I spent with Bill saved my sanity. He was my first true love, someone I could laugh and talk with and open my heart to and enjoy all my waking hours thinking about. I was deeply in love and during our time together Bill never made any sexual moves on me.

It came totally without warning - like a thunderbolt. My parents told me that I would be going back to Philadelphia to live with Aunt Virginia. No explanation was given but I was convinced that my stepfather had convinced my mother that something dirty was going on between Bill and myself. My stepfather was probably determined that if he couldn't have me, nobody could.

Saying goodbye to Bill was the toughest thing I ever had to do. It tore my heart out. I later heard that after we parted Bill had become a paratrooper. But we would meet again in 1950, in 1953, and for the last time in 1984.

I returned to Philadelphia with a heavy heart and some months later I met James Harlan Green on a blind date. He was twenty-one, over six feet tall, had a fine physique and was very handsome with really dark eyes. Extremely intelligent, he was a Chief Petty Officer in the Coast Guard. And the fact that he came from a fine, wealthy family and knew how to spend his money won him my Aunt Virginia's approval.

Jimmy was the living proof of her oft-repeated saying: "It's just as easy to marry a rich man as it is to marry a poor one," and she encouraged my relationship with him. We'd only been seeing each other for about six weeks when he bowled me over with a carat, blue-white diamond engagement ring which sure as hell wasn't too bad for a fifteen-year-old girl.

It was comfortable being with Jimmy. He was a romantic, had a good sense of humor and was very bright. We had some great times together, but that came to an end when he was shipped out to Recife, Brazil, leaving me lonely, engaged and forbidden to go out with other boys. As Aunt Virginia put it, "You're spoken for."

After school, instead of going home on the bus, I would usually spend time with some of my classmates in a sandwich shop called "Blue Skies." It was there that I met Joseph Ciocco, who had just gotten his army discharge after doing a stretch in Germany. This was in late 1947.

Joe was twenty-one, not bad looking and soft spoken - so I thought. His family was very much old-country Italian, and so was he. We started dating and when my aunt found out about it she was enraged. Even more so because she had already forbidden me to see him and I had defied her.

For the first time she struck me - a stinging slap across the face and then she practically ripped the blouse off my back. It was her ingrained prejudices at work. "Why," she demanded to know, "are you betraying a fine young American like James Green who is serving his country, for a foreigner who is nobody and has nothing?"

And then she grabbed my left hand and ripped Jim's engagement ring off my finger and strode out of the room still fuming.

If she had known that Joe and I had had sex - my very first time - she probably would have had me committed. Joe and I had been at a party and I, who was never a drinker, had three or four somethings that were sweet and potent and got bombed. And when we got in his car to go home he had me.

All I remember is the groping and the heavy breathing and the pain and my feelings of disappointment. "Is this what all the shouting's about? It's horrible!" And with that came the feelings of shame and embarrassment which I got over pretty quickly.

I was sixteen when the fumbling fiasco in Joe's Ford took place, and a short while later we decided to run away and get married. I had a strong feeling that I was making a mistake. That was in June 1949 and I was two months pregnant.

I remember thinking as we drove around Elkton, Maryland looking for a Justice-of-the-Peace, "Oh, well. If it doesn't work out, I can always get a divorce." It was not a great attitude with which to start a marriage.

And it didn't work out. We had a problem with our sex life. Joe had to have it all the time. This guy had a perpetual yen. Any time of day or night - you name it - he was ready. And he was never satisfied. I went along with it for a while but then I became one of the walking wounded. It became painful, it hurt even to walk, and I even developed blisters.

He had the idea that being a great lover meant making each act of intercourse last forever. I could handle twenty to twenty-five minutes - but for two hours! Come on, guy, give a girl a break!

For a long time he wasn't working, so he was always hanging around, following me and ambushing me at a staircase and banging me up against a kitchen wall. And when he wasn't performing he'd sit around and dream up new positions. Only they weren't very much different from the old ones - they just hurt more.

Since I didn't get around to learning about birth control until years later, I got pregnant. I was in my sixth month when my Aunt Virginia found out that Jimmy had returned from Recife, and she arranged for him to drop by and pick up his engagement ring.

Joe wasn't home and I was in our upstairs bedroom when the doorbell rang. I knew it was Jimmy. I had thought about him often and was eager to see him. And when I came down the stairs Jim's greeting was cordial and somewhat strained considering my obvious condition, so we looked at one another sadly.

I'd known from the very start that I'd made a mistake in marrying Joe and not waiting for Jimmy, but now in Jimmy's presence I felt the error of my ways even more so, but I didn't show it.

Aunt Virginia appeared, made some small talk and then handed Jimmy the engagement ring I'd been so proud to wear. Jimmy pocketed it and then said a fond farewell holding my hand in his. Our eyes met for a brief instant and then he turned to the door, opened it, and left me with tears in my eyes.

* * *

I saw Jimmy some years later when I went back to Philadelphia to visit my sons and while there, I called my childhood friend Rosemary Marley and learned from her that Jimmy was in town.

We met for dinner, we danced, we laughed and eventually went to a hotel and made love, and I came to realize that he was one of the better lovers in my life. It only served to compound the regret I deeply felt in not marrying him when I'd had the chance.

But it was too late. He was leaving the next day and I was already a part of the Hollywood scene, but I was deeply happy that our relationship had ended on a loving note.

Over the following years I looked for Jimmy and finally learned that he had gone to Honolulu and married a woman who had a number of children and was very happy.

When I went to Honolulu in 1971 I looked for him but could find no trace of him on any of the islands. I often thought of him as one of the brighter chapters of my life, and have looked for him ever since.

If our paths ever cross again, I'll tell him how sorry I am for having missed out on what might have been. If he hadn't been stationed in Recife for so long, we probably would have been married and how different my life would have been. C'est la vie!

* * *

Joe and I were the parents of Joe Jr. who was six months old when I was seventeen. That's when we separated - the first of four separations during our three year marriage. As usual I went back to live with Aunt Virginia and he with his mother.

Every now and then Joe would drop in and make a grab for me. By then any love I felt for him was gone and he pretty much turned me off to sex. He became the strikeout king, but not for long.

That's when Bill - Leo J. Valez, Jr. - suddenly showed up. He was still in the military - the airborne - and stationed at Fort Bragg, North Carolina. I saw him for about four months. He wanted me to divorce and marry him. It was during that period when I got pregnant and having a kid out of wedlock was the last thing I needed. It called for some pretty underhanded scheming on my part - which included getting back together with Joe after Bill was shipped to Korea. While in Korea, Bill was wounded in the famous Pork Chop Hill jump where much of his division was wiped out. It is with deep regret that I did not follow my heart and commit to a life with Bill.

Making up with "hot-pants" Joe wasn't too difficult. We were still married and we went out a few times and one night when he made his usual grab at me I played easy to get. It was a real quickie in a park standing up against a tree, and a few weeks later when he dropped by I said to him, "Guess what, Daddy?"

It didn't bother him one bit. He knew I didn't want another child so

13

he went out and bought some pills which only made me sick. When we finally ran out of options he called his cousin who was a doctor who lived upstate, and explained that we needed help badly. Fearing that we would end up going to some quack, he agreed to see us.

We took a train to his office which was out in the country, and we were both as nervous as hell. According to the doctor it was going to be quick and easy. It was horrible. He put me in those god-awful stirrups that I've come to know and hate, while Joe, looking a sickly green, held my hand. The entire procedure lasted three or four minutes, but each minute seemed like a year.

When I look back at that afternoon, knowing what I know now, I would have had the child. My thinking is that it's just laziness and stupidity that puts a woman in a position where she needs an abortion. Back then I was really dumb and placed my trust in luck. A month and a half after that abortion I had a miscarriage and then, four months later conceived a second time, a son who we named Dennis.

My marriage with Joe was an on-again off-again thing. His sex drive, if anything, increased and in order to save what was left of my female equipment I made the irrevocable decision to really break it off between us. This time I didn't go back to him, I'd met Bill Santell, a member of the very successful rock group "The Stardusters."

* * *

Bill was a good looking man who was very good to me. We began going out and when his work schedule called for New York and Montreal, he would take me with him. He was truly a beautiful man and what gave me the biggest charge was that everywhere we went the girls would look at him with their tongues hanging out.

I was nineteen and getting my first taste of show business and loved it. It seemed to me that show business people never got messed up with rules, and since I was always a rebel doing something I shouldn't, this definitely was going to be my way of life - my enchilada.

I'd go with Bill Santell to the after-hours club where he worked. It closed at 2:00 am and we'd get to my aunt's house at 3:00. It was my aunt's famous living room couch that caught all the action. And with Bill it wasn't quantity but quality.

He was truly a master at the art of lovemaking and he taught me many different techniques and practices that made me truly aware that for the first time I was experiencing sex at its most exquisite and exciting best.

* * *

Joe and I had lived with my Aunt Virginia during most of our married life which only lasted three years. He didn't work most of the time and she allowed us to live there rent free and fed us. Both of our sons were born in her house and she loved them dearly and used to help me take care of them.

Joe was very family oriented and visited his mother every day for an hour or so and then left her to spend most of the day chewing the rag with his buddies at the local pool room and beer hall.

That "neighborhood" was his life. He was born in the house his parents and brothers and sisters still lived in and when we separated, he had custody of the boys - which I gave him because I was going to California to change my life as he was harassing me all the time - he moved back into that house and lived there for the next sixteen years. And our sons followed in their father's footsteps - growing up there, too.

When Joe and I were still living together we would visit his parents every Sunday. His mother was very friendly but not very bright. She was only fourteen when she married Joe's father in Italy. She was very pretty but inclined to be a little heavy and could always be found in the kitchen. She had had ten children.

Joe's parents adored their grandsons and they did pressure me to have them baptized and raised in the Catholic faith. In fact, I had to go to the church rectory and sign papers saying that I would bring my sons up as Catholics. I did it all to please them.

However, despite my trying always to please them and to accede to their every wish, they never really accepted me as one of their own - not being Catholic or Italian. Quite often, particularly Lucy - a sister-in-law - would make disparaging remarks about my nationality which made for a miserable situation.

But mainly, one of the reasons was that I just wasn't good enough for their wonderful oversexed son. That was a big joke because at that time he was just a lazy bum without any ambition, laying around my aunt's house without contributing a penny for the upkeep of himself, his wife and his children.

After he moved back with his parents, three years after we were married, he got a job with General Electric and stayed with them for thirty-three years before retiring in 1988.

I was only nineteen when it became obvious that it was all over for Joe and me, and at that point with me in California, his family was more than joyous to finance a divorce.

With me out of the family - make that 'out of the picture' since I was never really considered one of the family - they had great cause for rejoicing. They were rid of me but they did have my two beautiful sons who they were bringing up as Catholics.

In retrospect I believe that if they'd given me only half a chance, accepted me as Joe's wife, we could have relaxed, perhaps even solved our problems and had a good life together watching our sons grow up. But what was past was past.

Once I'd shaken myself loose of Joe, Bill and I went steady for some six or seven months and it was long enough to change me - to make a tremendous difference in me. By then I knew what I wanted from my life.

Bill had turned me on to sex as I had never known it and I had discovered within myself a full blown sensitive, sensual woman who knew the full power that she possessed and now knew how to use it most effectively to get what she wanted.

He showed me the high life and introduced me to the exciting people who lived it and made me yearn to become a part of it. I now understood that there were people who lived their lives by letting things happen to them and there were the other people who made things happen. I was determined to make things happen.

From then on all I had to do was go onward, and I don't know anybody who was better at moving forward than me. And as a start I said farewell to Virginia Browne and welcome to Virginia Graham.

During my time with Bill Santell I'd turned full circle from my Betty Boop big bow period to the more subtle sexy look. Now I wore tight, short skirts; the better to show off my great butt and good legs. I wore nothing cut to the navel because I didn't want to come on too strong but just enough.

There was no doubt in my mind that sex was the most powerful weapon a woman had and a very intriguing one. All you had to do was play hard to get, hold back a little, and you could have anything. If you acted like you were available men would fall all over you. Ninety percent of the time I didn't come through.

And if they weren't interested and you were, that was even more fun. In my mind it was a challenge to change things around, to turn it in the other direction.

I knew exactly what I planned to do with my life. All I had to do was to think back and remember what it had been like, to remember the fear and the abuse, the disappointments and the unhappiness, and I resolved that nothing was going to stop me from achieving the good life, the better life, the opulent life. I was bound and determined. If it took balls, I had 'em.

In Philadelphia, one of the better after-hours clubs was owned by Frank Palumbo and was where a lot of entertainment people spent their off time. I'd been there many times with Bill Santell and after we split up I charged in there by myself and nobody seemed to mind. And if I say so, I looked pretty darned good.

It was where I began to meet people with whom I began to swing in places besides my aunt's couch. One night I ended up watching a big crap game at the elegant Warwick Hotel. I'd never seen so much money floating around in one place. One shooter who was winning big handed me $150 - with no strings attached. To keep the peace I had to call my aunt and tell her that I'd been playing cards and shooting craps all night. When I got home at 6:00 am I gave her half of the $150 I'd gotten. Under those conditions being out all night didn't seem to bother my well-bred Southern aunt at all.

In those early years, money wasn't a really big deal with me. What really appealed to me and gave me my highs was the idea that I was actually messing around with people who everybody else knew from their newspapers and magazines and the other side of the spotlight.

And I was following my game plan. For example, at one club I met Nick Ravell, a well-known dancer who just oozed that Latin charm and sensuality all over the place. He had that Fernando Lamas accent at a

17

time when women were going for it.

He was definitely my type and on my list, and the fact that he showed no interest in me at all turned me on even more. I'd drop in at the club and would somehow manage to show up at some of the other places he frequented. Finally, I just wore him down and when he became interested in me, I dropped him.

He came on like a real winner and to my astonishment he turned out to be a flop in the feathers - he really couldn't produce. And since then I've learned that a helluva lot of those glamorous hunks who are so hung up on themselves are absolutely unaware of what it takes to turn a woman on and, as a result, are complete washouts.

At the same time I was chasing after Nick I was also on the make for Dan Bucceroni, a leading contender for the Heavyweight Championship of the World who was a helluva lot better boxing in the ring than he was in bed.

But I still experienced a great feeling of accomplishment being with somebody everybody else wanted, and when Dan would slip out for a few drinks with me which was against training rules, I felt even better.

As I became more adept at this way of life, I went out with a federal judge whose name I can't remember. He wasn't just some plain judge, but Supreme Court or something like that. We'd go out for drinks and dinner and he'd send me presents. I remember the morning a solid gold cigarette case showed up in the morning mail. But he didn't excite me much and the gifts didn't do it.

If at that point he'd offered me $500 to sleep with him, I'd have slugged him. However, if he were to mention $500 a few years later, I'd have said, "Make it five thousand and we'll talk about it." But back then, the idea of accepting money was something I couldn't consider, not for a pretty long time.

After the judge, I went out with Al who had the most beautiful salt-and-pepper hair and a bookmaking operation that was an absolute gold mine. He was pretty lousy in bed and would apologize afterward. When I was really hard up for money, I'd let him give me a few dollars, but I felt real crummy about taking it.

I later dated Johnny D'Angelo, a gorgeous looking man but probably the worst lover I'd ever had. He didn't pay much attention to what he was doing and I had the feeling that he had his mind on something totally different. And he sure did.

One day he mentioned rather casually that he was going to introduce me to some girls and I was going to make lots of money. That really scared me and when I told him to shove it, he got rough and belted me. Just to get out of the car I agreed to work for him and then I ran like hell. I was so upset I even told my aunt.

Before leaving Philadelphia I'd had some twenty or so affairs. They were never one night stands. I would date a guy for a while and slept with him only if I really felt the need. Most of them proposed marriage but I was a real bitch, a spoiled brat and men would have had to put up with a lot to handle me.

I had more hang-ups than a superstitious Irishman. I didn't like to make-out during the day because there was too much light and I never wanted to take all my clothes off. I'd keep on my bra if I could get away with it. Also, I would avoid spending the night with someone when I could get home to my own bed.

I used to think that it all came about from a sense of guilt I was really never able to overcome. And I was right. It all stemmed from good old Aunt Virginia who had made me feel as though I was living in a nunnery with all her rules.

* * *

I remember an experience I had with Joe while we were still married. It was one of those spur-of-the-moment quickies. We were making love in the dining room at a friend's house where I was staying when we heard the door open. The grandmother of the house had come home early and was in the mood for a seemingly never ending session of small talk.

Joe was sitting on a dining room chair with the front of his trousers open. I had everything on but my panties and was sitting astride him - we were in the act. Luckily, I had on a taffeta skirt which was easily spread to cover our vital areas. And Grandma, never suspecting a thing, just sat there yakking while I wiggled around on Joe's lap so as not to injure him permanently.

* * *

It was in late 1952 that Joe began giving me problems. He would park up the street and watch the house and if I went out he would follow me. One evening I went to a place called the "Click" and was there just a few minutes, when Joe and a buddy came walking over to the booth where I was sitting alone.

He demanded to know what I was doing there in a loud voice and when I was too stunned to answer he slapped me in front of dozens of people. I was so embarrassed I ran out of the place and got into a passing cab and went home.

It was the first of what became a series of such harassments that became a commonplace thing, and even my Aunt Virginia with whom I was then living realized that the situation could become serious. Eventually, I only left the house on Saturday night just to get a break in the routine. I was only nineteen.

Finally, I called my mother in California and she advised me to come out there and that she would try to help me get myself together. It was then that I had made the decision to let Joe take care of our two sons, Joe Jr. and Dennis, for a few months until I could find a job and get an apartment.

The other alternative was to take the two boys with me and hope that my stepfather would allow me to bring the boys into his home. Perhaps if he saw what fine children they were and would come to realize how hard I was trying to make a real home for them he might soften up a bit.

But the more I thought about it and the more I recalled what a really hard-hearted individual he was, I came to the conclusion that I'd have to leave them with Joe until I was able to send for them.

I called Joe and we met and sat on a park bench near the house, where I told him that I thought it best that I go to live in California. I explained that my Aunt Virginia was in her 60's, that Uncle Horace had died and she wanted to sell her house, and that my living there prevented her from doing so.

Joe and I came to an agreement that he would care for the children for approximately three to six months - however long it took me to get settled - and then he would send them to me in California. He asked me if I would sign a paper giving him custody of the kids just in case they became ill and he needed legal authority to make any urgent medical decisions. I saw nothing wrong in being prepared for such a possible emergency, and a few days later when he showed up with the document I signed it.

It was an action that I lived to regret. I didn't come to realize until later how he had suckered me in. With passing time I realized how stupid I'd been in trusting him. He never at any time had any intention of sending the boys to join me in California. His entire ploy had been to get them permanently and it had worked.

During my last few months in Philadelphia I spent a good deal of time in the Shubert Theatre building where many theatrical agents had their offices. It was from these offices that Sammy Davis Jr., Frank Fontaine and Robert Preston got their step up into the bigtime along with strippers and frustrated models like myself.

I finally found an agent who said he'd try to get me work as a model, but I turned out to be too short and the Model's Guild turned me down. For someone with an ego the size of mine it was a pretty crushing blow. But instead of letting it get me down it lit all sorts of fires.

I had daydreams of becoming a high fashion model in California with my face plastered on every magazine cover. I'd marry a big star with money to burn and come back to Philadelphia. Only this time I'd be dripping with mink and diamonds and I would drop in on my former in-laws, my old nightclub hangouts and the Model's Guild and I'd say to them, "Okay suckers! How do you like these apples?"

* * *

It was in 1953 when I went to California, leaving Joe and the boys in Philadelphia, that I saw Bill - Leo J. Valez, Jr. He still wanted to marry me but by then I was deeply involved with Richard Lopez, an actor and sometime stuntman.

I was deeply torn between Bill and Richard and couldn't make up my mind which way to go, and then in a weak moment I told Bill I would marry him only to change my mind and marry Richard instead.

It was a mistake that I would regret for a lifetime and admit to Bill when I saw him thirty years later, when he was on his deathbed.

* * *

In California, my stepfather made it very clear that in no way could I ever bring my boys into his house with the words, "Your mother will not be your babysitter." And as always, he had his rules: I could date once a week and I had to be home by eleven. One night I was five minutes late and found the front door locked. I made up my mind that as soon as I was financially able I'd find a place of my own.

I found a job as a car-hop at a place called The Hula Hut in El Monte which called for me to work evenings and my stepfather objected to that because I had to work until 11:00 pm. "I just won't have you coming into my home at that ungodly hour!" That was the end of The Hula Hut.

Living under his tyranny became too difficult. I had some small savings and was desperate to get away from him. I remembered some friends from school, a married couple named Fischer, who lived in the Echo Park section of Los Angeles. We'd met when Bill Valez and I were dating. They had been his friends and had liked me, were happy to hear from me and invited me to stay with them.

Time was passing and nothing was happening. I was close to being broke when I found work at a place called The Sunset Cocktail Lounge which was about a block from where I was living. I was as nervous as hell when I walked in and asked for a job as a cocktail waitress. It was owned by a nice guy, an ex-boxer named Carmen Giorgino. When he asked my age I told him I was twenty-one even though I was very close to being twenty. He told me to come in and work a few nights a week as a start.

I went to work there and the second night that I was on the job I saw this white Cadillac with gold license plates roll into the parking lot and let out a fantastically handsome man. When he swaggered into the place I made a point of deliberately ignoring him and pretty soon he walked over and said to me, "I'm Art Aragon," and I asked, "Who?" "The Golden Boy," he replied, "the middleweight contender."

"Oh," I said, still pretending to be disinterested and it was either my ongoing refusal to be impressed or my tight pants, but he kept after me and we started going out. Before he even made a pass at me he began setting me up, trying to give me money when he ordered drinks. He tried to hand me $30, $40, $50 at a time. It didn't sit right with me but when I was really strapped I'd take it - but I still didn't like it and he didn't push until later.

When the great moment came, this leading contender for the Middleweight Championship of the World turned out to be just another washout. He would gaze lovingly at himself in the mirror and almost grudgingly come over to the bed and share the treasure. He was so hung up on his own body that he was really nothing as a lover.

He came into the Sunset one night when I was there with a girlfriend. We were both a little blasted so when he suggested that she and I both go to a hotel, I went.

But nothing had changed. He was still a disaster. I kinda felt sorry for him - he was such a beautiful male.

Working at the Sunset didn't help my bitchy ego any. With each passing day I grew more discontented until the day this guy drove up in a yellow Cadillac and one of the waitresses made a big fuss over him. It didn't take much to get his attention and cut her out. Looking back I think the conditions were just right for Richard Lopez to come into my life and take over.

* * *

An old friend wrote me from Philly to say that Joe and our two children were still living with his parents, three unmarried sisters and an unmarried brother in that old row house. I phoned often only to have them hang up on me.

It was a setup that pleased tightwad Joe. Since he had no job, he neither contributed toward the rent nor the groceries, but best of all he had a small army of built-in babysitters.

And best of all he had his evenings free for his role as God's gift to the hard up broads of Southwest Philly. And when he landed a job with General Electric he threw in a few bucks to pay for his meals at home. I remember thinking at the time, "Joe, how much luckier can a guy get?"

His oldest sister, Lucy, in her mid-thirties and still unmarried was the matriarch of the family who kept everybody in line with her poisonous tongue. She was the one who had taken over the raising of my sons Joe Jr. and Dennis.

Some years later Lucy became involved with Frank, a priest who served the local parish, and they fell in love and after a short affair he gave up his priesthood so that they could be married.

An act of that nature was considered by devout Catholics to be a terrible sin and therefore shameful and something that the Ciocco family never discussed. But nevertheless the newly married couple was accepted into the family.

Lucy took possession of the house after both of her parents passed away and she ruled like a Mafia matriarch. At her passing, the property was taken over by her husband who owned the place where my sons spent their early years.

I'd been in California for some eight months when I decided it was time to go back to Philadelphia and see my children. I didn't tell Joe I was coming. I didn't think it was necessary since he'd given me his word that I could have the kids back any time I said the word. So I flew back.

As soon as I checked into my hotel I called him. He was very pleasant and suggested that we meet in the cocktail lounge of the Warwick, where I was staying, for a get-together drink and to make arrangements for me to see the boys.

We were finishing up our second drink when I said, "Joe, what do you say we get moving? I'm dying to see my boys." It was then that he made it quite clear that there was no way that I could see them without going to bed with him first!

I reminded him that we had an agreement. He smiled and slowly shook his head. "You know something. You should never sign anything without reading it. I got full custody of those kids and there ain't any way that you can see them unless I say so. And I just told you the only way there is for you to see them. What room are you staying in?"

I was stunned and then I remembered. "That paper you had me sign..." He grinned. "One hundred percent legal. My lawyer... good man, outta' Columbia Law School... What did you say was your room number?"

I never was a hater but at that moment I became one. I never thought I could hate anyone as much as I hated this evil man. But that afternoon I saw my boys.

Chapter Three

For the first two months I went out with Richard Lopez I kept wondering whether I was a leper or if he was gay. All we did those first couple of months was go out for breakfast before dawn and talk, and drive around endlessly, all of which was sort of comfortable.

Richard could talk about any subject you could come up with. He knew a little about everything - just enough so you couldn't trip him up. If you said something, anything, he would give you twenty reasons why you were wrong and he was right, even if he was wrong, which he never was.

It was during those talks that I learned that he was the black sheep of a very jazzy show business family. He just never made it to the big time, but was still trying.

He was performing by the time he was three and was into Spanish dancing, singing and acting and later worked in films which starred Grace Kelly and Audrey Hepburn. He also doubled for Tyrone Power and Omar Sharif. He got his big break when he was signed to a major contract but then he was drafted and sent to Korea. By the time he did his hitch and returned to Hollywood, his time had come and gone. The bloom had left the rose - he was washed up. Finished.

All that was left was his photo with Grace Kelly, exchanging old-pal grins, and an old friend or two who threw him a bit part now and then.

Though Richard still had show business friends - Marlon Brando and Errol Flynn to name a couple - he had a lot of other things going for him. And his lifestyle showed that whatever they were they obviously paid well but there was no way to find out about them.

He played it very close to his chest. He went a little bit overboard with this cloak and dagger stuff. To watch him you'd think that the Bonanno family was listed after him on the FBI's most wanted list.

Grace Kelly and Richard Lopez, 1954

To give you an idea, there were always three or four places where he lived and no one ever knew which one was his real base. If you thought he was someplace you were usually wrong, he was someplace else. He stabled a fleet of cars and switched them at random. He'd often stop at a payphone and rattle off what he had to say in Spanish - he was Spanish - and weird guys would float up to him and quietly slip wads of hundreds into his pocket. I wasn't the brightest gal in town but I had a sneaking suspicion that Richard was not a candidate for California's Citizen of the Year.

And being young and impressionable, all this intrigue and charm excited me down to my toes. He was always late for dates, if he showed up, and he would come on like, "Why are you mad, I'm here aren't I?" I can never, ever remember hearing him use the word "sorry." But it was fun when he did show for a date, even if all it meant was cruising the freeways and emptying the fifth of expensive tequila he always kept in the back of the Caddy.

I remember one morning - it was about five when we pulled up to a motel and he said, "I'm kind of beat, why don't we lay down for a while." There were absolutely no indications that what he meant was, "Well, we're going in here for a little action," and I swear to all that's holy that that was the furthest thing from my mind. After all, in two months of solid dating, I considered it a miracle if he ever kissed me goodnight. And this time he was working on a movie, so I figured he really wanted to rest.

When we got the room I went into the bathroom and came out with a towel around me and - in bra and panties - hopped into what I figured was my bed. After he took a shower he got into the other bed and damn near fell asleep and that's when it happened. He came over to my bed and began kissing me - and it still hadn't dawned on me that I was about to be made by this guy.

Now first lays are usually never very good. Both parties are a little nervous and fast and you really don't know each other and they're generally pretty crummy all around. If you can make it past the first few times, you're all set but there's no judging before then. Those guys who blow off steam about how good some girl was on the first date are usually full of crap.

But for our first time, Richard knocked my socks off. It was a great ball. Not spectacularly long where time was concerned, but he was gentle, confident and well built. It was plain from the start that he was no amateur and knew where everything went. And he cared about getting it right.

It was absolutely great and when I figured his little surprise party was over I started to get up when he asked me where I was going and before I could answer he was making love again.

Now according to my past experiences, when it's over - it's over - and with most guys it takes at least twenty or thirty minutes to re-charge, right? Wrong! With Richard it was instant replay and I remember smirking about that and thinking happy thoughts.

Our first time was a preview of some great coming attractions. I was certain that his next performance would definitely be Oscar mate-rial. For one reason, he was always as sure as hell of his ground before trying anything. And too, because he couldn't handle rejection he had to be the one pursued and since by then I was good at pursuing, every-thing seemed to be coming up roses.

But that first afternoon, with my various hang-ups, it was a pretty funny scene that was played out in that motel room. I stayed in bed with the sheet up to my eyeballs. Every trip I made to the bathroom meant a careful re-draping of a towel with great gnashing of bra fasten-ers and slapping of panty elastic. I even kept a piece of adhesive tape over an old appendix scar which Richard removed right away. It wasn't until I really got to know him that I felt comfortable about leaving it off.

With our respective approaches about pursuit, we had an interesting few months after that. He didn't want to get bogged down in anything and didn't push very hard. And since I wasn't very big on accepting no, I did everything from going down a fire escape and breaking into his apartment to applying feminine black arts.

I'd wire my Aunt Virginia for money and then give it to him to hold for me, saying I was afraid of spending it too quickly. There's nothing like having someone keep money for you. It gives you a good reason for staying in close touch. And then I'd give him expensive little gifts, always insisting that there was no obligation on his part. And of course there was - always is - always has been.

I was always a great believer in gifts - if I had $100, I'd spend $99 on a present and keep the rest for lunch. Nothing too flashy, but always with a touch of class. He was Catholic, not too religious, and when I gave Richard a solid gold Saint Christopher medal it showed I was a good girl.

I always had good taste in men's clothes so I'd buy an expensive shirt which he would mysteriously find on his bed with a bow. Never with a card, but he always knew. The great thing about gifts, particularly the ones that cost money, is that guys always accept them and then even without realizing feel obligated to you.

Richard was a foxy character, and my plot was to nail him down like I was some general trying to storm a fort. And after a while he began coming around and I could feel that he cared about me more and more. His mysterious contacts would leave huge sums of money with me for him, and that helped seal a bond - at least psychologically.

During all this time - it was in 1953 - I was still working at the Sunset Bar and still looking over everyone who walked in the door. Art Aragon was still high on me and on himself of course, and occasionally fixed me up with friends. Once Art brought in his manager Jimmy Roach who started talking to me about going to Lake Tahoe. He was nice, rich and very insistent. Finally I talked it over with Richard.

Richard, though short-fused and Latin, had a pretty tight hold on his emotions. With him, showing how you felt was a weakness, and jealousy was out of the question for anyone with class. He didn't encourage me, but he didn't indicate he'd rather I didn't go. In fact, all he said was that if I went, he knew exactly what would happen.

What he was really saying was that once I got a taste of real money, I would be hooked on it. And he was right. I found out that money really is honey.

So Jimmy Roach and I got into his Cadillac and went flashing up to Tahoe where he got me a job at the Cal-Neva Lodge. And shortly after we got there he told me that he'd like me to sleep with one of his millionaire friends. He was appealing to my practical side when he asked me, "What do you have to lose?"

I was - are you ready for this? - horrified. "How could I?" I sniffed. "I mean what kind of low-life bitch would do a thing like that... take money from a man for...? Why, you had to be a dirty, filthy, rotten tramp..."

And I got to like it.

To get me around to it took a lot of hard work on Jimmy's part.

When the money approach didn't work he got me plastered. I'd graduated from screwdrivers to orange blossoms and got so high that I hardly noticed when he slipped in his friend. He was a big time Texas oil tycoon whose wife was fabulously-wealthy-in-her-own-right.

He turned out to be a nice, easygoing guy who liked me and treated me like a lady. After a while he even suggested that I quit my job, but I told him my two sons had to eat. Then a girlfriend and I decided to move into a really nice cottage in an exclusive section but we couldn't afford the rent.

The oil tycoon found out about it, so he would either give my friend the money for me, or have it quietly slipped under the door in an envelope. Gifts followed, straight from my own philosophy - gold earrings with pearl and diamond chips, clothes. He even had my teeth fixed. For a gal who had never seen too many hundred dollar bills, here was this guy barraging me with all this loot.

And it was very hush-hush, because he had a wife with one foot in the grave but eyes like a hawk. Then one day Jimmy Roach gave me the key to a huge suite he had rented, saying I was expected for "lunch." Well, after weeks of gifts and rent and things, I had a good idea of who was on the menu. I got pleasantly plastered on orange blossoms again, and staggered in.

I remember wearing a low-cut, cute, black knit sweater with white shorts and sexy shoes. When he saw me I thought he was going to have a heart attack. I don't know how we got from the living room to the bedroom, but even though I was loaded I wouldn't let him take my clothes off.

That was all right with him, because he was ecstatic about getting laid and was afraid I'd change my mind. Jimmy had informed him that I'd never been involved in such a set of circumstances before so he went along very easy, treating me like I was a virgin. I let him work over my thigh and slip off my shorts but he was so nervous that when he hopped on it was over in a flash.

Anyway, he wasn't Richard, so I went to the bathroom and washed. But he was obviously happily satisfied about the whole thing and slipped me some money - two or three hundred, I think - and suggested I go buy a dress.

All the while I was at Tahoe, the oil tycoon and I balled only three times, but the charge accounts and presents never stopped. Joseph Magnin's held their big deal fashion shows and he would go there with his wife. He would watch me, and if I saw something I liked, I'd wink.

The second time we had sex was in the back of a chauffeur-driven limousine. He had sneaked away and we had dinner on the north shore. On the way back we went to King's Beach and pulled off down a dark road. I jumped on top, I straddled him, with my full skirt, just like with my first husband Joe. Virginia rides again. And as usual all that came off were my panties.

Again it was over in a flash, but he was pretty pleased with himself and he pulled a pair of beautiful earrings out of his pocket.

He was on his way to the lodge early one morning when he stopped by my house, the one he was underwriting, for round three. Jimmy had been over the night before to announce the v-i-s-i-t.

I had a bathrobe on over a sheer nightgown. First he told me he wanted to take me to Palm Springs to meet some rich club owners and other "right people." These were some of the most powerful Texas oil people. Among his friends was Ray Ryan who owned the El Mirador in Palm Springs as well as some big gamblers like Allen Smiley, who was a former associate of Bugsy Siegel.

Finally he eased over and I let him take off my bathrobe but not the nightgown, which seemed to satisfy him. This third time was also very quick. But he was nervous about his wife and hurried off, saying he'd be back in a week.

He never got back. Jimmy came flying up in his car to tell me that the oil tycoon's wife had put a detective on him and had found out about me. I was immediately packed off to Los Angeles and given $1,500 for the trip.

That was fine with me since I was up to my ears in irate wives. I was working at the Cal-Neva when one of the owners got me bombed and we ended up in bed. He really liked me and opened a charge account for me at Magnin's. But there was a stupid screw-up - the store sent a bill for something I'd bought to his wife.

Virginia Graham, 1954

I walked into the club one night when a flock of my friends rushed over to say this broad was after me with knives and spears. Before I could do anything, she came roaring in.

Now she was a storybook Jewish wife with an approach I didn't believe. "I know my husband is faithful; I know he could never do anything wrong..." And I grabbed onto that line like a spare banknote.

"Oh, no, let me explain. I was out of money and needed some
clothes, and your husband was kind enough to lend..." And it worked!
But I just couldn't believe that she could look at herself and then at this
twenty-one-year-old babe, built like I was, and not know there was
some hanky-panky going on.

During that summer I stayed in Tahoe I also had an affair with August Busch of the wealthy beer brewing family. He was only 18 or 19
and I was twenty-one. His aunt owned the cottage I was living in in
Kings Beach and she introduced us. Making it with a young guy like
Augie was certainly a change of pace from some of the older guys I
was seeing.

Ten years later I was staying at the Beverly Hills Hotel when one of
the maître d's called. Some important gentlemen were in town and
wanted some company. I accepted the invitation and when I met the
group, much to my surprise it turned out to be August Busch and some
of his rich friends. With the passage of time he didn't recognize me or
pretended he didn't, and I let it go at that. While we did get together for
dinner I lied and said I had a previous engagement and left after dessert.

Tahoe made the change that Richard had predicted and of course it
was a lot of fun. I had gotten hot for a young golf pro who was a good
ball, and pursued him with the old Virginia tactics. He tried like hell
not to accept the sweaters I bought him with Ray's money. But he did,
naturally. The only thing was that he dropped me and since that didn't
happen very often it was a nasty shock.

But most of all, Tahoe was my turning point and it provided pages
and pages of names for future climbing. I learned that rich people are
no different from poor people except they drink more.

I felt easy among the rustling of currency, as if it were something I
had always done. So many people have the wild idea that millionaires
are superior, somewhat different. Hell, most of them are a bunch of
drunks, with twice the problems of working stiffs. Poor people might
have trouble paying bills, but the rich are usually so afraid that everyone likes them only for their money that they get neurotic. As a whole,

I've found them to be unhappy, superficial and, generally, pitiful.

My lucrative little stay at Lake Tahoe had left me practically nothing. I could never keep money, no matter how much I had. I'd gamble it, buy clothes, give a friend a present, anything. But who needed it?

I phoned Richard and told him I was coming back. He was pissed off that I hadn't bothered to call him all the time, but was tickled to hear from me. I asked if I could stay with him until I found a place. Actually, once I was in his place I had no intention of moving out.

Those first few months after Lake Tahoe were some of our best. We really got to like each other, and each of us found out what we were up against. I was anything from a loving obedient mate to a screaming terror who would drop out of arguments by overdosing on sleeping pills. He would range from gentle fingertip caresses to vicious body blows that would leave me sprawled over the bathroom tiles.

When things went well they were incredible. Richard would spend an entire evening making love to me. It would start with a perfect dinner by candlelight, always with the best wines and music. We would smoke a few joints and lie around the fireplace talking and giggling. He'd light incense sticks and put on a soft kabuki robe. We would lie on a furry rug, and he would lightly and thoroughly work over my body with fingertips and tongue for hours until I was scratching chunks out of the rug and out of him. And we would make out on the sink, on the bed, on the toilet, along the banister, against the door, on the dining room table.

He kept vibrators at each side of our enormous bed, and we'd use them until we were both screaming. Sometimes - just at climax - Richard would inhale a nitrate compound used by heart patients to dilate arteries and get the blood rushing. My own blood was coursing so loudly, usually, you could hear it. In fact, you could hear both of us all the way to Orange County.

Richard was a camera freak, with a Leica he knew how to use. After I wiped out my inhibitions with pills, we took roll after roll of pictures that would make a Danish censor blush. He would set the camera, push the self-timer, and then we'd scramble to enmesh the various organs that were to star before the camera clicked.

His secret was time and attention. It's something every man should know well. It was never OK - let's get laid. Never. Richard had to work up to it and do it right.

And during all this time I never forgot my children. I sent them money, toys, clothing, only to find out years later that they never received any of my gifts. It only added to their belief that I had given up on them - deserted them and that their loyal, ever-loving Aunt Lucy had taken my place.

This was the same Aunt Lucy who told me that inasmuch as I wasn't a Catholic I wasn't permitted to be present at the christening of my sons, and I was naïve enough to believe her. I waited at home during both ceremonies. What a poor, stupid fool I had been!

I later learned that she even forbid my boys to refer to me as "mother." She always spoke of me as "that woman" and time and time again would tell them that I had "left" them and then add how much she loved them. Whenever I called the house she would hang up on me and one time warned me to not even try to come to the house.

I don't know if Joe was a part of the conspiracy or not. I chose not to believe it although I'm sure he knew what was going on and never intervened. I do know that Aunt Lucy had succeeded in totally severing the ties between me and my children. She had wanted my children and had gotten them.

I decided to go to Philadelphia and see my boys, Richard's advice to the contrary. When I got to the city I took a cab to the house and knocked on the door. No matter what, I was determined to see my sons.

My former mother-in-law answered the door and I stepped inside. My Aunt Virginia was in the living room visiting with Joe Jr. and I was told that Dennis was upstairs with his Aunt Ann. Just then Frannie, one of Joe's sisters who'd always been very hostile toward me, appeared and began screaming for me to get out. I said I wouldn't leave without seeing my sons and with that Ann came downstairs with Dennis in her arms. Joe Jr. remained sitting on Aunt Virginia's lap.

I went to reach for Dennis when Frannie came at me and we got into a real fist fight. Little Joe Jr. started crying as did Aunt Virginia whose nose began bleeding. It was a terrible scene which fortunately Ann, who got in between us, managed to break it up. How traumatic, I thought, for the boys.

Fran had scratched my face, which was bleeding, and poor little Joe Jr. was crying, "Mommy, Mommy!" and trying to run to me. It was a heartbreaking thing and not made any easier with the knowledge that my children were being stolen from me. Since there was nothing else I could do I turned and left, resolving that I would never allow those people to hurt me again, or allow my boys to witness such violence.

I went back to California with the deep determination to be a success, make a lot of money and hire a top attorney to help me get my sons back. And every time I saw *Lassie* on television I would cry because the little boy looked so much like my little Joe Jr., which would only make Richard furious.

This time when I returned with my face all scratched up he started screaming at me about my "goddamn kids," saying that they didn't want me and to "get the hell out of their lives!"

I'm certain that the reason I took so much abuse from Richard and got involved with sleeping pills was to kill the pain and feeling of guilt of not being able to be with my sons. I loved them deeply but there were too many people standing in the way of my being with them.

I never gave up hoping and praying that when they grew up they would somehow learn the truth about our relationship, which was that their mother didn't give them up and loved them with all her heart. But it never came to pass. Over the years they were so thoroughly brainwashed by their father's family that the lie lived on for years.

And it's so very, very sad because I know in my heart of hearts that I would have been one hell of a mom to them. God, the love I would have given them!

I had trusted Joe when he said he would send Joe Jr. and Dennis to me when I got settled in California, but he had tricked me into signing that paper and now, unloved, unmarried Lucy who wanted children, had children, mine.

And me? I had Richard Lopez.

By early 1954, Richard and I were getting along pretty well so we drove down to Tijuana, Mexico and were married. I was completely turned on to him, mainly - believe it or not - to his mind. The entire time I was with Richard, I think the thing that attracted me most was his intellect. Of course a good roll in the hay helps, too.

When Richard and I were married I was in my second month of pregnancy, and one day a gal pal by the name of Sally Yarnell who was kept busy doing bit parts invited me to join her for dinner.

I wasn't expecting Richard home until much later that evening so I accepted, and when I arrived at the restaurant I was pleasantly surprised to discover that Sally had also invited Michael Rennie, the English star.

We had a very pleasant couple of hours. The food was good and the conversation was sparkling, and all-in-all I couldn't remember when I had enjoyed myself so much.

I arrived home to find Richard in a foul mood. He'd been drinking and made it clear that whenever he came home he expected me to be there, and when I tried to explain where I'd been he punched me in the stomach.

He beat me real bad and kept punching me in the stomach despite my pleas for him to stop, and as a result I began hemorrhaging and within twenty-four hours I was in the hospital where I suffered a miscarriage.

While I was married to Richard I tried like hell to have a child. We made love all the time and I even went through the agony of having oil put on my tubes. And afterwards I would stand on my head just in case. I would even insert a Tampax inside of me so that nothing that could possibly bring about a pregnancy could get away, but all I was actually doing was absorbing all those otherwise willing little sperm cells. Then, when I was twenty-three I had a hysterectomy and for a long time I suffered terrible feelings of guilt, like I was being paid back.

Even after we were married he still didn't take me into his confidence and kept his business dealings to himself. It was all very hush-hush. He kept two phones in the place, one I could use and one I wasn't to touch. Whatever he was engaged in - the money kept rolling in.

One afternoon I was so curious that I asked him what he was doing and he replied, "None of your friggin' business!" And he was right. As long as the bills were being paid and we were living well, who cared how he made his money? Come to think of it, it was none of my friggin' business.

That held true until the day I came home and had forgotten my keys, so I had to knock, only to have this gorilla-type answer the door pointing a huge goddamned pistol at my head. "You can put the gun down," Richard said. "It's my wife."

The place looked like it had been hit by a quake. A bunch of cops were tearing the place apart. There was garbage on the floor, drawers out, furniture upside down. My little dog was frantically trying to bite one of them.

The only thing they found was an embarrassing picture of me. Fortunately I'd hidden the heavy stuff in the telephone book. The FBI had been living across the street filming everyone that came in and out of our house and taking notes like crazy.

They took Richard downtown, questioned him and charged him with transporting narcotics. His Caddy was impounded after they found a single codeine tablet in it without a prescription. We got a good lawyer, a former FBI man by the name of George Danielson, who later went to the state senate in California. His fee was about $5,000. The case never got beyond the preliminary hearing, but it scared the hell out of Richard and me and really upset his family who were lovely and very fine people.

What had happened was that Richard had driven some guy to the airport where five feds nailed him with uncut heroin as he was checking into his flight. They had pictures of Richard driving with him. We lost the car but won a dismissal.

Richard was certain he was going to prison. He never told me if he was guilty or not, but it was the only time I'd ever seen him really let his hair down and reveal his emotions. And it was the last trouble with the law he ever had. I think it scared him into staying clear of anything they might hang on to him.

About that time I was doing a little freelance swinging on my own. I had gotten a job as an assistant to Dr. Lewis Morrill, the Beverly Hills physician who was then married to actress Rhonda Fleming, when Fernando Lamas, one of Dr. Morrill's patients, came into the office for a B12 injection. To my great amazement and embarrassment, the doctor asked me to give him the shot.

Lamas was both elegant and charming as he bared his magnificent rear end which was the site for the injection. Up until then I hadn't given too many shots and since this one was special, it was a struggle to keep my hand that held the needle steady. Fortunately I was able to control the shaking and everything went well.

I decided that after Richard's arrest that I would make a try at earning our money. I was convinced that with a little judicious wiggling of my well-built rear, we could clean up. A girlfriend had already been drilling me in the procedures, and I felt I was ready. Also, I thought I'd try modeling and film work.

It took one hell of an argument to sell this to Richard. He had really been training me for this sort of thing, but he was reluctant to let me go ahead. He eventually agreed but with the understanding that if I did it, it would have to be under his direction. He was going to play Pygmalion, mold me into something sleek and impressive.

"You're not going to be some goddamn fool screwing a producer for a day's work," he thundered. "No wife of mine is going to lay down for an assistant director or cameraman or anyone else for a lousy $50 or $60 a day when she can make many times that without working up a sweat."

I knew he was right. I've seen so many aspiring young starlets screwing their way to a limited success. If you want to believe the old American dream, go ahead, but very, very few girls get into films on their merits alone.

Richard steeped me in his philosophy: if you do anything, do it right. Drink the most expensive brands of booze. Wear only the finest perfume and choose it carefully. In restaurants order to impress. Dress rich but subtly. Above all, he would repeat many times, people don't know anything about you that you don't tell them.

Chapter Four

To start with, for the type of high class operation Richard had in mind we needed the right address. We found a place on Wilshire only a few doors down from Frank Sinatra.

As it turned out, I had already gotten to know my new neighbor extremely well.

I had just returned from Tahoe to live with Richard. A man I had met named Paul Rinaldi called and told me he had a good friend he wanted me to meet and asked if I could make it right away to Don the Beachcomber's. It was 11 pm and Richard wasn't home, and I didn't want to go. But I figured what the hell and took a taxi.

The headwaiter showed me to Rinaldi's table, and when I walked up, his friend had his back to me. I got there and the friend stood up, turned around, took my hand, smiled and said in that beautiful baritone, "When are we gettin' married?" And that's how we started. I'll never forget that I almost didn't keep a blind date with Frank Sinatra.

Talk about being "flabbergasted!" My never-failing mouth went briefly out of commission and was fairly silent at the start of the evening. I was nervous and afraid of saying something stupid... but as time went on, Frank was so gracious and down-to-earth that I soon relaxed and was able to be myself.

We didn't stay at Don's too long and when we left the place, Frank was mobbed by autograph seekers. He was gentle, patient and kind to everyone. Just being with him made me feel as though I was floating in the clouds and I tried desperately to stay cool.

Paul was with Irene, his girlfriend, when the four of us walked past the boutique shop in Don the Beachcomber's, when Frank eyed a dress in the window and suggested that we go in. Once inside he insisted that I pick out something for myself and I chose that same dress he saw, a very expensive emerald-green satin Suzy Wong dress with a high neck and matching jacket.

The shop also carried an interesting collection of Hawaiian artifacts and curios. Frank remembered that I had mentioned having two small sons and he bought a miniature outrigger canoe which he arranged to have shipped to them in Philadelphia.

From the very beginning of our relationship he was very generous and seemed to like the idea that I had children. He said that I looked a great deal like Judy Garland and Lana Turner.

We all went to Frank's apartment on Wilshire Boulevard - a beautiful place whose main color theme was orange and white both upstairs and downstairs. Fine paintings adorned the walls among which were smaller paintings of Ava Gardner. Although at the time they were separated but still married, it was obvious that he was still carrying a torch for her.

When we were all comfortably settled in his huge living room he explained that he had just cut a new record, "Day In, Day Out," I think, and we listened to it over and over. It wasn't an ego trip. Frank was a perfectionist and wanted to make sure that it was flawless. As I sat there, I couldn't help but see what a wonderful way he had handling small talk, being attentive to what you had to say and making you forget he was "Sinatra - the King." He was generally just a nice guy.

And that's the way the hours passed. And during all that time - it was 4:00 am - he never made a pass or voiced any suggestive innuendos. He was a perfect gentleman. And it was about four when he asked me if I would like to accompany him to Palm Springs the following week. I replied that it would be my pleasure but added that it was at that time of morning when I felt it best to be getting on home. He agreed and phoned for a cab.

When the cab arrived he gently took my arm and walked me to it, opened the door and helped me in, telling the driver to make sure I got home safely. And with that he handed the driver a $100 bill.

He then took my hand and pressed three one hundred dollar bills into it and told me to buy myself some good perfume. Since he had already given me a beautiful dress and an outrigger canoe for my boys, I told him he'd been more than generous and that I couldn't accept the money, but he was insistent and besides who could refuse "Mr. S?"

When I got back to my apartment I told Richard what a great evening I'd had with Frank and that he'd invited me to Palm Springs. All Richard could do was smile and say, "Don't hold your breath waiting for his call. Don't you realize he can have any woman he wants? He was just being polite."

A week later, Frank did call reminding me about our trip to Palm Springs and that we would be leaving in a couple of hours. Richard wasn't home when I packed a bag, grabbed a cab and went over to Frank's to find Paul Rinaldi and his girlfriend, Irene, already there.

We drove out to Palm Springs in Frank's long black convertible with me feeling pretty good in a sexy, white knit dress with a cowl collar.

En route we stopped for some hot dogs and some autographs. It was there that a carload of punk kids started smart-assing around and making cracks.

Frank ignored them at first but then they followed us, trying to cut us off on a dangerously winding road. Frank was getting madder and madder, until at one point when they got real close he sounded off.

He half stood up behind the wheel and bellowed in the finest Sinatra timbre: "You mothers! You get your ass…!" I can't remember exactly what he packed into the following three sentences but it had its desired effect. Their pimply little faces dropped about a foot, their mouths fell open, they quit hassling us and took off.

Jimmy Van Heusen, the songwriter, was host for the weekend at his place next to Bing Crosby's at the Tamarisk golf course. A half dozen people were in for the weekend and others kept dropping by. They were mostly just rich guys and golfing friends. Crosby was the only one I recognized.

It was a pleasant day and Frank decided he was going to cook up a full spaghetti dinner. And there he was in this kitchen, pitching tomatoes around, slopping sauce and turning out a tremendous batch of pasta. He was the typical Italian chef and the result was a gourmet's delight.

As the evening wore on people were slowly getting plastered, and Jimmy started playing the piano. Frank hopped onto the piano himself and ran through hours of his old stuff. By then there were some thirty to thirty-five people hanging around, having a pretty good time, but some drunken married woman who'd been trying to get to Frank at the pool was making herself obnoxious. He had a firm ethic about not messing around with friends' wives and she was no great prize, anyway, so he took her home and came right back.

I wasn't too big on staying up late, so I went in early and sacked out. Besides I was in no hurry to fling it at Frank and get crossed off his list as just another easy lay.

But Frank had decided there was no way I'd get away a second time. I was yawning and nodding, but he hung right in there with me until about four. When we had first arrived, the servant had put our bags in a large guestroom with big twin beds. So after we told everyone goodnight, I showered and put on a nightgown, and went to my bed.

Frank climbed into his, looked over and said, "Why don't you come over here?" It was nothing like a command: "C'mere baby..." or anything like that - Frank did everything with his special touch of class. I went over, and we lay there and talked and talked until it became pretty clear that I was going to be made love to.

I discovered that there was one large problem with sleeping with Sinatra. He was overly endowed. Girls had obviously told him about it. In fact, he always kept a jar of cold cream nearby. He whispered a warning just before the strategic breach, and he promised not to hurt me. He was extremely tender and gentle, carefully not charging ahead gung-ho but he wasn't terribly long-winded. It lasted about ten minutes, I guess, and all the while he murmured romantic things. He kept saying that he liked me a lot and that he needed me.

In the midst of the sex act, men often say things like that, things they don't really mean. But I detected a terrible loneliness, the honest emotion of a desperately lonely man. It was a tremendous compliment, I felt, and it brought us closer together. He was a man who sincerely cared for the woman he was with and who seemed to have the need to feel liked for himself.

Sinatra, always, was an affectionate, warm person - a toucher. He held hands, brushed shoulders, kissed cheeks. When he spoke, he fixed you with gorgeous sky-blue eyes and simply enveloped you. His gaze didn't flicker or wander. Nothing existed but you. He'd really screw up the electrons when he'd walk into a room - the kind of weird magnetism thing people talk about. And he'd see right into your soul.

After our first night in bed together, I woke up early and went to the pool. Jimmy had breakfast ready and I had eaten by the time Frank came out. He asked why I had slipped out and I said something about not wanting to bother him. Actually, it was another of my hang-ups; if I'd stayed we would have balled again, and I couldn't do it in the day-time.

On the way back to Los Angeles he asked if I wanted to go to New York. I said yes and he asked me where I lived so he could drive me there. That was a sweat. I didn't want him to see my place - and there was Richard. But he drove me to my building and insisted upon taking me up to my door - I was petrified that Richard would come out and raise hell - but Frank kissed me goodbye and left.

Fortunately, Richard was taking one of his two-hour showers. He came out and we didn't say much about the weekend. But I thought to myself, Jesus, how did ol' Virginia Browne get so lucky so quick? Browne was the name I used in California. I didn't use Graham until later.

I didn't hear from Sinatra for a few months until one day the phone rang and a voice said: "Hi, how are you?" I answered: "Fine, who is this?" "Frank." Again: "Frank who?" This time he wasn't as amused. He said he was calling as he'd promised and wanted to know if I was ready to go to New York in the next few days.

When I hesitated and said I didn't have any warm clothes, he sent his secretary scurrying over, and we bought a couple thousand dollars' worth of stuff for me. I tried desperately to get hold of Richard to tell him. Finally he rang me. When I told him, there was a deathly silence on the line. Sinatra was the only one who ever made Richard show any signs of jealousy, but he couldn't say no. Instead he asked, predictably, if it was worth any money. I lied and said sure. Actually I just wanted to go. So Frank's car took me to Union Station for the train trip a few hours after he had first called.

We took the train because Frank had some time to kill. It was great - Jimmy Van Heusen and a few Sinatra buddies were also going. And then Ronald Reagan came swooping up in a stunning off-white, vicuna trench coat. He was on his way back east to host the General Electric Theatre Series he was doing on television. Frank didn't feel too friend-ly toward Reagan - he even made a deprecating remark about him - however he asked him to join us.

It was a merry old trip and Frank was belting down Jack Daniel's on the rocks with a tall glass of cool water on the side. But I spent most of my time talking to Reagan. He had been one of my childhood idols and I mentioned this and, although Reagan was not too happy about the father image, he loved the attention.

If Reagan was pleased, Sinatra wasn't. But I could remember my mother flipping out over *King's Row* and it was a strange thrill talking to the guy who had starred in it. And he was charming in a sort of All-American, wholesome way. The longer it went on, the more pissed and pissed off Frank got.

Finally Reagan excused himself and left whereupon Frank pointedly asked Jimmy why I didn't go with Reagan inasmuch as I had been talking to him all night. Frank's show of jealousy was surprising to me. Not only didn't it please me, but I actually felt bad about it.

Things got nasty when we rolled into a town where the local columnist had insulted Frank, and he wanted to find the guy and belt him. The only way we could control Frank was to lock him in his compartment.

I started crying and Frank cooled down and apologized. It was the day before his birthday, so I gave him some cologne. Frank seemed touched. I didn't tell him I'd planned to give it to my ex-husband Joe Ciocco.

Frank blew up again in Chicago when some reporters kept asking him about a reported romance between Ava Gardner and Luis Miguel Dominguín, Spain's premier bullfighter, but that passed.

In New York we checked into The Sherry-Netherland and enjoyed seeing some plays and night clubbing. I expressed a desire to go to Philadelphia and visit with my sons.

Frank was very agreeable. He arranged for my flight and hotel accommodations at the Bellevue-Stratford, gave me several hundred dollars to cover any other expenses and insisted that I pay a visit to FAO Schwarz, New York's most famous toy store, and load up on toys for Joe Jr. and Dennis.

I remembered that during an earlier visit I had promised to get Joe Jr. a bike and I got the best one that Schwarz carried, among a slew of other things and had them shipped.

But beneath all the shopping and the traveling was the deep need to see the boys. How my arms ached to hold Joe Jr. and Dennis. I was impatient for the plane to land, for the taxi to get to the house. I needed my boys in my arms.

I checked into the hotel and called Joe to make arrangements for him to collect his "pound of flesh." We'd always have a drink first and then we'd go to my room for the "payoff." And through it all I found it impossible to keep my feelings of contempt for him from my face.

But when I saw my children I knew what happiness was. They were growing up beautifully and I knew that if I never did another good thing in my life, I had done well in bringing those two angels into the world.

That afternoon I told Joe Jr. that the bike he had wanted was on its way and it would only be a matter of a few days. The light in his eyes was something to see. His face lit up, he grinned from ear-to-ear, put his arms around me, kissed my cheek and said very quietly, "Thanks, Mom."

At that moment I knew in my heart of hearts that if I had to screw twenty heels like Joe in order to see my beautiful boys - it was worth it. Joe may have had full custody but I had carried them inside of me, they were the flesh-of-my-flesh and no matter how those mean-minded members of Joe's family tried to come between us, they could never take away from me the fact that I was their mother.

* * *

Years later I was talking to my son Joe Jr. and he mentioned that bike. He told me that he had waited on the front steps for days on end, waiting for that bike which never came - the bike that I had promised him.

In my mind's eye I could see that little boy waiting and waiting day-after-day and I could feel the terrible disappointment he felt and I cried inside. The only answer was that the bike had come when he wasn't home and his Aunt Lucy or his Aunt Frannie had spirited it away, along with all the other gifts I'd gotten the boys in New York. They had been busy painting a picture of me as a mother who had forsaken them, and getting gifts from me didn't quite fit their image. That a little boy had his heart broken didn't count for anything with such small, mean minds.

* * *

I called Richard from Philadelphia and, like an ass, I let him talk me into charging some clothes for him to Frank. How dumb could I get? Naturally, the bills had to be cleared because the stuff was to be shipped, so when I got home Frank's secretary rang me up madder than all hell. That tore it with Frank, I was sure, but I made up my mind to get back with him.

It took seven years to do it.

The East Coast trip with Sinatra was in December 1954, my first year on the loose in California. I didn't see him again until 1961 when he was doing his "Ring-a-Ding-Ding" show at the Sands in Las Vegas.

A friend of mine, Regina Harris - the most beautiful girl I've ever known - had been dating him on and off, but she wanted more than anything to meet Bob Hope. I told her I'd introduce her to Bob if she would fix me up with Frank.

So she called him in Vegas and told him this lovely friend of hers named Kathy Parness had come to town and was hot to meet him. He spoke to me over the phone, was as charming as hell and asked me up to watch the show.

Richard, who had been listening to the conversation, hit the roof and shouted, "Goddamn, why did you do that, for Christ's sake, because you're not going!" He was still jealous of Frank and was a bit distraught because Kim - the girl we took in as part of our operation - was in the next room slitting her wrists.

Richard took time out to go in and beat the hell out of her and then came back to argue with me some more. I stood my ground with him and finally won the argument. He'd been taking out his anger at Kim on me. But the wrist-cutting nonsense was something she did a number of times for attention.

Anyway, I flew up to Vegas and Frank's new valet, a handsome black guy named George Jacobs, drove me over to the Sands. Frank came out for a warm welcome, dressed in a bright orange shirt and a cute little white hat with a bumble bee on it. *Great!* I thought, *I pulled it off.* I'd even had a ring made for myself with the initials KP in diamonds. Later, I learned that he knew right off who I was but didn't let on. It was his way of saying that all was forgiven.

47

Our second go-round was a carbon copy of the first. We were out until 8 am and he showered attention on me, but I wouldn't make out with him the first night. Still, the conversation was interesting; I'd mentioned I was trying to buy a house, so he told me to find something in the $100,000 range and he would have his bank finance it.

I couldn't believe it. But no lousy hundred grand was going to buy me that night. When it got to bedtime, Frank lay down, and I went into the bathroom and piddled around for an hour until he fell asleep. I awoke at eleven and left. When he finally got up, he found me and announced: "You're not getting away tonight."

I didn't get away, of course. After he did the show that night we went clubbing for a little while and then he went to the Black Jack table and we were there until 8 am and he came out losing about $55,000. It didn't seem to bother him at all. Winning or losing, he took it all with his usual grace.

The Sinatra temper flared once that evening when the bouncers at one place tried to eject a disabled man who quarreled with a waiter. When the hotel security called the police and had the guy arrested, Frank flared: "Haven't those mothers got anything better to do than pick on a cripple?" He disliked cops on general principles, anyway. The disabled fellow never knew that it was Frank Sinatra who bailed him out.

I had discovered that his favorite perfume was Ma Griffe, and when we got back to our suite I was swimming in it. After putting on a wild blue negligee I came into the bedroom and he asked me to come over and give him a backrub. And we spent the night in his bed.

We were supposed to leave for Palm Springs the next day, but he had to rush off to Miami. He sent me home with some addresses for modeling jobs. And he had given me about $800 the night before as gambling money.

When I got home, Richard fumed about "piss money" and "bullshit money." We'd just gotten a call from some rich Texas guys who wanted to go out with Kim, Caroline and me - especially me - so I had no choice. My head was really in the clouds, and I was lousy company for the creeps. I wouldn't consider balling and had trouble even pretending I might. One of the girls told Richard what a drag I'd been, and he had one of his all-time explosions.

He began slapping me around the room, screeching, "You're never seeing him again... In fact, I'm telling him that you're never seeing him!" I yelled back, "I can see whoever the hell I want!" and he answered, "We'll see about that!" timed with a punch in the stomach that sent me to the floor.

He swung at my face, as usual, but I covered pretty well with my arms and then he yanked at my hair and dragged me around a while. All his pent up anger and jealousy of Sinatra poured out, and he told me how I was screwing up everything for nothing.

I called Richard a dumb mother and refused to give an inch. He could see I was looking directly at him, and suddenly he felt threatened. Here I was fighting back like never before for Frank - a man I obviously had deep feelings for - and he backed off. And with Kim, who had come in from the next room, yanking him away, things calmed down for a time.

Richard didn't do anything, but Lisa Kent did. She was a girl who fell crazy in love with Sinatra, to a point where she pestered him so much that he once had her thrown out of his house on Beaumont Drive. It was Lisa who got word to Frank that I had a husband who was a bad loser. Friends told me later that Frank wasn't looking for trouble so he dropped me. I put a few calls through to him at the studio, but I never got past his secretary.

* * *

I never saw Sinatra again. But as fate would have it, our paths would cross again in 1969 when I shared a cell in Sybil Brand Institute with Susan Atkins, one of the Manson Family cold-blooded killers who told me about her involvement in the Sharon Tate killings and their plans to murder Frank Sinatra along with other famous celebrities. She didn't know that she was talking to a girl who had slept with Frank and cared deeply about him.

I have never doubted that I was placed in that cell at that particular moment by a Higher Power for the purpose of saving the life of someone who had been very special in my life - the great Mr. Sinatra.

And to Regina Harris, who had opened the door so that I might have that second time around with Frank, I owe a special thanks.

Chapter Five

I recall another visit to Philadelphia when I spent two weeks in a suite at the Warwick. The Milwaukee Braves baseball team were playing a series with the Phillies and also staying at the Warwick.

On this particular afternoon, Joe had dropped the boys off and I met them in the lobby which was packed with members of the Milwaukee team. And as we walked among them with my boys, my little son Dennis was open-mouthed in awe as he recognized one player after another. He loved baseball.

We were in the elevator when a good looking gentleman got on with us and started a conversation with Dennis about baseball that ended when we reached my floor. By the time we got to my suite the phone was ringing. It was the friendly man from the elevator who introduced himself as Johnny Logan, who was a player with the Braves. He thought that Dennis would like to meet some of the other members of the team.

I asked Dennis about it and he was ecstatic. I told Mr. Logan so and five minutes later he appeared and took little Dennis to the lobby, where not only did he meet all the players, but they also signed a baseball for him. When Dennis came back to our suite he was ten feet off the ground. It was then that Johnny Logan asked if I would have dinner with him and I accepted, not knowing that he was married and that his wife was going into labor that very night.

It was during dinner that he decided to mention his wife, after excusing himself a number of times and going to use the phone. He then also told me that she was in labor at that very moment!

This was an astounding piece of information that really pissed me off. I was so angry I could spit. I'd heard about the low-down, crummy things that some men were capable of but this was the absolute lowest, the very bottom of the barrel and I decided to teach him a lesson.

So I went along as Johnny Logan, America's Mister Super Clean, our number one ballplayer, began turning on the charm, pulling out all the stops in his plan to go to bed with another woman while his wife was going through the most indescribable pain of giving birth to his baby.

I didn't know Mrs. Johnny Logan, but I was definitely on her side and I was going to show this bum-of-a-husband a thing or two, and when he went into his romantic mode and said that he was very much attracted to me and wanted to sleep with me, I played along with him and let him think that it was a "done deal."

But the night was young and I suggested that we stop at a very private club, the RDA, where the who's who of Philly and elsewhere could be found. But Johnny was so elated that I had agreed to a night of "fun and games" that he called a motel and made reservations.

We took a cab to the club where the doorman recognized me, and of course Johnny, and we were immediately given the royal treatment. We were given the best booth in the place and Johnny couldn't "buy" a drink.

The music was hot and heavy and Johnny asked me to dance, and when we got to the floor and I put my arm around him I was truly tempted. His body was firm and hard with beautiful muscles - a truly athletic body.

From the very beginning I thought that he was one real hunk of man, absolutely gorgeous and I was greatly attracted to him, but in spite of all that, when I realized that at that moment his wife was suffering through labor pains, I was completely turned off.

We were at the club for about an hour when he began to show signs of expectation for our night of ecstasy. He was also getting anxious to leave. The moment of truth had arrived. I excused myself, saying I had to go to the Powder Room and left him at the table with several male admirers.

But instead of going to the Powder Room, I went through the kitchen and out a back door to the street where I hailed a cab and went back to the hotel. I later heard that when Johnny got back to the hotel he was caught by one of the coaches and heavily fined for "breaking curfew." Not only did he not get lucky with me but it cost him, too.

He called me a number of times after that and I did talk to him and he even called me when he came to Los Angeles and was staying at the Town House on Wilshire Boulevard. But we never did get together and many years later I met Howie Goss, a former teammate and roommate of Johnny's when they played for the Pittsburgh Pirates, and he told me, "I heard all about you." Johnny had told him about the "disappearing brunette" and the heavy fine so I guess he never did forget me - or I him.

Chapter Six

Richard and I, now comfortably settled in Beverly Hills, went into the party girl business with a bang and we cleaned up from the start. Richard found the idea a helluva lot more preferable to working.

I used to follow up on old contacts and take my chances in classy cocktail lounges like the Beverly Hills Polo Lounge, but too often a promising prospect would screech to a halt when the man I had cornered asked if I had a girlfriend.

Besides, there are a lot of places you just can't go into alone, no matter how gutsy you are. And, finally, I had to come to the inescapable conclusion that two girls could easily bring in twice as much as one. So we found Lisa.

I asked Richard to find us some starry-eyed young chick from around the studios where a lot of girls were giving it away for a $22 job on the set. Hell, we could offer an awful lot more, like a nice house, and too, she wouldn't have to screw if she didn't feel like it.

Richard argued, saying that he didn't have the time to be playing footsie with some dumb broads. I don't think he realized the manly duties involved in keeping a girl interested. It took some convincing and he finally agreed to look around.

He spent a lot of time in a restaurant he owned in the suburbs, and girls always hung around the place flirting with him. One day he found a girl who needed a lot of improvement but was kind of cute.

First we decided to tell her that Richard and I were still married but separated and considering a divorce. He took her to Salem's, a very nice place and snowed her from the start.

He had been coming on to her with the standard approach she wanted to model, and yes, he could probably help. I then showed up in my best clothes, perfumed and cool.

This girl was such a hayseed, it was unbelievable. She had on a little lavender sweater and skirt with a plastic flower pinned near her left breast. Her English was abominable, and because she spoke so softly, you had to lean so close to her that you saw her teeth needed fixing. She bit her nails and her badly applied make-up emphasized her small eyes.

But she was the perfect subject. She lived at her mother's with her little boy from a broken marriage, and it was a hassle she hated. Clearly she was extroverted because she had worked at dance studios, which no bashful girl would do. And she was obviously interested enough in Richard to want to keep after him.

We moved in on Lisa slowly but completely. There was no way we wouldn't sew her up. I dropped a few names like Sinatra's, and tried to be as sisterly and motherly as I could, feeding her lines like: "Why don't you move in? If you're really sincere about modeling and film work..." and "Gee, I've got this extra bedroom and I am sort of lonesome... I mean just until you get it together." Easy but never forceful.

From then on it was up to Richard. He took her around Hollywood and turned on all his gentlemanly Lopez charm. She told him she couldn't believe someone like me would help her. Oh sure, Richard said, Virginia would love it. And he added that it wouldn't be a bad idea since Lisa said her ex-husband and mother were bugging her all the time.

The first thing I did was hustle her into Gene Shacove, a high class hairdresser in Beverly Hills where you had to step over June Allyson and Marie McDonald to get a seat. Lisa watched the celebrities there and her eyes were bugging out.

Gene was trying to date me and was a pretty good friend, so he made a special fuss over Lisa. I told her I'd pick up the tab until she could pay me back. You must always be careful of giving away something for free because people get suspicious. And I had to use a little diplomacy, telling her that her hair color, which was a mousy shade of swamp water, wouldn't come across well in photographs.

By the time Gene and his make-up artist finished with Lisa, she was literally someone else, with tawny sun-streaked hair, peach-glow complexion and round innocent eyes. And she was hooked cold.

Richard went with her to meet her parents and get her clothes. She said she was moving in with an actress who would help her find work. As usual Richard made a good impression on the parents, reflecting the image of a businessman, a nice fellow helping out. His line of patter was magnificent. There was no one that good... except maybe me.

We still took it easy because you never drop something like this on a girl too quickly. She got settled in her room, with her own bathroom, and I picked out Lisa Palmer as her name. Her real name was something uncool, and - take my advice - you shouldn't use your own name for this business, anyway.

I figured about three or four outfits would get her going, so we invested another $1,000 on her, after the hairdo and make-up. If she was going out with me, she had to look good. That is the key: anyone can go anywhere if they look like they belong there. If they're a misfit, forget it.

Pretty soon, it was time to start earning some return on our investment. A wild oil promoter we called Harry the Hat lived across the street and used to throw tremendous parties at the Mocambo between 5 and 8, just before the big shows started.

He always had big money oilmen flying in from all over, as well as a roomful of top starlets and other charming young things. I was one of his favorites, so one week I took Lisa.

Often at Harry's parties guys would ask you out for dinner afterward. I told Lisa if anyone suggested it, we should go because they might slip in $300 or $400. She couldn't believe men would pay if you didn't put out, but she went along on my assurance that it was simple.

After all, if a man is attracted to you, you just give him the attention and affection he wants. What other way can he show his gratitude? You're a poor struggling - and if you can manage it - virtuous girl, and he plays the white knight in shining armor. He helps out with the bills while you're trying to further your career.

All you have to do is make him believe that something else is coming, whether it is or not. That way you're totally in control. Why become a beat-up whore when the guy will happily pay more if you don't go to bed with him?

Anyone good at this approach can tell what sort of story a man will buy, and how to get into it. First you drop a few broad hints, and if he picks up on them, you get more specific. If he lets the hints go right over his head, it's time for a graceful exit.

The longest strictly vertical relationship I can remember was with Walter the Roach. It never got beyond the hand-holding stage, but it brought me a fortune.

Poor Walter. I met him through girls who had already milked him, and there were an awful lot of those. He carried his generosity to a ridiculous extreme. I don't know where he got all his money, but he must have had plenty. Walter was really creepy, but for some reason he considered himself a real lady killer.

Before I knew him, he used to get loaded and call over four or five girls at a time, paying them hundreds of dollars each just to hang around and keep him company. The drunker he got the more girls he rounded up and the more he gave them, to the point where he sometimes passed around blank checks.

A few girls would be timid in cases like that, afraid of overdoing it, but others would find out exactly how much he had in his checking account and then clean him out.

Sure enough, two fellows from Chicago invited us out. I knew they were loaded simply because they were at Harry's party. No one who wasn't well heeled got into that crowd.

We ended up at the Polo Lounge in the Beverly Hills Hotel, where they conveniently had a suite upstairs. When they eventually asked us up, I started to go but hesitated and went into a star performance for Lisa's benefit.

"Well no... I have to get up early to shoot some pictures... You see, I'm trying desperately to get my university degree and I'm modeling to pay for it. I just have to make something of myself. And it's really tough, see, because my mother has been living with me - in failing health - since my poor father passed on. And modeling is so rough because guys always try to take advantage of you. The bills keep mounting up and it's really a vicious circle because you have to dress properly, live in a good area, maintain respectability... you understand."

Now, number one, the guy always wants to get in your pants, especially with a few drinks in him. He's heard your pitch before, but he really doesn't care, since he knows damn well that if you don't come through this time he'll get you on the second. What he doesn't know is that there is no second time.

All I did was play out a little twenty-minute routine and my guy said, "Here, honey, here's some cab fare," and handed me $300. And all Lisa did was look like she was going to faint, and her guy says, "Here, honey, so you'll have some cab fare too…" and handed her $150.

She was aghast. A good party, tremendous dinner with Mel Tormé performing, and all at one of the finest places in Beverly Hills, and she's getting paid for it. That was nothing I told her. I could have laid it on and gotten three times that much, but there could have been some payback.

I told Lisa how easy it was - just trot out a sick kid, or a grandmother with a heart murmur, anything, but just believe it. Lisa had that baby-girl innocence, like she couldn't lie if she wanted, and the technique was beautiful with her.

Once we had her in with us, we had to nail her down solidly. That depended mainly on Richard. He and I were perfect - never any indication that we were anything more than friends. No touching, no soft words, no glances. After a while she started complaining to me that Richard wouldn't make a pass at her. What was wrong? I spoke to him and told him he'd better make his move.

He dragged out the vibrators and the amyl nitrate, and gave her a jump that loosened her toenails. Later, Richard took her aside and said that I was giving him money to hold since I spent it like water. She knew that was true. I had done that, Richard said, because we were old friends and I trusted him.

He actually made her insist that he do the same for her. He refused a few times and she was furious. Wasn't her money as good as mine, she demanded to know. So he obliged her.

Lisa held on with us for two years. Finally Richard started kicking her around too much. He would hardly sleep with her. When he did, about once a month, she'd be dancing around in heaven for the next three days, happily waiting for the next month.

Actually Richard couldn't stand her because she chased him so much, and each session was so splendid because he was always looking for something unusual to pull off so he could have an orgasm.

He kept her around simply by bullshit and promises. You name it, he said it. Part of it was his father image and part of it was his unavailability. But eventually he started abusing her too much.

One day she went to visit her mother and son and never came back. A month later she married some guy working for the phone company who she knew before Richard came into the picture.

She didn't take any money; she just wanted out. After two years she took off with nothing. She had brought in about $100,000. She had never seen that much money in her life and spent it like there was no tomorrow. She bought closets full of clothes, a fine car and was very generous helping her mother.

Poor Lisa, everything she did was wrong. She scared Richard off by chasing him. No matter how much money she brought in, no matter how hard she tried, she was always wrong. But in the end she was smarter than me. It took her two years to get away from Richard's hold. It took me ten.

After Lisa left we needed another girl right away - our overhead was high and included leasing two houses and an apartment. We had a house in Malibu that was right off the Pacific Coast Highway that ran $850 a month in 1959 dollars which would likely be equal to several thousand in today's dollars.

We kept an apartment on Wilshire and Westwood in a building called the "Marie Antoinette" for which we paid $1,000 a month, and finally there was a house in Benedict Canyon.

When I spoke to Richard about another girl he gave me some more of his "I-don't-need-any-more-goddamned-bitches-around-here" line, but eventually he produced a Western Union teletype operator who turned into good old Kim.

Kim, when she first appeared had obvious possibilities. I had dark hair with large brown eyes, and we needed an opposite, since men usually like one type or the other. Kim was very German looking. She was a little lumpy around the hips but with a much better figure than Lisa. She had large blue eyes, slanted like a cat's, with a full mouth and a square jaw. Her teeth needed some attention and her hair was a mess.

We put her through the routine, from the classy restaurant to a session under Gene's scissors. She emerged as one of those cool blondes with sex just ready to boil up through the smooth surface. And Kim had plenty of other added features for bait.

One night I was having a lot of problems about different things, so I popped a few pills to get some sleep. I schemed so much I got headaches. Still do. Anyway, we kept separate apartments for appearances, and Richard happened to call that night.

I told him about the pills and he ranted on so long about them that they took effect, and I dropped off in mid-harangue, with the bottle stuck in the pocket of a jacket I had on. Kim happened to show up at his apartment while he was screaming about sonuvabitchin' pills and she saw a chance to save a life.

The two of them rushed over and managed to get through the chain latch on my front door. They found the pills and really freaked out. They took me to Richard's place, unconscious. When I awoke, Kim was on the bed, all concerned.

Richard, meanwhile, had her spellbound. I don't know what line he laid on her, but she decided to move in and give us a try. He had gotten some hot clothes, so he gave her a mink and a few dresses which she thought he had bought.

I took her to meet another oil tycoon friend who had a fabulous house with a pool where you could jump out of your living room chair and swim outside. For kicks he used to fill the pool with naked girls and watch them from a glassed-off room underneath, like in an aquarium. Anyway, he considered himself my testing ground, so he took Kim on a tour of the house that ended in the bedroom.

His verdict was that she had a fine bust, and wasn't too bad, but she had a big ass. That meant she went on an immediate diet. He tried to give me some money, but I told him it went to her. I didn't want to be a madam. I suppose I was, but not really.

He gave her $200. I was discouraged, since he was good for $300 or $400 if he was really pleased, but Kim couldn't believe it. She had to sweat her ass off on the swing shift for two weeks to earn that. And she considered screwing no work at all.

Western Union had lost her for good.

I took her to Big Jim Houston, another of my testers, and he introduced her to a lot of important people, including some of the famous astronauts.

Kim stayed four years and was really the only girl I trusted.

She picked up tricks as fast as we could teach them, and before long she was inventing her own. We were a tremendous team, and we liked each other.

Pretty soon we had people coming in from Spain, England, Mexico... more than we could possibly handle. We traveled the country together, absolutely cleaning up. Finally, we decided to get a third girl, whether Richard wanted one or not. He didn't complain bitterly. But I think he just wanted it clear that in case things screwed up, he could say it wasn't his friggin' idea.

So we changed residences and names - I became Romney Ames and Kim went from an earlier name to Kim Van Kory and we took on Caroline.

I met Caroline when I was with a United States Air Force General. She had been a registered nurse, but got fed up with doctors chasing her for a free ride. She had done a little screwing on the side for money and liked it.

Caroline was tall, blonde and blue-eyed. And she was a Texan, so I figured she might not like Mexicans. However that turned out not to be the case. Caroline was snowed by the house and the operation and went to work.

With Caroline, we really had to get organized. She loved her screwing with or without money, and it was hell lining her up for dates. She would sail out by 7 pm, promising to be back by 10. Someone would phone, and I would make an 11 o'clock appointment for her. And then she'd show up, broke and screwed out at 3 am.

That had to stop fast. I could see what was coming with the other girls, too. Most of them wanted to do a little screwing for cash and keep a boyfriend or two on the side. That was out. It just didn't fit in with the system and was no way to make money.

So I worked out a master plan and Richard loved it.

All of us would pool everything we earned and stick it into a common pot for six months. We would only take out living expenses... money for clothes and perfume and the hairdresser and stuff. At the end we would split it three ways.

I waited until Caroline had blown all her money to spring the plan on her. Wouldn't it be better, I asked her, to keep your money in some safe place, like Richard's back pocket instead of pissing it away as fast as it comes in?

I told her after six months she could go back to Texas or buy a mink farm or stick around and make more money. All she had to do was follow the rules.

It turned out to be a great system, and we worked it like a corporation - unregistered, of course. As each new girl came in, we signed her up for six months at a time. That way we all worked as a team. If one girl made money, everyone benefited. There was no jealousy. If she farted around, we all jumped on her.

Each girl got the money she earned and it was up to her to hand it over to Richard.

At first, I sincerely meant for the plan to work, they deserved to make as much as me. But in practice, it made Richard and me a fortune. Girls who left before six months got nothing. And there were a hell of a lot of girls who took off after a few months. They just couldn't hack the discipline, or they wanted some corny boyfriend or something, and they just went.

Eventually I decided that if they were that dumb, somebody was going to screw them out of their money anyway, so it might as well go to a good cause - us.

Things got interesting around the place with our fourth girl, a terribly cute little Mexican chick with a bad complexion but a knock-out style. We called her Vicky. She liked to drink but she couldn't hold it, and she got awfully sloppy sometimes. She also liked to spend too much time with customers and Richard's vibrators.

Vicky was a nympho if I ever saw one. Her mother was a hooker, and for a while they were a mother-daughter team. Vicky was available any time of the night, morning or day. She'd come home from a date, gasping and walking slightly sideways, and the phone would ring and she'd be off again, like Native Dancer after the Derby Stakes.

I know it wasn't for money. Vicky would just pack her vibrator and a can of whipped cream and gallop out grinning from ear to ear. The whipped cream because she was always hoping to get a guy who would do her all up like a hot fudge sundae and eat it all off.

She was so hot that I always worried that some guy might wind up with a heart attack - and how could we explain that? A few guys complained that she was too much. It was done in a joking way, but they wouldn't come back. They couldn't handle it.

Most people have the idea that if you really put out and do everything - you'll have guys all over the place. Actually the reverse is true. If men can't come up to your standard, they feel inadequate. You de-ball them, in a sense. Vicky took away their masculinity. She was always the aggressor and that's a very, very bad thing for a woman to be.

61

By the time Vicky showed up, Richard was having some real problems with his masculine obligations. Only some things turned him on, and he hated to be pressured.

We also knew that to hold on to these girls he would have to service them. They were getting plenty on the job, but they had to feel like they could just relax and be with a man they liked.

He was a father-confessor, too, and listened to all their stories about some of the weirdos and some of the far-out bedroom games they were asking for. The girls asked his advice on make-up and clothes; it was as though he was everybody's husband.

Kim, particularly, was insanely hot to ball Richard but he just wasn't having any and she wouldn't give up. She tried everything. And when Vicky came, she figured out a great system.

Vicky was as aggressive as hell with Richard and drove him straight up a wall. He would bring her to orgasm as often as eight times, but she would still be trying for one more time. Caroline, too, was happiest when Richard gave her a ride.

It was Kim who realized that Richard loved his sex in groups and was susceptible to a mass sneak attack, and two or three times a week after everyone came back from dates, she staged some beauties.

Kim, Caroline and Vicky would go in and start undressing Richard, then they would all splash into our gigantic Roman tub after which the four of them would roll into bed for a round-robin with everyone doing everything to everybody.

Richard had a habit of continually comparing the girls to me, and it would send some of them into fits. He would ask Kim to get me to fix her make-up and she would explode: "Goddamnit, haven't I got any taste?" That just made Richard clobber her. But Kim was a good friend, and she and the other girls acknowledged me as the den mother.

He would just flop down anywhere when he was tired, so every girl in the house had a chance at him. I accepted the fact early on that there was no way that Richard and I could play the happily married couple and keep the other girls around.

Despite his occasional lapses, Richard's screwing was what kept everyone in line. It was exactly like Charles Manson without the violence. I think that's why I understood the Manson Family so well when Susan Atkins began laying it out for me. I had been through the whole thing before... for years.

Vicky got to be too much for Richard to handle and he was frantic to get her out. Finally she had a screaming fistfight with Kim in the kitchen, after about three months with us, and he threw her out.

Caroline left early, too. But we had a steady supply of new ones. Big Jim sent us a lot of girls. One lasted about a week until Richard picked up that she was a hype, druggie and she was out on her ass that morning.

Sherry was probably the oddest one we had. Richard had more in the boob department than she had, and she had legs like a football player. Her chin not only receded, it never existed.

She had great big, pretty blue eyes and gorgeous red hair, but she dressed like a typical whore. Just outrageous. She went for satiny, brocady, slinky dresses, slit up the side, and though she was the titless wonder of the world, cut low. And she would top this with imitation fur. But even a girl like that can make money.

Sherry was convinced that she had it all together, and I never really completely made her over. One reason is that she was the only girl who really didn't go wild for Richard. She would jump into the groupies and work away with the best of them, but she wasn't as turned on to him as the others. And she was the one girl whose money we never got.

She lasted a month under our system, but then she came to me and asked if she could keep on living with us while working on her own, just paying expenses. By then we were making so much money it really didn't matter. She helped us out because often her dates would have friends who needed servicing. Sherry didn't stay long, but she was one of the few who left on good terms.

One thing Richard did with every girl who moved out was to put the fear of God in her. He said that if she ever mentioned his name and blew the whistle, or let any of our dates know he existed, he'd ram a gun up her ass and blow her mouth out. And he was convincing. They had seen him throwing shit fits and they believed him. I knew all along that it was just talk. He was sheer pussy. But he talked well.

So Vicky and Caroline were gone, and Sherry was leaving. It was back to Kim and me. But we had a home in Malibu, an apartment in Westwood and a house in Benedict Canyon.

By that time, picking up new talent was nothing, and we had no worries at all.

* * *

I've always considered it very unladylike to take your own pants off. And that's how we ran our business. Like ladies.

The trick was simply class. We had a house right out of *Architectural Digest* with dressing tables groaning under all the bottles of Jasmine and Joy and mounds of jewelry. Each of us would stay at the hairdresser's for entire afternoons, spending more in a day than most call girl types, even happy ones, could earn in nights of hustling.

We had some fabulous houses, but the best was one we found after turning down the place on Cielo Drive that Roman Polanski and Sharon Tate eventually rented. I shudder to think of how close we came to renting that house - it was magnificent, set back by itself with split-rail fences and trees. I can't even remember why we didn't take it.

But we did settle on a tremendous ranchy place on Cherokee Lane, right over Coldwater Canyon, in a neighborhood where houses were worth up to a half-million and selling today for many times that much.

It had a gigantic living room that looked over the Olympic-sized pool. A fireplace ran along an entire wall, open to the living room on one side and the den on the other. There were lots of bedrooms, each with its own bath, all around the house. Some even had a mossy interior fountain between the entrance and the walkway to the patio.

The house sprawled all over the lawn, behind a little brook crossed by a wooden bridge. Cherokee Lane was hardly ever used, and our place was far up a private road. Thick trees on Ward Bond's personal mountain shielded it from behind. A dozen people could walk around the pool nude and nobody would notice - and that was what we were after.

Also, it was seven minutes from the Beverly Wilshire Hotel and four minutes from either Frank Sinatra or Marlon Brando, depending upon which way you went.

We entertained there just like we were a bunch of girls, maybe a little hornier than most, who enjoyed cooking dinner for guests. And even though we were piling up money like crazy, we really did have a lot of fun. I mean, partying isn't always work, even if you get paid for it.

After dates were arranged, men would drive up, and I'd greet them at the door like a loving wife. It took hours of planning. Did they like long hostess gowns or casual shorts? Were they allergic to fresh petunias or Japanese incense? What kind of music did they want on the stereo? It took real talent figuring out that sort of stuff beforehand without asking. But they paid for it.

It was terribly important that the atmosphere be perfect. You couldn't have a man walking into a cold house - lights had to be right, the fire burned down far enough, everything spotless. I was an antique nut, and the place really looked great. We had our own furniture, good stuff in shades of gold and white. The carpeting was thick and furry.

The big difference between our operation and those whorehouses run by women who consider themselves big-deal madams is that we entertained men as though we liked them. Hookers are clock watchers, and that's why they never make any big money.

On a typical evening, maybe three or four guys would come over about cocktail time. The bar was always stocked with Grant's 12-Year-Old Scotch Whisky, Ambassador, Jack Daniel's... none of this Old Crow or Old Shit. We'd light a fire inside and maybe barbecue steaks on the patio, with a big green salad and fresh strawberries. Later we would dance and usually go for a swim, talking and laughing and teasing.

Then, if everything went well and no one got obnoxious, couples would start disappearing unobtrusively into the bedrooms. If it was a wild crowd, everyone would disappear very obtrusively into the bedroom with the adjoining Roman bath big enough for nine.

Orgies were available upon request, but the girls always knew beforehand what was coming.

Money was never discussed. We had a lot of guys who came over and never knew a dime had changed hands. They were usually business contacts brought over by regulars who were trying to snow them. Sometimes the "host" would catch me in the kitchen and say, "Please, let me help pay for the champagne." I'd say, "Oh, don't be silly." Then I'd wait a few tactful seconds and accept a few thousand dollars.

Payments varied, since you can always get more if you don't mention a figure. Sometimes a man would ask what the tab was for the steaks, and if it was good beef I'd say something like $1,200.

I would always give the girls a few hundred each and keep the rest. After all, it was my party and my contacts. But if the girls were in our little corporation, of course, they'd get an even split. I gave them the money, and then later each would casually drop the full amount into our common pot. It was important to make them feel they were voluntarily taking part in the sharing arrangement. Of course I'd hate to be the one to try holding out on old Richard.

One strict rule we never broke was that no one spent the night. For one thing, where were we going to put poor Richard? And for another, it was too much of a problem to wake up with some guy hoping he would get lucky again. We were also firm about men drinking too much. If someone got too plastered, we would point him down the hill and say a polite but final goodnight.

Once in a rare while you'd get a nickel-and-dime guy who wanted a signed and witnessed contract before setting foot inside the door. They usually ate and drank the most, stayed the longest and tried to bargain. Now I would just not haggle, and I wouldn't discuss money at all, so they were difficult for me to handle.

But nine times out of ten, this type of guy would show up and ask bluntly what he was going to get and how much it was going to cost him. "Supposing I want to stay longer, what's the deal...?" He'd also sometimes ask, "Is a blowjob extra...?" Wow.

Kim always took charge in those cases. She could do that hooker stuff and she loved to hassle the bargain basement types. It was beautiful, if embarrassing to watch her operate. "Now look, baby, are you interested or aren't you? Like I can be busy someplace else. It's a couple of hundred if you want to stay, and we'll see that you have a good time. But I think you'd better give it to me up front."

I fought with her over that approach, and she eventually slipped into a pretty hard life from it, but she could argue with the nickel-and-dime guys toe-to-toe and crack up over it later.

Most men who came over weren't interested only in sex. For them, it was just like they had made a date with a starlet or model who liked them and showed them a good time. And the food was good.

If we went to a hotel, or to someone's home, it was about the same approach. We wouldn't stand for any unlady-like action - just good wholesome partying around. Even Richard, outrageous as he was, remained firm on that point. He told all the girls that if anyone got unreasonable or sloppy drunk, they should put on their clothes and split without taking a penny.

Our biggest moment was always the cocktail hour. A few of us would go down to the Polo Lounge or the Luau or someplace for a few drinks. It was invaluable for finding people who had lost our number or for making new contacts. After a while, when we were seen with the right people, we got to know maître d's and hotel people who could put us in touch with rich, lonely men.

We had one tremendous contact at a hotel. Occasionally men would ask him discreetly if he knew a warm and unattached redhead, or a brunette with big boobs, or an Eskimo chick with a cold nose, and he always called us.

He had to use a payphone and handle things very carefully because he might not only lose his job but also land in jail on a felony. The next morning he would drop by and pick up twenty percent of whatever we got. We were scrupulously honest with him. Guys like that were worth a fortune to us, and we treated them right. Often our contacts would refuse money, but we never failed to deliver a small but expensive gift.

Once, after some big orgy arranged by some politicians who had bought protection, an assistant manager started eyeing me. I began talking to him because I figured what the hell, guys like this can be a lot of help. If he puts you on to somebody, it has to be good. He's not going to jeopardize his position. I found it a really good idea to cultivate managers and executives of the better hotels, even if only as friends.

But I never said anything more than hello to the help. For guys like the parking lot boy, the doorman, the bell captain, just a quick nod on the way past. They will often try to start a conversation because if they see you around with a lot of different men, they pick up on it. And, of course, they want some of the action. But they don't usually know what they're doing and they can get themselves arrested. And you with them.

Never, not once, were we hassled by the police. It was a question of looking like ladies and acting like we belonged, and going exclusively to the very best places. There were cheaper hotels where hookers hung out hoping for a $25 or $50 score, and those places were crawling with vice-squad creeps.

You can always tell a prostitute, anyway, not only by the way she dresses. She has that hungry, desperate look, eyeing everyone who walks by. By being selective, we led a completely different kind of life. We made a hell of a lot more money for a lot less work.

When we partied, it was usually fun and relaxed and classy. We practically never worried about venereal disease or later hassles from former customers because our contacts were men who avoided stuff like that like cholera. If you just pick some guy up at random, even somebody with his hair combed and his tie knotted, you're asking for it.

The key to the whole operation, of course, was the telephone. It's more important than your car, your clothes, anything but your snatch. Without it you're dead. We had at least three phones and an answering service. That's how I kept the girls in line when they had ideas about setting up some action on the side.

I answered the phones myself, and if I wasn't there, the answering service took all calls. There was a code for our operators which only Kim and I knew. And no one was allowed to hang on the phone blabbering to a bunch of dumb friends. Our monthly phone bill was always deep in three and four figures, but the phones were our lifeline.

A lot of our action came through guys like Big Jim. Not that there were many like Big Jim - who weighed 200 pounds, was 6 feet 3 inches tall, and lifted weights at age 72. He never drank coffee or booze, and he wouldn't smoke. He just fucked.

He retired at 24 to make millions in land, cards and other things I never understood. He came to California and immediately began moving in top show business and money circles.

He once noted, humbly, his I.Q. was in the genius category and he used to talk about his World War II secret-agent days. But anyway, he was wild. Jim's thing was organizing orgies and kinky pair-offs. He never made any of the money. He just liked grateful friends and screwing for free. Horny guys called him up from all over the United States and flew in for his parties. He was so successful the cops were after him for procuring.

Jim's specialties were the Pink Pal and the Green Monster. They were ten-inch dildos, as thick as German knackwurst and dyed in rich colors, which he would spring on unsuspecting young things to inevitable roars of laughter. And he kept a closetful of vibrators, the good kind like the beauty salons used with wires that fit over the back of the hand.

Orgies were really Jim's forte. He was the world's best icebreaker. People would just be sitting around and he could talk anyone's clothes off. He'd just start talking corny but persuasive, "Let's see your goodies... Those legs, just like a Vargas girl... Ah, it should be revered like the Virgin Mary..." He sort of put you in a corner, on stage, where you couldn't say no. It worked.

Richard and I were clearing quite a bit of money when our Hollywood Screw System got going. I can't remember what we took in altogether, but we went through a hell of a lot of Dom Pérignon champagne, Ma Griffe and fancy underwear.

I was given more expensive clothes than I could wear in a decade, but we had to buy a few things for Richard... If we had bothered to save or invest, we could probably be earning more than some of the guys who spent money on us.

Really, cash was nothing. If we needed a Cadillac, we handed the car dealer the money and drove away.

And it was a great life. We went to sleep at about four or five in the morning and stayed in bed until noon. We hardly ever cooked, except for guests, and we did more partying in a month than some people do in a lifetime. I was sleeping with men that other girls couldn't get autographs from. It was exactly what I had dreamed about when I left Philadelphia, and it was fantastic.

All the job amounted to was getting very good at living well and pampering yourself. Buying nice things wasn't a luxury, it was a business expense. We bought the most expensive perfume by the pint and never considered trading down to Danish caviar.

The hours we spent in the beauty salon were great for meeting other girls with contacts and for finding out who was in town, but the beauticians kept us looking pretty good. You couldn't find a chipped nail or a split end on any one of us for years at a time.

And I was my own boss, so if things were dull, I could move the whole operation to the Bahamas or Costa Brava. For a girl who enjoyed a good meal and a good screwing, it was the ideal life.

But sometimes it was a hassle. Richard could get unbelievably impossible, and the pressure was sometimes too much to handle. I had a whole range of escapes. For minor things, I simply freaked out on pills... anything, but usually sleeping pills since they made me high before knocking me out. Supply was no problem at all. I could call up my doctor at night and talk him into prescribing me things over the phone.

Occasionally I'd just check into a hospital. That was just as easy. First I'd take a few drinks and then pop some pills that didn't mix with booze, after which I'd call my doctor and feed him some long story about a pain somewhere. Most doctors can't be bothered to go out on night house calls, so they'll just call and have you admitted sight unseen until morning. By the next morning the pills would have worn off, but they give you so much medication when you're admitted, it keeps you off balance for another three days. By then, I would be generally ready to go home.

Other times I would storm off and hide, calling the answering service and cutting off the phones so no one could make a nickel until I came back. I could hide out at a gay friend's place.

Richard had a very short fuse. He would go wild when I took pills, but he blew up at almost anything. And he would have delayed reaction fits, sometimes bringing up things that happened months, even years, earlier and yelling about them as if they happened minutes before.

I remember once when the maid was off, I was sweeping the floor, and he grabbed the broom to show me how to do it. Short sweeps, he said, not long ones. I remarked that was kind of silly, and he exploded: "You dumb motherfucker..." It went on for hours.

Once I said something insignificant while he was putting on his shoe, and he threw it at me. The bastard had good aim, too. Another time I overcooked a chicken and he threw the pot at me. He would drop the argument and then hours later start all over again.

He had one hang-up that caused terrible problems. He hated the word "wife" and never let me act like one. He wouldn't even call me by my first name. I had always wanted a husband and a home, and it was a fight. My two sons were in Philadelphia, and although I could visit them, ours was hardly a home that they could come out to visit.

Once, on our anniversary, I gave him a cute card that said "To my husband" or something, and he went crazy. "You lame-brained piece of crap, you're just like all those shithead housewives, you want a fucking ring and every goddamned thing…"

But you would never know from one minute to the next how he would be. There was no middle of the road with Richard. He was either a charming, laughing, loving husband or a flaming prick.

One incident was a good example. He had been pestering me, not letting me sleep and storming off and on, about some idiotic thing. So I took a few pills to get some rest. He came in and found the bottle. Richard went absolutely raving berserk. He grabbed me by the hair and dragged me into the bathroom. I bounced around pretty hard on the marble floor and he shoved my head into the toilet.

I was trying desperately to throw up, but he kept pushing me down into the toilet. First I tried to defend myself by blocking him, but with Richard you didn't do that. He always hit you where it wouldn't show, usually between the bust and the stomach. When you get hit there, you go down fast. Which I did.

I crashed onto the tile face first and he hit me again three times. I kept trying to get up, but each time I fell. Later I found out I had a few fractures, a hematoma in the left eye and a crack in the bridge of my nose.

Finally he cooled down and took me back to the bed. By then my face was swelling terribly, and he had suddenly changed completely. He was cool and efficient, applying ice and saying gentle things. He was my Jekyll and Hyde.

I think it was mainly due to the fact that Richard always faced strong-willed women in his family. His mother was very forceful, and he had seen his father completely dominated and he was striking back unconsciously. That's what my professional friends said. He couldn't stand strong women and had to react, but at times he hated himself for doing it.

The whole scene was hard on Richard. While he himself had missed out on a career and wanted to create something through me, he had to pull me back at the same time because he feared I would leave him.

But it was real hell when he got going. He was worse than a half-dozen cops because they take a break. By the time I encountered the police, I was ready for anything because I had had ten years of first class training.

Richard was the same lovable shithead to the other girls, and some-times our place was a regular nuthouse. Kim, especially, took an enor-mous amount of crap because she was so hot for him.

Once when I left Richard, in 1961, he knocked up Kim. I came back when she was a few months pregnant, and she stayed with us. At first I wasn't too happy about it, but I love children, and I figured it would be the baby I couldn't have. Also, I thought for Richard that eve-ry man ought to have a son.

Kim, out of commission for the screw system, took charge of our little dog kennel and looked after our Chihuahuas, Yorkies and Dober-mans while she carried her baby.

Richard, being the prick that he was, wanted Kim to blame the baby on a well-known Hollywood actor/producer. She knew it wasn't his - she hadn't been seeing him when she got pregnant and there was no doubt it was Richard's - and she wasn't having any part of it. But Rich-ard made her life so miserable, she finally called and told him over the phone that he was about to be a father. Richard had counted on five or ten thousand out of it.

Instead, the actor/producer got furious and told her to piss off. An-other girl had just pulled that on him. Kim was relieved at his reaction, but Richard threw a classic Lopez fit.

Kim had a cute little boy. Richard took the boy to his mother's on a promise it was only a temporary arrangement, and Kim could see him whenever she wanted. Naturally he had no intention of keeping his word. Every time Kim brought up the subject, Richard came up with a million reasons why it wasn't the right time.

The boy grew up without knowing who his mother was, and it broke Kim's heart.

Most of the girls had thinner skins than Kim or me, and Richard usually ended up scaring them off. The turnover was pretty high and, although it made us richer because of our corporation system, it took a constant round of training and grooming of new girls.

At one point, during a changing of the guard, I decided it was time to find a really super-knockout broad. We were doing a tremendous business with what we had, and I thought some solid talent would put us out of sight. By then we knew an awful lot of people, so I quietly put the word out. And a friend of mine who worked for an exclusive dress designing company told me he knew a gorgeous redhead with a forty-inch bust, a twenty-one inch waist and great legs.

She called me up and, with this beautiful Marilyn Monroe voice, made an appointment. Her name was Laura and I thought that if she looked a quarter as good as she sounded, she had to be fabulous.

Laura rolled up in a pink Cadillac convertible driven by a dark, curly haired kid of about nineteen. She was fantastic, absolutely magnificent... flawless chiseled features and eyes like a Keane painting. I didn't like her dress much, but she had a body Raquel Welch couldn't touch. She was eighteen.

"Romney," she said, "I'd like you to meet my husband.

"Fuck," I said to myself, "a husband."

Laura said about twenty words after that, and then he did all the talking. It was funny as hell. He was trying to talk me into coming with them. He told me about their big home, and how she never took less than $500 or $600.

Apparently he was a musician with a struggling group and she gave him $300 to $400 a day to get it going. I was really cracking up listening to this little creep with his sales pitch.

So we set up a business deal. Laura didn't know I had a house, a husband, or an operation far bigger than hers. I introduced her to Kim and right away I saw a problem. Kim knew that men would take one look at Laura, and Kim wouldn't exist. She left us behind in every way. But I argued that was an asset for all of us.

Laura had a way with men that I have never seen since. She was soft, completely feminine and the greatest lay in the world. A total actress, with the groaning and the moaning and writhing and hanging on. The minute a man walked in the door she was holding his hand, talking in this baby girl voice and looking up with huge blue eyes. Wow, I figured this bitch has got to make a fortune.

We got to be friends quickly, and she opened up to me. She wasn't getting along with her husband, Nick. He blew the money she gave him, and he belted her around and wanted to hear the most intimate and intricate details of every sexual relationship she had. It was something she didn't like to discuss with him. He hit her when she didn't tell him, and he hit her when she did.

Nick used to hang around when she was entertaining and peek in the window or hide in the closet. If a call came at midnight he'd stuff her with speed and send her off. Then when she came home, he screwed her all night. The poor kid was getting about two and three hours of sleep a night, since he wanted to show her off to his musician friends in the mornings.

His furniture-magnate father had cut him off because he married a girl out of their religion, so he had to continue living in the style to which he was accustomed when he had his daddy's money. Laura came to me in tears one day and asked what she could do.

I told her I would help on one condition - she had to ditch Nick for good. I wasn't getting into any husband-wife beef, giving her my trade secrets and having her cut out. If I hid her, I knew I was going to have trouble with Nick. But I figured it was worth it.

Just before that, Laura, Kim and I had taken a penthouse for entertaining. I had just paid the first and last month's rent and had the telephone hooked up. Laura said she'd think about it all and let me know.

A week later she called, sobbing, and asked me to come get her. Nick had beaten her, and she was taking the baby and splitting. I told her somebody would pick her up in fifteen minutes - she knew nothing about Richard and didn't know we lived a few minutes down the hill from her.

Richard didn't mind the kid - we all had children - and he went to get her, diapers, bottles and all. She left a note for Nick saying she wouldn't be back ever.

Two hours later, Nick's on the phone: "Listen, she hadda have help, are you sure…?" Thirty minutes after that he was over quizzing the doorman at the penthouse. Kim and I drove damn near to Santa Barbara that night to shake him before going home to Richard.

Meanwhile Richard had explained the scene to Laura, and she was interested. We knew we couldn't give her only a few hundred dollars for action, she was high money. So we rented another house just for her, the baby and Richard - in case Nick picked up on us - and she was to lay low for three or four months.

To me it was an investment. We had already blown the rent and the phones on the penthouse and then there was the new home. We were into this new chick for maybe $7,000 already, so we thought we might as well keep her on ice, no dates or anything, until the heat was off.

After a while Nick eased up, and I started giving our new numbers to a few regulars. Laura felt she was mooching and insisted on making a few bucks. I introduced her to a Hollywood producer who went wild over her and immediately sent her to Estelle Harman, the best drama school in California, and wanted to put her under contract.

Laura was starting to waver at that point because she was still hung up on her husband. Richard had gotten her a divorce lawyer and was working on her himself as hard as he could.

But Kim and Richard were having some incredible scenes - just the usual battles, but badly timed. He chased her down the driveway and she tried to run him down with the car. He threw a shoe - I mean, some very bad things were coming down. We tried to keep it from Laura, but how quiet can such rumbles be? We were afraid she would think Richard was worse than Nick, which he had to be.

So Laura went off to court for the divorce case. Richard gave her the cab fare, and that was the last we saw of her.

She called at five the next morning to say she and Nick were back together again. She was crying, really upset at the trouble she had caused us. I liked her so much I didn't even care about the money we had blown on her. I told her to just do what she had to do. After all, what's $20,000?

And of course, she did exactly what I was afraid of in the first place, clever me. The last I heard, not too long after she left us, she was still with Nick and doing a fantastic business in Brentwood.

She had learned the routine from Richard and me and then did the same thing with her husband and a bunch of girls. They've bought a million dollar home, so I guess Laura's doing pretty well for herself.

It's nice to know that the Hollywood Screw System still works.

Chapter Seven

Even for someone who loved balling like I did, sex with a gargoyle could be a drag. So if I didn't feel moved, I would just keep my pants on and collect anyway.

Some men aren't even hot for sex - they just want pretty girls around them. Everyone, I think, figures that eventually he's going to get lucky. But it's amazing how much patience some men have.

Sometimes it's easier than others.

There was this Texan named Stanley who I had dated a few times. One day at lunch he asked me if I had a girlfriend, and he suggested the three of us have dinner that night. God knows what he had in mind, but since the girlfriend I picked was Kim, we never found out.

At the table he was coming on like a well-heeled but liberal thinking big cheese from the oil country. He got drunker and drunker and progressively louder and more obnoxious. He kept talking about all his money and how he loved to spend it.

Kim suddenly blurted out of the blue: "You know, you're just like some Jewish guys I know."

With her Geiger-counter eyeballs, Kim had seen the weak spot I had missed completely. Stanley was super sensitive about Jews. He was pretty loose about things in general, but he was a raving anti-Semite.

He turned the color of a maraschino cherry and sputtered for a full three minutes.

"What in the hell do you mean?" he gurgled, yanking out his checkbook. He scribbled out a check for a thousand dollars and handed it to Kim.

"That's just what I mean," she said airily, flipping the check back at him. "Cheap."

He thundered: "Well, how much do you want?" and Kim pushed it to the hilt. "Oh, hell, that's another thing those guys do, they haggle."

By then the veins in his neck were writhing around like rattle-snakes, and I was starting to get a little worried. But he tore up the old check and wrote a new one for $5,000.

With the check in hand, I decided we had better split before he changed his mind. Which he promptly did. He asked Kim if he could have it back.

"Brother, you are really a first class cheapskate," she said, eyeing him like she might a lizard on her Caesar salad. "One minute you give it and the next minute you want it back..."

That settled that, and we left.

The next morning at ten minutes after ten Stanley rang up, of course.

"Um, uh... you remember that check last night? Well, I was a little drunk, see, and uh, I'm not sure there's enough in that account to cover it..."

Oh, yes there was.

The bank opened at ten, and good old Kim was out there standing in line at 9:30. She even paid for the call to San Francisco to check on whether it would clear.

There was a tremendous groan over the phone and we didn't hear much from Stanley after that.

It was pretty clear we had reached the limit with him, so I simply passed his name and address, with a complete account of the story, to a gorgeous actress friend of mine from San Francisco. Over the next year she got about $40,000 from him, and on a few occasions she returned the favor.

* * *

On all my dates, I'd ball if I was in the mood but would put them off if I wasn't up for it. I mean, what the hell, I wasn't selling my body - I just offered a fighting chance for it at a good price.

I had my period more often than any girl in the United States. But there are a lot of ways out of that situation. One of my favorites was always, "But, but... it's not in my horoscope."

Girls who say they model can always say they have to wake up early, looking fresh, for a shooting session. And there's always the handy headache that wives across America can generally develop at a moment's notice.

77

It's the easiest thing in the world. As soon as a guy puts his arm around you, give him a sweet look, wait a few seconds, and say, "Oh, God, have you got an aspirin?"

Much of the time, though, sex didn't come up. Basically, there are two types of guys. Some are extremely generous and others need a stick of dynamite under them to dislodge a dollar from their wallets. I could tell after fifteen minutes of conversation what a man was like, and if he looked tight, I'd bow out. If he was generous, it was easy.

I know a girl who bought herself a thriving telephone answering service purely with money she got hanging around Walter the Roach. Another would get checks for $200 and change them into $1,200 before cashing them.

The next morning, Walter would moan and complain that girls were taking advantage of him - which, of course, they were - but then he would do it all over again.

You'd think Walter would learn, but it went on and on. He lived in a building owned by his sister-in-law, an ex-madam, which was famous for always being stuffed with call girls. Whenever he came back from a trip, girls would see his car out front and not even wait for him to ring.

They knew all they had to do was sit and talk and pour booze into him. If they took the phone off the hook and got him really stinking, the money was fantastic.

After a while it got to be too much even for Walter, and he started giving one girl $1,000 to distribute to the others. Under no circumstances, she was told, was he to be allowed near his checkbook. But the minute he got drunk, it was a superhuman task to keep him away from the checks. Some girls really made an effort, but others just handed him the pen.

When I met him, I was working at the Beverly Hills Doctor Hospital as a nurse's assistant on the 11 pm to 7 am shift. From time-to-time in California I took jobs as a grip-on-sanity, and because I enjoyed normal work for a change, and that was one of them. Walter had been given my phone number and called just as I was leaving for work. He said he wanted badly to meet me. He tried to talk me out of going to work and finally settled on coming over to drive me there.

I had already been told about him and I knew that if he liked a girl, she could really clean up. So I decided to play it straight, and I went into one of my best goody-goody routines.

He came over to drive me to the hospital, and we stopped off at Robb's restaurant on the way. Walter begged me not to go to work that night, but I was squeezing the role for all it was worth. I hadn't been working there long and you just couldn't call in like that when so many patients depended upon you, I told him, adding with fluttering eyelids, that I couldn't afford to lose the job.

Look, he said, picking up on it immediately, what could I be making, $20, $30? He would give me $150, he'd go much higher, so it would be stupid to settle for that. It wasn't the money, I told him, it was a question of what was right. But I would love to have dinner with him later.

The next morning Walter phoned and a few days later he drove in from Santa Barbara to see me. He thought I was real nice - just the sort of girl he was looking for to keep.

He was tired of getting ripped off and of giving away hundreds without a thank-you. So when we went to dinner, he didn't even try to hold my hand.

He had a yacht that he entered in the San Diego-Honolulu race, and he asked me if I wanted to go along. I'd love to, I replied, but just couldn't get away from work. Finally, after four dates, I decided to hit him up for something. I mentioned that although I enjoyed helping people, I had always been interested in art and wanted to study it full time. But there was no time to do it.

"Why?" Walter asked. Heh, heh, I thought, now I had him.

I replied, "Well, I couldn't just quit my job, see, because I was supporting my two sons and needed a steady income. And there was no Prince charming around."

That was like King Whoever sounding the trumpet. Walter galloped up on his white horse and asked me to figure out how much it would cost. It still wasn't a firm commitment, so I had to keep pushing. But I had two more courses and brandy to work with.

Pretty soon Walter volunteered to bankroll an apartment I said I wanted but couldn't afford. "Oh, no," I said, "that sort of relationship wouldn't be right."

"Don't be silly," he argued. "I can afford it. You're a sweet girl, and you should have nice things. Let me do this. Make a man happy."

That was the key, of course. You must really make them think they want to do it. So I told him okay because I wanted to go to art school and make something of myself instead of ending up as some Mrs. Joe Lunchpail. He was giving me the chance to use my potential and I would show him what I could do and make him proud.

With that, Walter told me to find something the next day and call him in Santa Barbara. The place I found came to $1,200 for a month's rent and deposit - it was 10620 Wilshire Boulevard, just down from Sinatra. Walter paid it without batting an eyelash.

But who just wants rent money - you can get that from anybody. So I said, "Walter, it's not just the rent. I've got to fix it up and all. I mean, I might just as well stay where I am. So the $1,200 became $2,000 and this was after four dinners.

Walter said he wanted to come around at the weekend to see the place, so I had to oblige him and be there. Actually, I was living down the street with Richard and only needed the extra apartment for entertaining.

It took some careful planning. I'd give Walter a certain time to phone me, saying I would be in and out the rest of the time. But don't call late I said, because I keep a pillow over the phone so I can sleep.

He came over often, but he was never allowed to spend the night. After two months, he was up to the hand-holding and goodnight kiss on the cheek stage.

He came through with money for school, but I made excuses about having to straighten things out before starting. Then I told him my grandmother got desperately ill and there were a lot of bills, naturally, so I didn't have any money left for school. Walter bought me groceries, and I would load them up in Richard's car and take them over to the other apartment.

That lasted quite a while. The apartment was handy for some pretty lucrative side action, but I was always careful not to let Walter catch on. He tended to be a little unreasonable.

I don't think I would be too hot on being kept again. It was a lot of work. Walter never gave me large sums but only $300 or $400 twice a week. Then I'd let a week go by and hit him up for $700. I think he felt that if he gave me a whole lot at once, I would dump him. So there was always enough, he thought, to keep me dangling.

And he liked me to ask for money. That was a problem because I didn't like to do that. I'd hassle him, telling him if he didn't want to give me money, he should just leave. Otherwise I would go back to work. If he ever took the bluff, I probably would have had a heart attack.

Pretty soon he started getting possessive, like a husband. He asked me to stay up late so he could call, and it meant going to the apartment and waiting around. I felt I could make more money without the aggravation. And then he even wanted to get laid. I mean, the nerve of him. That took a lot of balls.

So I decided to break it off. The final straw came when he ran into a guy leaving as he was coming in, and he gave me a hard time. But that was the time I needed a hysterectomy - I was twenty-three - and it would be $3,000 for the doctor alone. So I figured I had better stay nice to him a while longer. I called to tell him the bad news, and he wrote a check. But he made it out to the doctor, mistrusting son of a bitch that he was.

After the operation, Walter and Richard came to see me in the hospital on alternate days. Once Walter showed up when Richard was leaning over my bed. But this sharp old lady in the room with me, a real gas, saved the day. She said to Richard, "Now you come back over here, honey, you've been over there long enough. You know I don't like you talking to those pretty girls all the time..." Afterwards she and I laughed so hard we almost burst our stitches.

Richard had been bugging me to dump Walter because the rent and the $2,200 a month just wasn't worth my time. But since I was going to be laid up for a while, I hung on a bit longer.

When I got out of the hospital, I went to stay at Richard's. Then I did a pretty dumb thing. I called Walter collect a few times, not realizing the phone bill would list the number I was calling from. No one ever called us collect; how was I supposed to know? So pretty soon Walter rang and Richard answered. Man, I caught shit from both sides that time, and everyone was furious.

But I explained away Richard to Walter on the phone and asked for more money. He wasn't too happy about it, saying he had given me $500 on leaving the hospital, and where had I been to spend it? Besides, I had pulled a disappearing act on him.

81

I said, "Walter, I need money and you're either going to give it to me or not, but I'm not going to go through all these explanations. As soon as I get better, I'm going back to work because you're starting to make me feel obligated. I just won't be tied to any man, and you have to accept that. I told you that from the very beginning. That's the way I am. In fact, come to think of it, don't give me the money. I know where I can get it."

It came in a flash. He wired it.

But my cover was blown, and it had gotten to be a genuine pain in the ass. I told Walter that we were getting too close and I was afraid because my husband, who was divorcing me, was trying to catch me at something, and he could be dangerous. I said we should stop seeing each other for a month to see how things go. If he really cared about me, I told him, he would go along with it. Then I simply moved out of the apartment, moved back in with Richard and changed the number of the phone that Walter knew about.

He was frantic, calling around and looking for me. Eventually he got the number of my answering service and kept phoning. But I didn't call him back until eight years later... and he didn't get laid then either.

For the longest time, he went around badmouthing me like crazy. He was really pissed off. "If she was lying in a gutter dying," he told one friend of mine, "I wouldn't give her five cents."

But the next time I saw him, I got $750 in less than a half hour.

A girlfriend ran into him eight years later and invited him over. She told him she was staying with me, and he was still hostile. When he walked in I threw my arms around him and kissed him and said I had wanted to call but heard he was really mad at me. He had to understand, I said. I was married to a skunk and under terrible pressure.

But everything worked out. In fact, I went on and told Walter that my friend and I had found the most magnificent house just above the strip on Doheny Drive. It used to be a big gambling house and then some famous person shot her husband there and jumped off the balcony and it was supposed to be full of ghosts... If I could drum up a little more money - hint, hint - I would buy it.

All the time we were sitting on the couch, with me bouncing and giggling and holding his hand. He took his first few drinks after being on the wagon for six years, and we were pretty merry. "Gee," I said, "I wish we could go back eight years, but not like before because I was so unfair…"

And I went on to tell him that I'd done him a big favor by getting him clear of all the trouble with my snake ex-husband. And then I teased him… he was a sly old fox… he knew I had someone in the background and I knew he knew… by then it got to be a big joke, and we were both chuckling.

The conversation went on and then I said, "Listen, Walter, you're a smart businessman, let's go take a look at this place." Up the hill I said, "Look, here's what I've got planned." I explained the whole operation with my girls and all. I hinted broadly that a houseful of grateful girls might be very handy. Without another word, he said, "How much?"

I wanted to say $12,000 but I honestly didn't have the nerve. So I said $7,000 or $8,000. The funny thing was that I had no intention of buying that house. So that was the end of Walter.

* * *

Once in a while collecting without putting out is so easy it's embarrassing.

I was working as a model for Ruth Matthews, one of the finest designers in Beverly Hills, and I met this guy who I used to see a lot in the Beverly Wilshire Hotel. He would smile and nod, and one day he asked me to dinner. He was a bit on the gargoyle side, but I checked him out with friends and found out he was loaded, so I accepted. Callous? Sure, but that's the name of the game.

At the Brazilian Room of the Beverly Wilshire, I told him I was disgusted with modeling because so many men were always propositioning me and it was disheartening. I said I wanted to try interior decorating, but the schools were so expensive. I'd only been with him an hour, spilling out sad tales of young girls against the cruel world, when he suddenly whipped out his checkbook.

"How much is that school?"

Even I couldn't believe that one.

"What are you doing?" I asked, knowing damn well what he was doing.

"Let's get this straight. I'm doing this because I think you're a sharp, pretty nice girl and, baby, there's no strings attached."

"Oh, no, if I had thought you would do this, I would never have said anything, I don't even know you. What would you think if I accepted your money?"

"Okay, let's call it a loan, and someday if you get famous, you can pay me back."

So I said I'd think about it over a drink. I thought very carefully. Why, yes, I decided after touch-and-go deliberation. But, I told him, he would get it back the minute I got lucky. He wrote a check for something big - $5,000 - I think, but there were so many checks I can't remember.

"You're gonna need more," he said. "When you need it, just ask me." He really felt like he was doing a big thing, and I was melting inside with all sorts of soon-to-be channeled gratitude. He went off without trying a goodnight kiss, playing it super cool.

We went out two or three times after that and he gave me a little more, maybe $200. On the last date he started coming on affectionately, trying to put his arm around me. I couldn't stand him and I remember thinking, this one is going to be no fun whatsoever, so I ditched him.

Leaving is easy, if you're careful. I would never give out my personal telephone number, just my answering service. My name changed all the time, and Southern California is a big place.

This guy called for months, and I wouldn't ring him back. One day I came home and found a letter in the mailbox… very businesslike. He had loaned me money in good faith and it should be paid in a reasonable amount of time or legal action would be taken. I almost hemorrhaged laughing at that one. He called a few times more and then finally hung it up.

* * *

Then there was Jim from a very well-known razor blade company who couldn't get laid in a whorehouse with thousand dollar bills in his hand. It was sort of pathetic. He was small with dark hair, thick glasses and pimples. And a whiney voice. Jackie turned me on to him. She had lunch with him when he was in California from his New York headquarters.

One day she came in so loaded down with packages she couldn't walk. She and Jim had been at the Beverly Hills lunchtime fashion show, and every time she saw something she liked, he bought it. She never went to bed with Jim - I don't think anyone did.

Jackie introduced me to Jim and by the next lunch hour I had $900 worth of clothes. I said, "Oh, Jim, these are lovely, but I don't have anything to go with them..." The lunch cost him $1,400. Then he asked me to dinner, which was cheaper... only $1,000. I gave him my art school routine and he had the check signed by the time I got to the part about men taking advantage of poor working girls.

Jim was timid, and that's where the girls had the edge. He had been ripped off so many times it was a pattern. I saw him off and on and came away with at least $800 each time. He didn't even let me tell my stories. I'd just get going and he'd say, "Okay, how much do you need?"

One night I was at his place and this girl breezed in. She said, "Hi, Jim, I need $500 right away." Before he could say, "Luisa, this is Virginia," she had reached into his pocket, peeled off five bills and disappeared. She did that about once a month, it seemed. She died later in a plane crash on her way to screw a Mexican senator.

Anyway, after a while Jim finally made his pitch to me. Until then, I had been going to his apartment where he played music and cooked dinner, but we always ended up discussing politics and smog. He never came on. This time, though, Jim was going to get it on.

He had a fire going in this fantastic place full of Oriental art and antiques. He disappeared into the bathroom, and all of a sudden swooped out like Superman coming out of a phone booth. Two spindly legs stuck out from under a terry cloth robe. He came over and sat by me on this sectional in front of the fireplace. Then he put his arm around me and kissed me. I had kissed him before, but only at my door where I could run in. But this time he tried to get super sexy.

"Jim, what are you doing?" I asked. His whole face dropped, and he stammered and stuttered that I was so attractive... I really felt sorry for him and didn't want to be cruel. But I certainly wasn't going to screw him, either. So my period started right then, for the third time that month. I told him I would like to go to bed with him sometime, not only because he gave me things, but also because he was a nice guy. I said

I felt sorry that so many girls were ripping him off, and he seemed to appreciate the concern and backed off. I later gave him expensive little presents, lighters, jewelry…

Actually, I really got to like him in a strange sort of way and started backing away from taking money. I'd never let him get close to me, but he really was a sad case. He called hookers once in a while at $100-a-night and wanted to make an evening of it with champagne and a good dinner. Then he'd get them into the bedroom but would usually ejaculate prematurely.

The most I ever took off him in one whack was around $1,900. It was for rent or I was being sued or something. The biggest rip-off for Jim was by a girl named Joan who later married a famous actor. Jim wanted to marry her, and he came up with a house and a five carat diamond and a lot of cash - I heard about $18,000. Two days before they were to be married she took off with everything to be with another guy. Jim was so crushed he went back to New York and stayed a while.

* * *

There were lots of others. Two of them were just like Walter. One owned a top professional football team and a racetrack, and the other owned an oil company. The sporty one was an incredible boozer who was also on pills for his gout.

One night Kim and I visited him in Riverside and in the middle of the night we heard a blood-curdling yell: "Giirrllss!!" We thought something terrible had happened and rushed in. The drunken fool had fallen into the bathtub, and we had to pull him out. We brought home $1,000 each for that night, not counting the jewelry Kim got off of him.

Another guy was president of one of the ritziest country clubs in California and he used to stuff envelopes full of money under my door.

Every time you collect money like that you really have to come on like the nice girl who is only taking it because it is being forced on her. You can't let them think you expect it, even though you fully intend to break their arm if they don't come across. And when you dry up one guy, you pass him on to your friends like a revolving charge account.

At high levels of Hollywood culture, it's just the standard. Most of the guys are married, blue-book types, and they have to be discreet and convincing. They can't afford to get kissed off as second-raters. And besides, what sixty-year-old drunk is going to be able to ring up five knockout broads to come over and hang around just because he's sweet?

If men called me up from a reference, there was never any problem. With my reputation, money didn't have to be mentioned. It was understood. When I went after someone myself, it was only after careful financial research.

Some awfully nice guys paid out heavy cash for the privilege of being turned down in the bedroom. But looking back, I honestly can't remember a single case where money was given out of pure goodness. If I had been collecting for the March of Dimes and I was a real dog, the figures involved would have been a little different.

In the back of his mind - if not closer to the front of it - a guy who gives money to a good looking girl wants to get laid. And he usually does.

Chapter Eight

I was always turned on by famous people. It was lots of fun, for example, while millions of Americans knew that George, the well-known toastmaster had a fantastic, articulate tongue, I knew personally what he could do with it besides talk.

When I first got to California, my little heart was all aflutter when some bit player off the lots walked into the Sunset Bar for a drink. By the time I left, I wouldn't have flexed a dimple if he was the real Jesus Christ Superstar, unless I checked out how he handled his money. It wasn't that I was mercenary - which I was - it's simply that stars are like everybody else, only worse.

Fame and new money do weird things to some people, and Hollywood isn't exactly the town for developing mental stability. Of the hundreds of big-name show people I met, and of the dozens I bedded, there were only a few who really had a solid personality of their own.

Some were simply losers when forced to talk about anything besides themselves. Others were among the kinkiest freaks I ever met. And many turned out to be real surprises.

George, I was astonished to discover, was a magnificent lover and a very beautiful person. I used to hang around the Luau in Beverly Hills at cocktail time. One night George came in and sat down across from me. He wasn't the most bashful of men, and he offered me a drink. We had a few and exchanged telephone numbers. A few days later, he asked me to dinner.

He arrived in a chauffeur-driven Rolls, and we went to Jack's on the Beach. George was so interesting I completely forgot he was no double for Cary Grant. We sat cracking lobsters and watching the waves, and he talked on and on.

He told me about his travels around the world, his political friends, his views on life. He also explained Judaism. As he described it, it was such a beautiful religion that I decided to take a long look at it.

After dinner we went to his house on the Pacific Coast Highway in

Santa Monica. George was a real romancer, always telling you how lovely you are... very affectionate. His house was filled with pictures of Presidents and stars and politicians and he could crack you up for hours talking about the people in them.

George wasn't the type to ask you if you wanted to go to bed; he'd been around too long. There was no "Are you or aren't you?" or kissing around. He just took me by the hand and led me into the bedroom. I knew from friends that he was generous, and he's so fascinating you just forget that he's homely, so I followed him without two thoughts.

I think he was interested in me because I was a dead ringer for a girl who he was going to marry. He told me a lot about her as we were drinking brandy. Apparently she took too many pills after a night of drinking and died in her sleep.

George's bedroom had two adjoining bathrooms, so we each went into one to take off our clothes. I came out and climbed into bed. He had an amazing magnetic way about him - it made you feel relaxed and easy, but I can't really explain it.

Believe it or not, he was one of the best lovers I ever knew. The son of a bitch is as well-endowed as Sinatra, almost. It's unbelievable. Men who are built that large usually run into problems with women. Even though guys are terribly competitive about the size of their organs, those with the biggest often had bad complexes because most women are too small for them and they can never really let themselves go. George was aware of that, obviously, and knocked himself out with foreplay.

George was definitely a pleaser of women, and that's where he got his satisfaction. I climaxed quickly, lubricating everything in sight, and then we balled. He was slow and careful, and he didn't spend too long at it, maybe five or six minutes.

Afterward he went into the bathroom, and he came out in a pair of gorgeous silky red Chinese pajamas. He took a few sleeping pills and his driver took me home.

He always wore a toupee in bed, in the shower, it was never re-moved. When he was really freaking out between my legs the first time, I felt something furry and opened an eye. His toupee had slipped. It was so funny - because he was such a nut about it - that if I hadn't been tearing the sheets to shreds I would have laughed.

I saw George about ten times while he lived on the beach, and he always gave me a check for a few hundred. Eventually we stopped going out because I got so busy, but I fixed him up with other girls.

* * *

At the other extreme was Peter Lawford, the White House in-law. He had to be the biggest flop in the United States. I met him when I was with a musician and another guy. He spent a long time on the phone in the other room, and when the two guys left, I found myself alone with him.

He walked in with his velvet-type loafers. I saw him on television several months later and he was still wearing them. While looking at him I was thinking, my God, what a magnificent looking creature. This was a long time ago, and he was slim, with no gray hair at all and a beautiful body.

We were both a little loaded, and before we knew it, we were both stripped on the bed. He had a fantastic body, smooth with very little hair, and I remember being awfully turned on.

But I can't remember anybody having as much trouble performing. After about two hours of horsing around, giggling and boozing, nothing happened so we decided to leave.

Peter and I went over to the penthouse that Walter the Roach was paying for, arriving just as dawn was beginning to break. We stripped down and tried again, but no luck. He was apologizing madly and blaming the alcohol, but I later heard similar stories from other girls.

Finally, I just decided, Jesus Christ, this is ridiculous. I don't care if he is beautiful, he's not worth it. I went to bed with him because he turned me on and there was no money involved.

Celebrities were often my downfall on our profit and loss statement. Although I got some of my biggest money from stars, I put out the most free for them. It was mainly because handsome men really turned me on.

I had this incredible thing about a rising young actor named Bob something, really hot property then. We'd see each other once in a while, and I loved to make love with him. Besides, it was a break from going out only when money was involved.

One night Kim and I and three girlfriends got a call from a maître d' at the Beverly Hilton, fixing us up with some moneyed guys from Chicago. We were just having a last drink at the Luau before going over there when in walks Bob. I mean, he was gorgeous. I took one look and figured, screw the money, I'm going with him.

First we made a few plans and phone calls to a motel, and then we left. The five of us went over to the Hilton for our date. When we got there, I broke my longstanding rule about accepting money beforehand, and collected $1,000 - $200 for each of us - from the men. Then I excused myself to the ladies room. And straight out the door.

Kim was raving mad after that one, but I figured there were four of them left, what the hell. She phoned Richard, and he wasn't too happy as I was cheating on him and pissing off our customers at the same time.

Bob and I piled into a bed at the Tropic Palms Motel, giggling and laughing and about to really get it on when all of a sudden the door flew open. Guess who? We had left the car in an obvious place out front and forgot to lock the front door, so old Sherlock Lopez tracked us down in about zero minutes flat.

I almost died, but Bob, with more balls than anyone I've ever met said, "Hi, join the party."

Richard deflated slowly at that and all he did was snarl some and walk out, feeling a little silly. I was furious at that little bitch Kim for squealing, but I was so plastered by then I forgot. I had drunk so much I passed out and missed the fun. What a waste.

* * *

A lot of times my experiences with actors were more amusing than anything else. My finest hour was putting down a handsome, slender young actor.

Hughie had one approach that was almost a Hollywood legend. He would ask a girl to dinner, hinting at real classy stuff. Later he'd call and say, "Sorry, honey, but I've really got to work on a script. Why don't you come over here for dinner?"

And then on a second call: "Listen, it's really late, and I haven't gotten out yet. Pick up a few steaks on the way over, will you?" The girls would arrive, paying their taxi and carrying their steaks, and they were lucky if they got a free drink in return. That happened to five girls I know.

So one day Hughie asked me to dinner, I waited, and right on schedule, the first call came. "Sure," I said, "I'd love it." On the second call, he asked me if I'd bring some steaks. "Of course," I said, "I know how it is with busy TV idols." I rang up a butcher who delivered and sent him a dozen of the best steaks in the place C.O.D., and I went somewhere else.

* * *

One good giggle came during a minor orgy in Las Vegas. It was a golf tournament - and we were in a suite with about six club owners. Vicky was there, so pretty soon we all had our clothes off and she was screwing everyone in sight, grooving on the stir she was creating.

Then someone phoned up this aging comedian who everyone knows well but I won't name. This guy was a peek freak, and he just came in to watch, fully dressed. Finally he whipped out his little pecker and had Vicky give him a blowjob. Then he did one of his little gestures and walked out. No one saw two cents from him. People who work for him tell you they don't come any cheaper.

I got to know Rory Calhoun, who has to be one of the most amusing human beings alive. One day he just knocked on the door and started clowning. Kim and I were home at the time. We asked him in and almost collapsed at his jokes and gags. We were never intimate, but it sure was fun to have him around.

Some of our wildest scenes were with a well-known Hollywood actor/producer. He just couldn't make it as the great Latin lover, but he never stopped trying.

He would call over seven or eight girls, always at least four, and hand them each a few hundred dollars as they walked in the door. He was a fantastic cook, I remember, and he would generally make a good meal for everyone. He was usually pretty nice before he started the night's boozing. Then, as he got drunker and drunker, things got ridiculous.

First he would put on cha-cha music and start mamboing around, shedding clothes. When he was really plastered, he'd sing. After a while, here was this hairy Don Juan, without a stitch on, jerking around and singing at us. He liked to parade around nude, although I could never figure out why… he had nothing to advertise.

Party time would start with all of us in the bedroom, but by that time he was so stinking drunk he didn't know what he was doing, and one by one the girls would sneak out and hide. Pretty soon he would be all alone on the bed yelling, "Where is everybody?" in between the singing and the cha-chas, and then stagger off on a search.

I mean, picture this: a half dozen girls hiding in the closets, behind the beds, under the beds - all over this huge apartment - and this naked guy with a played-out pecker groping around trying to find them.

It was hard as hell not to giggle, but woe be the girl who gave away her hiding place. He'd come crashing into the closet, for example, bellowing with laughter, and try to screw everyone inside. He thought it was a big joke that the girls were playing hide and seek.

Kim was one of the girls who liked him, and she would get angry at us for hiding. But you know Kim's tastes. We didn't feel too guilty about leaving him alone. He was too drunk to notice who was there and who wasn't. I was never too nice to him because he turned me off, but I kept getting asked back.

Eventually we would decide to get it over with, so we'd venture out and ambush him. Someone usually had a vibrator to finish the job in a hurry, but that didn't always work.

The gatherings at his place were much like the one I went to at the house of this big Hollywood writer. He kept one girlfriend around on the understanding that she would line up four or five women for him whenever he felt like partying. The trick here was to get paid in advance because he would always end up too wiped out to handle business later on.

Anyway, one time we were all running around naked like a bunch of idiots trying to avoid this obnoxious drunk who was leaning in the doorway holding his sawed off pecker. He staggered over to a couch and passed out.

After a few minutes he was up and horny again, when all of a sudden we smelled smoke. This lunatic had set fire to his couch with a cigarette. So we all rushed to the kitchen for water and came back to find him standing on the couch peeing into the fire. At least he put it out.

Chapter Nine

For people who like to hero-worship and think stars are really like they are on the screen, Hollywood is a pretty sad letdown. It's hardly news to say that the place is phony and impressed only with money. But I never really realized how bad it was until I missed getting my elephant from Ibn Hur, the son of King Saud.

I was at one of Harry's rich oilman-type parties at the Mocambo. Remember Harry the Hat? Pretty soon word started buzzing around that King Saud's son was in town and, in fact, was right around the corner at Romanoff's. Then Harry, beaming with pride, passed around the news that the Arabian Prince was coming over to his party. And in a few minutes, this guy sweeps into the room.

He was incredibly attractive, not too tall but with striking features. His eyes gleamed under an Arab headdress, you know, with those kinds of bands around the head. But it was strange because his eyes were very, very blue. He had an FBI man with him as a personal bodyguard.

Well, the way I am, I figured immediately if this guy's a prince and filthy rich, he's gotta be good, right? Naturally a few other girls in the room had the same idea, so it took a little elbowing. But within twenty minutes, I was up to him and trying to start a conversation. It was hard as hell, I remember, because all he could say was, "I am keeng's son, my land very reech, you speak Arabic?"

While I was standing there this FBI guy, Frank, was telling Harry that he and Ibn Hur had just come down from Santa Barbara where they were staying with some phenomenally wealthy people. The prince was working his way down the coast and, because of who he was, Frank was saying, all doors were open to him. And it was true. People were literally bowing down to him.

He went to Romanoff's and Mike Romanoff himself came flying out. Dinners were free, everywhere, simply so owners could say, "Yes, the king's son was here."

After Harry's party, about a dozen of us decided to take the prince around town. He and I had been eyeing each other very subtly, and I was pretty excited by then. Each place we went Harry would make sure it was announced King Saud's son was in the audience.

There was always wild applause, and Ibn Hur would stand up and bow graciously. He would just sit there, very quietly, as if he were trying very hard to understand. Harry kept saying, "Virginia, talk slow to him." Lisa was there as Frank Sinatra's date, and she was working on Ibn Hur, too, for all she was worth.

The round of parties continued and I'm expecting this huge white elephant to be delivered, or at least a great big ruby. There was no discussion of money, but I had heard about Arabian royalty and their generosity. By then we had gone out three nights in a row. They would drop me off at home and then we would meet the next night at the Mocambo.

On the fourth date, we decided to go over to Frank's apartment on Norton, off the Strip. It wasn't elaborate but it was very nice. We were all pretty jolly and we started playing bullfighter. I got a red sweater and we put on loud Spanish music. I'd yell "Ole!" and Ibn Hur would charge after me like a bull. We were all laughing and having a wild time. After a while Frank disappeared into his bedroom with Lisa. And Ibn made his move with me.

He was very gentle. Very carefully, he helped take my clothes off and then pulled out a studio bed, and we climbed in. What followed was nothing spectacular, but I was so impressed by the thought that I was making it with a famous, rich Arab prince that it didn't matter. Again there was only broken conversation and he spoke in a thick accent.

By now I was certain I was going to get a diamond or maybe two elephants. He said he would soon be going to the United Nations to represent his father, and would be calling me regularly. Over the next few weeks we caught every party in Southern California. I introduced him around at the Beverly Hills Hotel and the Beverly Wilshire, and everyone was falling all over the place for him. Lines of girls were after him trying to get lucky, but he stayed with me all the time.

One night he called and said in his broken accent that he wanted to meet me at the Beverly Wilshire. There was a problem, he said. I remembered seeing something in the paper about trouble in Arabia, so I figured that was it.

When I got there, he fixed me with his eyes and said in flawless English with no trace of an accent: "Virginia, please don't be mad at me, but I have to tell you. I'm not King Saud's son. I'm a writer doing an article for *Reader's Digest* about how phony Hollywood is, and how people are impressed with royalty. Don't be angry, but I have to tell you because you're such a great girl."

It took a few minutes to sink in - I mean, this had been going on for a month and a half and everyone in town was drooling at his feet. Then I cracked up with laughter… so loud that waiters were hovering around waiting to call for help.

"Mad?" I said, choking. "It's fantastic!"

He was obviously a struggling writer who had managed to con everyone. I had been sleeping with him for weeks and, through the whole thing, he kept up his accent and no one suspected for a minute that he wasn't the real thing.

He asked me not to give him away, and I decided not only to keep his secret, but also line him up with the best girls in town and make certain he scored until he couldn't stand up.

I didn't see him for years until one night I saw him on television. He was on the Johnny Carson show, where he was introduced as the controversial young author of a bestseller.

They also mentioned that he was a great jokester. They were telling me!

I never got my elephants, but Ibn Hur sure as hell taught me something about Hollywood.

* * *

I'm the world's greatest secretary getter-through. Once I got the President of Mexico on the line in minutes simply by dropping the right name. It always worked… and after I got a guy on the phone, the rest was nothing. If a man had a telephone, I could have him.

Telephones were without a doubt the most important things we had going for us. Without them, you're dead. Really, if anyone had thought of it, we probably would have kept a bust of old Alexander Whatshisname Bell on the grand piano by the fireplace.

In every place we had, there were always at least three phones. All but one were the hands-off lines. Those were the numbers we gave our contacts. They were also the numbers we could change if things got tough with anyone in particular. No one was allowed to touch those phones - only Kim or I could answer them.

The last phone number was strictly private. No one got it but our closest friends. The girls could use it to call out. They could give the number to girlfriends, but never to men. Richard used that line, and it was the only telephone he could use to call in on.

The idea, of course, was that we didn't have anyone yakking about fingernail polish when some rich guy dying to spend $3,000 was trying to get through. If you miss a call like that, you've missed it. The man may call someone else that he ends up liking, and you've lost him for good.

Every time we moved, all phones had to be uprooted and changed. We went through a week-long process of getting hold of everyone in my blue book, telling them where we were going and giving out our new numbers.

It was really work - calling a half dozen European countries, most of the East Coast and Mexico. Our monthly bills under normal circumstances ran well over $500, but moving cost a fortune. It was, of course, money well spent.

No matter what, the incoming lines were always Crestview or Granite numbers, indicating Beverly Hills and Westwood. One time I was in a hotel room with a bunch of people and one of the guys got a note to call some girl with a Dunkirk number - from some raunchy area. "If this broad thinks I'm going to call her in a no-class dump like that..." he said, crumpling up and tossing out the paper. I got the message.

The answering service was the greatest thing going. Most of the time, they would automatically take all calls and ring me up to pass the message. Then I could decide whether to call back or to say a quiet prayer of thanks for the answering service and quickly leave town.

There was no better way of ditching some creep than to stonewall him that way. Since I never gave men my private number, and I only gave out an address when they were approved by our little board of good housekeeping, it was easy.

The operator could call me if I was at the hairdresser's or she could page me at a hotel. If I was at a cocktail lounge and nothing was working, I could ring up and find out who was trying to reach me. If things were promising where I was, I could simply assign one of my girls to the guy or put him off until later.

We never missed a call and we were never hassled in the midst of a good evening by some jerk phoning up for a quick house call.

The best thing was that the answering service was my sole protection against any of the girls cutting out on her own with my contacts. I made all the dates and all the plans. The service would talk only to me, or Kim, because we had a special code.

All the names and numbers went down in my thick blue book, which I kept under tighter security than the Bank of America keeps the combinations to their safes. I still have that book today, one of the few things left from my Hollywood Screw System days. It has names, with notes on what they're likely to pay, but nothing compromising about their habits. That's a bad policy.

Occasionally one of our girls would strike out alone, taking a few guys she met through us, but thanks to the answering service, she never got many.

Of course there were a few drawbacks. Some guys, especially over-sensitive married men, didn't like to leave their names with an operator. Some would get around that by giving a pet name I would recognize. Others just left a number on the assumption I would be interested enough to find out who it was. They were right... I almost always called mystery numbers, even though I was cagey until I found out what was on.

The trick is to find a professional service that is careful about hiring cool girls. You simply can't have some crusty old broad snapping into the phone. The girl who answered had to sound as sexy and soft as anyone likely to be part of our little operation.

The other thing is that answering services are legally required to keep a record for a certain length of time of all calls that come in. I've heard stories of weird guys, and probably cops, going into services and demanding to see lists of callers.

That never happened to me, but it was always a danger. One way around it, which we took, was to go in every month and take out the master list of our calls which just made it harder for the vice-squad goons to get anything on you.

In Hollywood, they're like the gestapo. We never had any problems, but lots of my friends were plagued with guys snooping around because any time a few girls live together and have a lot of men over, it looks suspicious.

There are a couple of other problems involved. Sometimes a girl at the answering service has a boyfriend who has girls in the business. Or a broad might work for a month or so just to collect numbers for herself. It doesn't take long hours working on a switchboard to find out who's getting the action. I've also heard that some operators sell numbers.

But for the most part, having an answering service was fantastic. Most successful models and actresses used them, so it was really no great put-off to men. In fact it just showed them we had some class.

A lot of our dates were made from incoming calls, but our operation really prospered from the calls I made out. Although I changed my name a half-dozen times, I nearly always took a name that could be either a woman or a man: Romney Ames, Sloane Meredith, things like that. It's an enormous help when calling a man at his office or home.

When you ring a man at his office, the trick is to sound extremely businesslike, never super-sexy or feminine. Secretaries tend to get overprotective and like to think they're screening their boss' calls.

Sometimes they have the hots for the guy themselves and don't want any new talent messing up their game. And generally the man himself doesn't want his office to know he's getting calls from a hot-sounding young babe.

The most important part is the first line. If you sound all breathy and timid and ask if you can please speak to the guy, you're dead. I would usually come on like this:

"Mr. Harold Holmes, please."

"May I say who is calling?"

"Romney Ames, Ames Incorporated, and I'd like to speak with him in regard to an important business matter."

"Well, I'm sorry, Miss Ames. May I take your number and have him return the call?"

"Yes, have him call Mr. Ames. He knows what it's in regard to."

Or if I didn't have the time to mess around, I'd sound more like an operator than usual and say:

"Ma'am, the party on the other end prefers not to say where the call is coming from... May we speak with Mr. Holmes, please?"

At this point you've got the secretary on the spot. She either has to check with Holmes and risk cutting off an important call, or let it through. It's no great secret. You just give the secretary as little information as possible and sound like you have urgent business.

And if I was really in a panic to talk to the guy, I'd say:

"It's a business call. Mr. Holmes knows the corporation. He asked me to call at this time on a very urgent matter."

"I'm sorry, he's in a meeting."

"Well, he did ask that we call at this time, so I suggest that unless it's a very important meeting, you let him know we're on the line."

Of course he might be legitimately busy and not able to talk to you, but at least he knows you've called. Occasionally you run into a smart secretary, but if you sound businesslike and determined, you can't miss.

One time I was in a hotel suite of a rich guy I'd been dating, and overheard him talking business with a man named Ron Sanders. Sanders was big stuff; I had heard how generous he was and had wanted to meet him for some time.

There are some men you can ring up cold and say, "Marie Spencer from New York suggested I call." They won't remember the name, but they'll be intrigued enough to call back and that's all you need. But Sanders wasn't one of these, and I hadn't been able to get through to him at all.

I memorized the conversation and where to find him. After Harry left town, it was a snap. I called up and said, "Mr. Sanders, please. Romney Ames calling."

"Who did you say?"

"Romney Ames, a business associate of Harry Richardson."

I knew that was the right name to get me through and it worked. He came right on the line.

"Yes, Miss Ames, may I help you?"

"Hello, Mr. Sanders. I hope you'll excuse the call, but I was having lunch with Harry yesterday, and he was talking to me about you. He said that you and he were doing business. I'm relatively new in town, and Harry suggested I give you a call. Maybe sometime if you can spare the time we can get together and have a drink. I've heard a great deal about you, and I'd really like to meet you."

"Why don't you leave your number and I'll give you a ring."

And he did, the next day. We had lunch at the Beverly Hilton and were off... It was worth $500 that same day.

Sometimes a man may sound curt with you over the phone, but that's usually because he had someone in the office. When you get him alone, he's generally pretty happy you called.

Overall, I'd guess about 95 percent of the men you call and offer a cocktail date pick up on it, if only for curiosity and their egos.

Some of the calls that came in were really wild. We had guys calling from Italy to say they would be in town the next week, and then they'd cable a thousand dollars just to let us know they intended to show up.

One guy called from Majorca and placed his order down to the most minute detail... a blonde, blue-eyed, busty athletic gal in her early twenties with a short nose and good teeth... I kept a catalogue as big as Montgomery Ward's with notes on girls' personalities, speech habits, abilities to adapt to weird situations, favorite perfumes.

There was also a notation on whether she had a pimp, and if she did I would call her only in sheer desperation.

* * *

The phone was good for a lot of other things. I used to keep up my supply of sleeping pills and other drugs simply by ringing up my doctor. It was so easy I could never quite believe it.

The first trick is to call late, between midnight and 2 am, when you know that no California doctor is going to bother getting out of the sack even if you have rabies, cholera and a broken neck.

First I would call the answering service and say I had to speak to, say, Doctor Brown, urgently. The operator would ask why, and I'd describe some intriguing symptoms. I'd be careful to pick things that made sense and fit together, and since I had worked at a hospital, I knew what to say. When the doctor returned the call, I sounded all scared and ran down my past medical history, mentioning an operation or two.

"Doctor, I don't believe in pain pills... can't you make a house call?"

"Well, there's not much I can do for you at home, but I can have you admitted to the hospital... do you have anything for pain?"

"I have so many allergies that I'm really afraid of pain pills. Can you prescribe something that will get me (and him) to sleep?"

This doesn't seem too unreasonable to him, since I've already ruled out heavy drugs, indicating I'm not some freak. He really doesn't want to go through the hassle of arranging hospital admittance, and he certainly won't come over.

"Well, do you have any preference...?"

At this point, it's just like getting money from a man. If you don't ask for anything, you clean up. I've had doctors give me twenty and thirty pills that way. I'd never settle for just two or three, since I always took at least six, but doctors never waste their energy prescribing only a few pills at a time anyway. Doctor Brown would call an all-night pharmacy nearby, and I'd get my pills.

Of course, if I wanted to get into a hospital, that was no problem either.

There was one doctor I got to know who had a phone in his car and he would drive over at 5 am to give you a shot of Demerol if you had the $50. He knew there was nothing wrong with you, but it was a little game to him; and so long as you paid, he didn't give a shit.

Every so often I'd find a doctor who liked my voice and decided to make a house call for his own reasons. One very famous surgeon came roaring over when I was really sick. He gave me a big enough shot to subdue Jack the Ripper, and when he thought I was knocked out, he took off his clothes and got into bed with me. I was awake just enough to ask him groggily what the hell he was doing, and he split fast. He was arrested six months later after many patients reported him to the police.

Over the years I guess about six or seven doctors tried that with me, one way or another.

I don't remember ever really getting into trouble over the phone, but our lines were tapped at least twice that I know about. Once after I spent some time on Trujillo's yacht, a private eye friend of mine called to warn that the FBI was watching me.

About a week later we were having a new phone installed and - something I learned from Richard - I was watching the workmen like a hawk. I was sitting right next to the phone man and noticed a little thing on the bottom of the telephone that looked like a black spool of thread covered with plastic. I asked him what it was, and he got all flustered and said he had no idea. He brought another phone from the truck, and surprise, no little black thing.

The other time I was bugged was when I was going around with a gangster named Manny. But nothing ever came of it. All in all, the telephone is the working girl's best friend. Everyone ought to have a few.

Chapter Ten

One night Big Jim called me at home to say he'd arranged a blind date for me, and he asked if I was ready to go meet the guy right away. He was in Miami.

I can't remember how many times I went on dates in an airplane. It was just part of the scene. In fact, I would guess about 20 percent of my business was outside of California, counting Las Vegas and Mexico.

After all, most of the men I knew were from somewhere besides Southern California, and they were just as horny at home as they were in Los Angeles. If a man's wife was away on a trip, he didn't want to waste time and take risks by messing around looking for entertainment in his hometown.

And if he had to go to New York or somewhere for business, he wanted to make sure he had something handy to decorate his hotel suite.

And then there were always pussy tournaments - golf tournaments - and conventions where most men would sooner come without their toothbrushes than without a good looking girl who might improve their status and keep their joint occupied.

Often men sent private airplanes. The more disadvantaged ones provided first class tickets on regular airlines instead.

I usually felt away-from-home trips were a hassle. If I wasn't absolutely positive the money was more than $500 a day, plus a few hundred extra for magazines and stamps, I wouldn't even consider it. Packing and unpacking is such a bother. Even a slow weekend at home was worth $400 or $500, and I could go home and sleep in my own bed.

But generally guys who are hot enough to send for you will think nothing of dropping a few thousand for long distance cab fare. And some are even more generous.

Before going anywhere, I always made sure I had a round-trip ticket. I wouldn't go to Santa Barbara one-way. You never know what's going to happen. What if you show up on the same plane as the guy's wife? Or you might have some disagreement with the man before the first drink. Those things don't normally happen, but a girl can't be careless.

And I always made sure I had at least a few hundred dollars in advance for expenses. Most men who do this sort of thing get around, and it's understood that they give the girl something when she gets the ticket. But if not, it would be one of the few times when I would ask for money up front.

There are lots of ways for a guy to handle it - men often paid for tickets from their end and cabled money, and others worked it out through a friend. If there was time, of course, many men preferred to send a check big enough to take care of everything. That would commit a girl to coming, unless she wanted to rip him off - which only a dope would do under those circumstances.

If I knew the man very well I might pay for the ticket myself, but only if I was sure I would be paid back within ten minutes of the hello hug.

When a guy I didn't know well wanted me to meet him out of town, I would put out a few feelers, just to check him out.

Let's say someone wanted me to fly to Boston. I'd say, "Well, I'm not sure I can because I've got some modeling lined up for the next few days..." If he was cool, he'd pick up on it and ask how much the job paid. Then, of course, I'd name a rate that would send the Models' Guild into spasms. With that system, you're on solid ground. If he hesitates, stay home. But even if he says, "No problem, I'll just make up for it myself," you had better not spend the money until you see it.

Packing is a vital part of making trips pay. You should take the right kind of clothes, but it's stupid to take too much. With an obviously hurried packing job, you're bound to be short a few things. So what if the guy gives you a few hundred extra to buy your eleventh bikini or your thirtieth pair of slacks?

It's usually understood that right after checking in you are sent out to pick up a few things you need - cocktail dresses, furs, incidentals like that. If you need some luggage, that's the time to get it. Of course some girls overdo that angle.

I knew several who would go off on a trip with a tube of lipstick and a nightgown, automatically assuming the man would outfit them completely. That marks you and cuts your earning power. Not only will it take away from the cash you get, it will dull the guy's generosity.

Whatever I had in my suitcase, I made sure to wear something with quiet class on the plane. The cover of respectability is extremely important, especially if you're going to see a man in his hometown.

You never know who he will have to introduce you to, and he'll have a hard time calling you his secretary if your boobs are hanging out of a shiny dress that stops above your thighs. Anyway, no girl with brains ever goes around looking like a hooker.

The first thing I packed, always, was a vibrator. You can get by without underwear, shoes or perfume. But forgetting your vibrator is asking for trouble. If you can't nail a guy one way, you can certainly get him off with a vibrator. You might run into a raving fuck-freak who wants to get lucky nine times a day.

At home you're in control. You don't even have to ball a guy if you don't want to, and he will still come through with money. And if you do go to bed with him, it's only for one or two times, and then you can duck out. But on a trip, there's no other place to go. You can make excuses and have your period, but it gets tough to keep that up.

Believe me, it's not easy surviving a Labor Day weekend with some idiot who takes the name literally.

An important part of any trip away from home, as far as I was concerned, was to keep your eyes open for future prospects. Nearly everyone with money gets to L.A. at some time or another. And if you've already planted your number and a few modest winks on him, you're way ahead.

And most of the time, you don't even have to wait until a new contact gets to California before he starts to come through for you. After all, you're usually on a trip with a guy doing business and you have to do something besides spend his money and read dirty books when he's meeting with people. So if you find someone else interesting who's worth going out with, you can do it then. You just have to cover your tracks.

The most significant trip I ever took - in fact, a hell of a lot more significant than I ever would have believed - started as a simple run to New York to see a few shows with a pair of rich young men from Phoenix.

These guys from Phoenix asked Kim and me if we had the weekend free to fly back east with them. Something big was opening on Broadway, and there was another play they wanted to see.

Richard dreaded it every time I got within a thousand miles of Philadelphia because he knew I would always angle a side trip to see my sons - and Joe, my first husband - and Richard was sure that one day I would decide to dump everything and stay there, but the prospect of a stop in Philadelphia was exactly what was attractive about the invitation. Besides, Kim had never been to New York, and it sounded like a good idea all around.

Though Richard never stopped us from taking trips he didn't like, this time he was pretty sour about it all. But we told him to stuff it, and went.

Naturally, the minute we reached New York I started calling old contacts and friends to see what was happening. We spent four days in New York and then an ice cream tycoon who might well be your kid's favorite person brought us over to Philadelphia. He put us into a ritzy hotel, very discreetly, and it seemed like we would be there a while.

When people play in Philadelphia, they do it extremely carefully. It's an entirely different sort of society from California - staid, conservative and fifty years behind. There's a whole system of class consciousness that is vital to their way of life. It exists in California, of course, but there status isn't how straight a life you pretend to keep but rather how wild you are.

Anyway, we went out with the ice cream man for a few days, but meanwhile I met a gentleman I will name Tony. He was head of a prosperous insurance company and, although he lived in Pittsburgh, he spent a lot of time on business in Philadelphia.

I knew after twenty minutes I had fallen into something good. Tony had been told by someone about my relationship with Sinatra. He figured I was some sort of starlet or model, and he was snowed.

Tony had taken almost an entire floor of this hotel for sales meetings, and his own suite was a palace. We went up there, and he kept running to the phone to order things. He called for two bottles of champagne and then rang back for another two.

He asked me which perfumes I liked and had big bottles of each sent up. After another half hour of talking, he phoned a jewelry store to bring up a tray of rings. By the time we left for dinner, he had already given me a fantastic diamond and turquoise ring, flasks of Ma Griffe and Joy and the clear impression that "You ain't seen nothing yet."

Tony knew what he liked and went after it super fast. He was Italian, not too tall and fairly chunky. He didn't turn me on much, but then he had other attributes... like a fortune he was obviously willing to share.

His vice-president, Gary, flew the company plane, and he was nearly as open handed as Tony. Kim and I went out with them the first night for dinner, and we all had a pretty good time. Tony gave me $400 which wasn't very much, but considering everything else, it seemed reasonable for starters. And, right away, he tried to talk me into staying.

The idea wasn't bad. When I mentioned I had mortgage payments and a new Lincoln and couldn't possibly meet my California bills without a job - giggle, giggle - that paid $3,500 a month, he didn't even flinch.

He had an office-apartment in a classy area of Philadelphia, in Jenkintown actually, and he wanted me to have a place near that. I could stay there for a while and see my children and take it easy, I thought, and then leave later.

Tony was a jolly sort, if no great lover. Philadelphia was pretty slow - we had to go to Cherry Hill, New Jersey for dinner and to find anything that resembled action - but then I had grown up there.

This came about a week into our brief trip to New York, and Richard hadn't heard anything from me by then. I called him to say I was on to something big, but he didn't seem too impressed.

"What makes you think he's such a big score?"

"Well, just my instincts - they've been pretty good so far."

Good old Richard didn't think so.

"If he's so fucking good, how come he gave you all that crummy jewelry and shit? What about money?"

And that, by the way, was my continual hassle with Richard. He would get furious if somebody gave me presents. "Get the money!" he would always say. "For Christ's sake, get the money!"

But I mean, what the hell do you do? You can't tell someone, "Thanks, but I'd rather have cash." That marks you as a two-bit hooker and turns off everything, now and later.

Finally we agreed - or at least I agreed - that I would stay a little longer and see what happened.

The first thing was for me to do a little shopping for my new apartment. I wasn't sure I'd be there for more than a week, but why do things halfway? The cheapest thing we bought, I think, was a snaked mirror to cover the back bedroom wall for about $1,400.

We - or he - spent $5,000 just for the drapes. The bedroom furniture was gorgeous white hand-carved stuff from Italy which Tony got wholesale for $4,500. We paid $12,000 for two rooms of furniture, with some fantastic antiques and a few incidentals.

And the apartment was already furnished when we took it.

Tony also got me a new Mustang, and he made arrangements to start paying my nonexistent commitments in Los Angeles. All this was within a few weeks of meeting him and I was beginning to think the situation was looking up.

Kim had been going out with Gary during this time and was living with me. Tony gave her a job as his Philadelphia secretary, just answering phones and things like that, and Gary gave her a lot of money. She was anxious to get back to California, and Gary was scaring the hell out of her by getting too serious, but we decided to stick around to see what developed.

Tony traveled all over the country, and I usually went with him. That was about the time that President Johnson was urging everyone to see the United States and spend money at home. He would have loved us.

One afternoon Tony rang up from Pittsburgh to ask if I'd like to go to New Orleans with him. I didn't really since I was involved with someone else - still on this brief New York theatre trip - but finances had to come first. So Kim and I went.

Tony and Gary flew over in their plane to pick us up at the Jenkintown airport near my apartment. It was a great trip, bumpy part of the way and long as hell. I must have flown in dozens of small planes on trips, and I always enjoyed it. You get a feeling of closeness to God, and you're at peace with the Universe.

After landing, we went straight to the Prince Conti Hotel in the French Quarter of Bourbon Street. I think of all the beautiful places I've seen, that was the nicest. It was plain from the outside, but when you walked in, you lost 120 years in a blink. The whole place had been beautifully restored, and each room was decorated with antiques which were available for purchase by the guests... for enormous amounts of money.

Our suite was magnificent. It was all in massive French furniture. The king-sized bed had a hand-carved headboard about four feet high with cupids shooting arrows at each other. I had never seen anything like it in years of looking at beds. I found out later it was available for only $7,500, and I mentioned it to Tony. He, or course, made arrangements to buy it.

Tony had some business to take care of, so Kim and I strolled up Bourbon Street spending money. They had given us about $1,500 each, which lasted us until they came back. We all went to lunch at Brennan's, an incredibly posh place, which we finally left after four bottles of champagne and three hours of talking with Tony's business friends. That night we went to the Roosevelt Hotel for roast duck, afterwards stopping at Al Hirt's, a theatre and a few clubs.

The chief of police was a friend of Tony's and was supposed to meet us the next day. He couldn't make it, but he sent an aide, so we all toured New Orleans in an unmarked cop car.

Tony had to meet Rocky Marciano, so we left New Orleans after a few days. It had really been fun. Altogether, I guess, I had gotten a $2,500 antique diamond ring, a $500 Dresden clock and a few thousand dollars in spending money. It wasn't bad considering that I balled Tony only once the whole trip.

Anyway, that kept me going a few days longer.

Sometimes short trips were the nicest. I liked to go to Palm Springs. It was close to home, and the money was usually pretty good. A few times I went to meet Texans there, and I really had great times. When you're dealing with Texans, you're in a different element. These are your spenders. With Texans and Mexicans, money is no consideration at all. They'll send private jets to Burbank just to take you to Palm Springs. They don't mess around, and that's my kind of person.

Texas oil men, especially, were my favorites. There was one who had a habit of giving me blank checks and sending me off in the direction of expensive shops. I don't think he ever really paid attention to the checks when they came back, but he had so much money he never missed any of it.

Regardless of who I was with, the mechanics of a trip remained fairly much the same. I was met at the airport and taken to a hotel where I was already registered. If I arrived at the same time as the man I was with, I would always stay in the car or wander off shopping while he checked in. Before anything else, the man would usually give me some money for "essentials."

I can't remember any really embarrassing situations with wives or families. The men I traveled with had their reputations to worry about and they were smooth. It was always amusing to be sitting on the bed doing my nails when some guy was on the phone to his wife saying, "Yes, dear, no, dear," and promising to be a good boy.

With all the traveling I did, I never really took a vacation the whole time I was with Richard. Occasionally he and I would go to Palm Springs or Vegas for a few days. We'd ride horses or swim during the day, but it was always business at night.

I guess I just figured it wasn't worth it to take myself out of circulation for too long. The girls used to call me Miss Cash Register Heart. I suppose they were right, but as long as it was ringing, what the hell? Besides, my out-of-town trips couldn't exactly be considered hard labor.

Chapter Eleven

Every politician I've ever known or heard about was a player, from Jack Kennedy, Adolfo López Mateos and Rafael Trujillo on down. If you didn't see it on the surface, it was only because they did it in private... and from the bed looking up, I was in a position to know.

I came out of the 1960 Democratic Convention firmly convinced that there couldn't be a single American politician who wasn't a first class asshole. I found Mexican politicos a little smoother, but only because they were elegant about it.

No matter where I met politicians, I found them incapable of paying their own way. They were among the greatest liars and con artists in the world. Lots of people have suggested that if we put the politicians in jail and let the criminals out, we'd be in better shape.

That might be true. At least with crooks you know where you stand, but the elected servants of the people just nod and smile and then shaft you. They wheel and deal, sometimes illegally but often just unethically, and all that happens is they get richer. I've seen this happen a number of times.

But the convention was too much. I went to the Santa Ynez Hotel on the beach near L.A. three or four nights, usually taking some of my girls. Delegates were falling all over the place, totally nude, chasing around the pool after girls. Some were even propositioning wives and women guests in the lobby who hadn't even come for the party.

The convention was in downtown L.A., and I guess they chose the Santa Ynez because it was about half an hour away from the convention center, and they could party with no problem. A friend of mine who was related to Lyndon Johnson arranged for us to come down. I was with the fantastic looking gutsy little broad who traded me Frank Sinatra later.

The first thing we saw was a lot of naked butts running around. The place was full of top level politicians, and they were acting like little kids who escaped from their counselor at summer camp.

Here they were, about to choose a nominee for President of the United States, and the minute they got back from the meetings they started drinking and screwing until they passed out.

It was a circus. I couldn't believe it. There were all these little Kennedy buttons, Kennedy lighters, Kennedy hats, and these guys running all over blowing horns like on New Year's Eve.

There were naked broads everywhere - blacks, Asians, everything. Most of the guys thought each girl would handle three or four of them at a time. Some girls did but I wasn't having any of it.

The guy I ended up with was a congressman from a Southern state. He was filthy drunk and kept apologizing for being so loaded. Then he started talking about his state and its girls. I got the idea that not only was a lot of hustling going on with full knowledge of the authorities, but that they encouraged it and made money off of it. He told me about one sheriff who lined up topnotch girls. They were really beauties, the congressman said, and they got $20.

I almost fell off the bed. "But Ah guess things are a little different heah, honeh?" he added. I said, "Honey, they sure are."

The Santa Ynez was a gorgeous place overlooking the sea on the coast highway between Santa Monica and Malibu. But it was a shambles. People running in and out of rooms, glasses breaking, bottles lying everywhere.

Of course, any time politicians are involved, they have a totally free hand. If anyone else tried it, the whole police force would be down there in minutes. I got about $300 or $400 from various people the first night, and I wasn't too hot to go back.

But since these guys were the moochers of society and they were so used to taking, I had no reluctance at all about discussing money and setting fixed prices with them.

The following nights were the same. I came away with a thick pile of cards and phone numbers from virtually every state in the country. If I had followed up on them, I'm sure I could have worked myself into a powerful position anywhere I wanted to go. But I threw most of them away.

I mean most of these guys are cheap creeps anyway, and the whole idea turned me off. You figure these are the nation's leaders, the people you're trusting your country's future with, and they're spending public money and acting like freshmen at their first fraternity party.

Of course some similar things were going on at other hotels where delegates were staying. Kim was called over to a big downtown hotel to meet some governor. People like governors don't do their own soliciting, of course. They have top aides and friends do their scouting for them.

Someone called our number, and Kim was available, so she went. Kim said she never saw this governor pick up a tab, and she couldn't believe the way everyone was falling all over him. She was told straight off not to think of money as it was such a great honor to sleep with a man of his stature. She told the go-between to shove it, and that was settled, but I can't remember the figure.

The governor was staggering drunk when she walked in and he had just made it with two other girls. But he figured he'd try again. Though he never got it up enough to ball, he messed around long enough to pass on gonorrhea to Kim. There was no doubt who it was because Kim wasn't around anyone for days before or after. She was pretty upset, but probably not half as mad as the guy's wife.

Throughout the whole convention, I was always hoping to meet Jack Kennedy. For the longest time that was my ultimate goal, to ball Kennedy. It was not so much for any hero-worship thing - I'd pretty well gotten over that - but I figured it would do incredible things for my status.

A lot of rich and powerful men I saw were really impressed by other big-timers that they knew I'd been with. And, of course, if a guy you're going out with knows that you've been balling the President, he's hardly going to risk getting away with slipping you a lousy $200.

Also, I had heard he made fantastic love.

There's no doubt in my mind that I would have gotten to him. I knew enough people who could have set it up. Twice I was supposed to be introduced to him, but I screwed it up by having to leave town.

It was well known around Hollywood that Kennedy was a great player, and I heard some incredible first-hand accounts.

One funny story I heard from an executive at the Beverly Hills Hotel happened during the 1960 convention. Someone had fixed Kennedy up with two girls in his suite, and he was in the bedroom with them. Somehow the Republicans had found out about it and had alerted the reporters.

Pretty soon a bunch of newsmen were outside of his room upstairs, and he must have figured he was trapped. He went out the window, pants in hand, and damn near killed himself doing it, my informant said.

I suppose it would have been a little rough on him to get caught with two call girls in his suite on the evening of his nomination.

After that, I'm told, he was very careful but still gave the Secret Service minor fits.

The law certainly didn't try to stop any of the other distinguished leaders from getting their rocks off after hours, but they didn't take many chances. I met a broad named Margo who said she supplied most of the girls for the 1960 convention.

She described the screening she went through by the FBI. Some heavy contacts of hers phoned from Washington to order chicks before-hand and they all had to be carefully checked out to make sure they wouldn't blackmail guys later.

That 1960 convention was the only one I went to. I couldn't stand that many politicians up close, and the money was lousy. But I dated a hell of a lot of legislators and officials singly and at parties. Most of them fit my general picture.

Sometimes I'd be asked to entertain important people by friends of mine who wanted favors. One man I knew gave me a lot of money to make it with a Superior Court judge in Pasadena because he wanted something big.

This judge was a heavy drinker, and he hassled the hell out of me. He must have balled me for an hour but couldn't climax because he was so loaded. I don't know if my friend got his favor but I got my money and was sore afterwards.

The guys who were a lot more fun - and enormously more generous - were sort of borderline politicians who didn't have to con voters and government auditors.

* * *

On one July Fourth weekend, Ramfis Trujillo, son of the former Dominican Republic dictator, brought his huge yacht into Los Angeles harbor. It was an unbelievable boat. He had taken a warship and converted it into a floating palace. Each stateroom was decorated differently, with thick carpets, rich brocade and full length mirrors.

Ramfis was in the country to study at some military academy, but he was more intent on studying Kim Novak, Zsa Zsa Gabor and Lita Milan - whom he later married. It looked like every press photographer on the west coast was there trying to get pictures of who was coming and going out to the boat.

I had met a big-shot Dominican and another Latin politico at a party, and one night over cocktails they asked me if I wanted to go on Trujillo's yacht. You know how long I had to think that one over.

It was an astounding party. We were on deck, in a bar with a long, dark wood table. Underneath, I remember, was a huge fantastic Persian rug that someone told me took a man an entire lifetime to make.

Porfirio Rubirosa was one of the guests, basking in his reputation as the number two Aly Khan and the playboy of the Latin world. I was terribly disappointed with him. He was nowhere near as attractive as I had imagined. His brother was also there - an interesting guy with kinky red hair who looked nothing like Rubirosa.

In fact, Rubirosa was one of the first guys I balled on the boat. He was really pretty cornball, drinking brandy out of a snifter and standing there like Señor Cool.

There was a jukebox in the bow but one night Andrés Segovia was on board to play. Everything started relaxed and cool, and Segovia left before any of the wild partying began.

We were listening to Segovia, and when I walked by Rubirosa, he grabbed me by the rear. I was pretty pissed off, and whirled around and asked him what in the hell he was doing. Very ladylike, you understand, I mentioned that gentlemen don't do that sort of thing. "Ah, but you have such a beautiful body," he said.

We started chatting about guitars and bodies, and we got romantic pretty quickly. I had beautiful eyes, he said, and I made his selective little heart quiver. Hmmm, hmmm. And we danced quite a bit, with him whispering chili recipes in my ear in Spanish. There was some sort of aphrodisiac floating around the ship, and he dosed both of our drinks with it liberally.

A few minutes later we slipped down to one of the sumptuous staterooms. He was coming on very, very romantic, and he was built like a stud. I guess he was a good lay, but I didn't like him. He had too much ego. I mean, basically a lay is a lay. If there's no feeling, you really don't get much out of it, no matter how technically adept the guy is with his equipment.

But we were flailing away and all of a sudden, in the midst of this Latin passion, I got sick from whatever it was he put in the booze. He was throwing his heart into a down-stroke, and I had to excuse myself to go and throw up. It was a flop all the way around.

Porfirio was a leg man, and I had wild legs, so he asked me back the following evening. I came, but I ducked him and had a girlfriend go with him instead, and I ended up with Trujillo. Ruby was a real Latin bullshitter and not bad in the feathers, but that was about it.

After I had attracted and trapped Trujillo, I was on the boat for a long weekend. We sailed out to Catalina and tied up there, where the partying got serious.

The first night I spent with Ramfis everyone was drinking absinthe - wormwood - which is supposed to turn you on. It was a disaster. As Trujillo was gracefully guiding me downstairs, I caught my heel on the carpet and fell head first. I got up all right, though I had really bounced my head on the deck, and we went to his cabin.

I guess Ramfis' stateroom was pretty sexy looking, but I didn't pay much attention. I went flying into the head and barfed. When I came out, looking a little ratty and fairly embarrassed, he was already in bed. What the hell, I figured, it's his boat, and I got under the covers with him.

We were both so loaded that I can't remember whether it was a good ball or not. I doubt it because every time he climaxed I leaped out of bed and went in to throw up again. I was positive I was going to die.

The next morning I hung around on deck sipping Ramos fizzes, which settled my stomach. From the number of people doing the same thing, it looked like it was just that kind of a party.

Ramfis gave me a jade and diamond bracelet that must have been worth $2,500, just as a little token of his esteem. After four days, I end-ed up with about $600 cash as well, but I would have gone even with-out the loot.

That was one of the perfect things to have in your past, almost like screwing Kennedy. My whole trade was based on name dropping and that gave me more door opening possibilities than six months of hanging around the Polo Lounge.

It worked, too. I'd call up all sorts of Latin diplomats, dignitaries and visiting politicos and casually say, "Hello, I'm a friend of Ramfis and…"

There were an awful lot of people worth knowing at the party itself. Couples would be around dancing and drinking, and then they would mysteriously disappear. You would see them later, looking very pleased with themselves, coming up from below.

There were maybe 100 or 150 people on board over the long weekend, with continuous recorded music in the bow and usually somebody playing live in the stern.

Someone told me there were a lot of FBI guys hanging around, but I didn't see them.

* * *

Of all the politicians I met, I liked the Mexicans best. It wasn't that they were any less crooked. They just had more class about it. And with Mexicans, money was no object when they saw a girl they liked. So you can bet I was on the phone fast any time I heard Mexican politicians were in town.

It's funny by the way that most people think that if you're a blonde in Mexico, you've got it made. Hell, if you're anything in Mexico, except a Mexican, you've got it made, as long as you're halfway pretty. For some reason foreign women, any foreign women, are wildly popular. I loved it.

Miguel Alemán Valdés, the former president of Mexico, used to come to town and rent a big cabana by the pool at the Beverly Hilton. I met him there at a big party he was throwing where Miguelito Valdés was singing.

I was asked to join Alemán's table. It was jammed with the finest hors d'oeuvres and booze that money could buy. I was glad to know he was up to my standards… It was a pleasant evening and couples began discreetly disappearing. I was left with El Jefe and didn't fight it. A lot of girls had tried to infiltrate the fort, but I held on.

He was a courtly old gentleman at the time, always in a conservative business suit but with immaculate white silk shirts. Miguel had no quirks at all. He just wanted a good old screwing, and I gave it to him.

I don't know why, but I rarely met a Latin lover who didn't want it straight. I mean real Latin Americans, not Mexicans living in the States who can be the most perverted cats ever to hit the mattresses. Very few real Latins ever went so far as to give you head, and a lot of them wouldn't even think of asking a girl to go down on them. They were years behind.

It was probably part of the old-style ethic. Only a whorehouse broad would do something dirty like oral sex. But a Latin was generally pretty good at what he did.

Miguel was the complete gentleman. He gave me $500 on the first occasion, paying it himself. I saw him a second time, and it was the same thing... a fine dinner with champagne and a rocking Mexican party with romantic music and a long buildup.

He gave me $400 that time. I guess he figured he was entitled to a discount by then.

The parties with Alemán put me on to a lot of suave Mexicans. I walked around at one party until I collected ten invitations to visit Mexico. American politicians have a lot to learn from these guys.

Like Americans, the Mexicans give you their card, but they also offer to send a private plane to pick you up. And almost to a fault, they do it with class. Not only lovemaking, but everything they do.

The sex part is done with dignity and tact. I can't ever remember feeling I'd done anything dirty or mercenary. They made you feel like a woman, not just a body.

* * *

I met Adolfo López Mateos when he had a meeting with President Johnson in Palm Springs. I can't remember exactly how I got down there, but I think it was with a good friend of mine who knew the guy who was arranging the meeting. This cat had sent a plane for us without much warning.

Frankly I was hoping to meet Johnson, but he had left by the time we got there. Lopez was still around with dozens of top aides and officials. We were whisked up to the house in a Cadillac limousine.

The first thing I noticed when we arrived was a big attaché case lying by the television set. A colonel, who I was told headed Mexico's secret police, was there and he noticed me looking at it. He laughed and said, "Mucho dinero" - $200,000, I think he said.

I didn't know why it was there or who had brought it, but it was very clearly changing hands in a shady way. He told me it was for a chunk of acreage in Mexico. I got the distinct impression the money was from some American for a prominent Mexican and I knew it was illegal for an American to own land in Mexico.

The colonel also showed me his shoulder holster, and I noticed a few other Mexicans hanging around packing pistols. We got along famously, and pretty soon he opened the briefcase and showed me the stacks of crisp notes. I went to the bathroom, and when I returned it was gone.

Ah, well.

I talked with López Mateos, but nothing came of it. He was in a hurry to get back to Mexico. The colonel stayed and I sort of became his date. I liked him, but I never went for super-fast sex. I preferred dinner and conversation first, getting to know a guy and then deciding if I'd ball him.

The colonel picked up on that and didn't push. We were spending the night away and had lots of time. The next night I screwed him, but it was no memorable evening.

The guy who had brought us to Palm Springs was very emphatic that we were not to collect any money from the Mexicans. He was picking up the tab. I got about $800, I recall, and I was very disappointed because I had wasted two days on the trip and should have gotten much more. He later put me on to some winners, so my hunch was right.

I had a few other things going with Mexicans, like a well-loved governor of Sonora. For some reason, I had a great understanding with Latins though I couldn't speak Spanish. They considered me simpatico, and they could tell I was impressed with their cool. I almost never turned down an invitation to Mexican parties - I would usually go flying over with visions of money dancing in my head.

Richard never wanted me to go to Mexico. He was afraid I'd get to like it too much and settle down with a checking account from some rich politico. He was probably right. In fact, if I had had any brains I would have done just that and saved myself a lot of hassle later. But then I remember Rory Calhoun once warning me that the absolute thing I should not do was to get tied up with a rich Mexican.

He said he knew girls who were complete prisoners in Mexico. One girl, he said, tried to get away from the man who was keeping her, and he cut one of her breasts off.

I never did much traveling in Mexico, though, except for a few whirlwind trips.

* * *

One of my buddies was a racetrack king with all sorts of mysterious connections to President Nixon. He was nailed by the Feds for his tax and betting practices. His dog tracks and bullrings and other holdings made him fortunes, and he spread it around among his favorite politicians and influential friends.

It was a treat to watch him work. I read later that after he went to prison the guards caught hell for letting him go out screwing and hunting.

He wasn't a politico, of course, but his friends certainly were. He was a very heavy dude. I don't know how much money he dumped into the Republican Party, but judging from what he spent on our parties, it wasn't small.

The scandals that came down around the racetrack king and his San Diego pals apparently caused the Republicans to move their 1972 convention from Southern California to Miami. He knew Nixon, he knew Reagan, he knew everyone.

He was really a good guy, but he had a hang-up that drove me absolutely bananas. He insisted on my talking baby talk to him.

It was ridiculous. He would come over and I'd have to say, "Ooo, hwwo, Daddy, how's my itty-bitty-poopsie-woopsie-snookums… oo is my baby waby going to see me now?" And then he'd bounce me on his knee and go off to see the governor.

This went on all the time. Sometimes he would phone up to have me call him "Daddy" in this disgusting infantile tone of voice, and he really grooved on it.

When it came to regular talk, he would clam up and was secretive about everything. Once we went to a hotel for a weekend, and it was like we were filming a Japanese James Bond thriller.

He headed for the reception desk while I slipped into a phone booth. Then he came by and casually went into the booth next to mine. After messing around and pretending to call, he passed the key to me when no one was looking.

Another time we met in Yuma, and it was like two colonels of Russian intelligence were handing over plans for a missile base or something. I mean, I can understand being embarrassed to be in Yuma, but what the hell?

But I learned a lot about him over the six or seven years I knew him. He was an Italian-American, born of a poor family and reared along the Mexican border. He was a smart gambler and a wise investor. He could see directly into people, and he knew how to cultivate and befriend the right ones.

He was a gorgeous dresser, always in the most expensive, well-tailored silk suits. God knows how many alligators died to keep him in shoes. His diamond rings and gold watchbands left no doubt that he had taste - well, my kind of taste - and money.

I first met him in Tijuana when I went down with some friends and ended up with a Mexican chief of police. This cop gave me $700, by the way, and I still don't know who he took it from.

Anyway, my racetrack king seemed to flip out when we were introduced. I had long black hair then, all sun tanned and made up, and he immediately asked for my number. He couldn't stay because of some crisis at one of his six million properties. But he called me soon afterward and we started going out from time to time.

I liked him a lot, but it was hard sometimes. He was tremendously active in bed, and he could go seven, eight times in a couple of hours. That leaves scars, and it gets to be no fun at all. He wasn't overly charming in bed either, and the constant stream of "Daddy-Waddy" nearly drove me crazy.

But he was extremely generous, not only in what he gave me when we balled. Whenever I needed help - even if I hadn't seen him in months and months - I knew I could count on him.

Once he stood bail for me when my own mother wouldn't. Another time he paid my tuition for real estate school. He even gave me the money so I could get married a third time.

That was part of his personality - he gave to orphanages, friends and Presidential campaigns. And he did it with a smoothness, so you never felt he was buying you.

Everything about him was class. It showed all over, all of the time. And he always traveled in the highest circles.

I was surprised when he got sent up because he had some extremely powerful friends. But then I guess someone more powerful was after him and made it stick.

That's politics and politicians, isn't it?

Chapter Twelve

Mickey Cohen and I went out for a long time, but I ended up dumping him because he was cheap. I mean, he could pull $50,000 out of his pocket during a picnic. He just didn't share it with his women.

Over the years I spent a lot of time with hoods and some pretty nice guys who weren't exactly popular with their local police force. I'm not even sure why, although I was fascinated with the James Cagney type from the time I was a kid. Also, most crooks live the sort of life I was after - class, lots of money and good hours.

My outlaw friends caused me a hell of a lot of problems, especially when I was a public enemy myself, but they had some of the warmest hearts and best manners of anyone I knew.

Ed, the burglar who wanted to marry me, had spent twelve of his thirty-two years in jail, and was working as a short order cook in a dump when I met him. But he gave me more in six months than all the big spenders I knew did in years.

When I was nineteen in Philadelphia, I started hanging around with some pretty big hoods without even knowing it. Johnny Dio and Blinky Palermo were two I remember. And there was a place called Palumbo's. Both were pretty notorious for having a lot of Mafioso around.

I was absolutely intrigued with these guys right from the beginning. They were always in huddles looking like George Raft. Maybe I saw too many movies when I was young. But I have always considered this type as the most masculine.

It took me the longest time to realize that the men who were buying me drinks and taking me out were big-time gangsters. I never heard anyone ever say anything about putting out a contract on a guy. No one ever talked about making hits or anything.

People - me, for instance, until I learned better - seem to think that hoods sit around talking about heists and heaters and hot rocks out of the corners of their mouths. They just don't talk. They can't. If they're not jam-up people - guys who can keep their mouths shut - they don't last. A Mafioso's wife might have a pretty good idea something funny is going on, but only very rarely will she know what her husband is really into.

Only the punks talk about their action to impress people. These guys are dangerous because if they'll talk to me about it, they'll talk about it to other people, and that's what busts them.

I remember one guy - Jesus, I was at a girlfriend's and all of a sudden there's a screech of brakes and a slamming car door. This cat comes flying in the door, shirt open to the waist, a pistol stuck in his belt and money coming out of his back pocket.

"This is Jimmy," my girlfriend announced, and he said, "...yeah, yeah, the cops are following me." He used to pull this all the time. I mean, he's cool? We called him Jesse James. He got busted, of course. A big mouth will do it every time.

A lot of guys who blab about how they knocked off this place or how they packed a rod - a heater, for God's sake - psychologically want to go back to jail. And they usually do. The professionals, if they ever had any business to discuss, would politely ask the women to leave.

I really never knew anything. That's why when police questioned me about guys, I could never answer even if I wanted to. No one had to write me a letter to tell me they were up to some shit, but details... I sure didn't know about it.

There are always lots of jokes about how dumb the cops are, but that's nothing unusual for anyone.

I found that gangsters mostly feel they have a real image to live up to. They have to be dangerous, evil and conniving with other men, but soft-hearted with women. Money has no real meaning to them so they usually shower their women with gifts. In bed, it's the same thing. They want to please you because they have to live up to their image, and want to feel good from sex themselves.

What I mainly dug was the constant undercurrent of excitement, guys talking secretly in corners and rushing off. Since a gangster never talked business to you, you never knew what was up, but there was always some suspense about it.

Really, I guess it's corny, but I thought it was thrilling to be around some of those guys. They were honest-to-God outlaws - daring, dangerous and beautiful. They had enough balls to go against the system, and I liked them for it. I wasn't too big on violence, but I never saw any of it.

* * *

Mickey Cohen was sort of interesting because while he fit some of the pattern - he was really big stuff - he was a drag in some other ways. I met him in the 1950s when I was living on Wilshire and working at John Robert Powers Modeling School.

A girl there who had been Miss Belgium knew him and several times invited me to come along with them to dinner, but I was always busy. One time when she asked Richard had gone to Cuba to invest in property, and I was free. So I went.

It turned out to be a great evening. We hit the Mocambo, Ciro's, every place on the Strip. Those were the days when you didn't go to those clubs unless you had lots of money and intended to spend it. Everywhere we went, people fawned all over Mickey, taking him to special tables and bowing from the waist. He'd pull out a wad - $60,000, $70,000 in cash - and strip off $100 bills as tips. Unfortunately this didn't carry to his girls.

That night, and the whole time I knew him, Mickey never let anyone say a foul word when women were around. He was a door-opener and chair-puller-outer. He was short and balding, with a New York accent, but I was weirdly attracted to him. I guess it was mostly that I ate up all the attention I was getting by being with him. It was really exciting being in the middle of it all, with this perfect gentleman carefully taking my elbow and lighting my cigarettes.

I didn't want to ball him and played hard-to-get for a long time. And he wasn't sexually aggressive at all. Finally he chose a night to make it with me at his apartment. I knew when the appointed time came there wasn't much point in being cool. Mickey wasn't too great in bed... he was really fast. And he was a nut about cleanliness, always taking showers and washing his hands.

There were always crowds of people around Mickey wherever he went. I didn't know who the paid bodyguards were, but he had some awfully muscled pals who never left him except for a few intimate breaks. No one carried guns, at least obviously. The big-time guys are much too smart for that. They're much more afraid of the FBI pinning some cooked-up charge on them that might stick.

And, naturally, Mickey always had a tail. The cops had stopped being subtle with him, and it was one of his favorite jokes. He would flip a finger at the detectives following him and laugh like crazy. One time we rolled out of his driveway in this big black Cadillac and an unmarked car pulled out right after us, almost touching the bumper. Mickey yelled, "I'll be at the Beverly Wilshire in case you lose me," and drove off, roaring with laughter.

He would never use his own telephone except to order a pizza. Just like Richard, he'd pull up to a payphone, say a few words in a low voice and drive off. Even if he called for a date, it was always, "How about dinner, sweetie? I'll pick you up at 8:30." That would be it. He never had big parties at his place, although his friends were always around.

The whole thing was a big joke to Mickey. I didn't mind all the cops around at first, but after a while it started to worry me. A girlfriend of mine who knew Mickey had a visit from the FBI asking how much money he carried and other questions about him, and I wasn't too hot for that.

And the scene was getting pretty bad anyway. Mickey would give me a few hundred dollars from time to time, but I usually had to come up with a story and ask for it. His conversations were pretty dull and it was getting boring just watching television at his place during those long card sessions.

Finally I figured the money wasn't worth the hassle, so I gave him the answering service treatment. After I didn't call back a few times, he found another chick and I was delighted.

* * *

The police never gave me any trouble when I was dating Mickey Cohen, but with Manny, who was another well-known gangster, they were a real pain in the ass.

I met Manny much later through a guy I was dating, a well-known Hollywood agent. This agent is the one who used to write blank checks to me until I cashed one for $800. Well, he did say buy a dress. Anyway, one night the maître d' at Jerry Lewis' restaurant on the Strip called, saying the agent wanted me to come down to meet some people. I knew him well enough not to hesitate a second. He was a great man, and if he had someone for me to meet, the guy was worth meeting.

When I got there, he hadn't turned up yet. But at the bar was this small, stocky, curly-haired, rugged-looking type who was talking too loudly but seemed to be having a great time. He was one of the agent's friends. I didn't pick up that he was syndicate or anything. He just seemed to be some guy with lots of money who enjoyed blowing it.

He was a little obnoxious and a braggart, but I sort of liked him because he was outspoken and frank. We talked about astrology and he was a Taurus. We hit it off famously.

Pretty soon I had half a dozen girls down there all spread around a table full of Manny's buddies. He slipped me $300 ten minutes after I sat down, and I remember thinking that wasn't bad for starters. He told me he didn't think I was his type when I first came in, since he liked blondes, but that would pass. Nice guy. But I wasn't at all offended. A lot of men are like that. I just put Kim on the poor bastard.

Actually Manny and I got to be pretty good friends. We never balled, but I would fix him up with girls and we often had drinks and dinner together.

That first night I noticed two guys at the bar occasionally eyeing our table. Later they got up and said something to one of the men in our party. Then he walked over to Manny and said something to him. "Okay… see you tomorrow," Manny said, and everyone burst out laughing.

It was the FBI, which had a permanent and very obvious tail on Manny, and that was the first time I knew something was a little strange about him.

As far as I knew, he had a big hotel called the Riviera outside of Chicago. Suddenly it dawned on me - these guys were all big hoods who had just come in from New York and Chicago, and the police figured something big was about to happen. It wasn't long before it was too goddamned clear that the cops were interested in Manny and his friends.

After the place closed, he asked if there was some place we could all have a drink. I suggested my house since it was as impressive as hell and certainly secluded. We went off in Manny's chauffeur driven car, stopping only for two cases of Dom Pérignon champagne and enough Scotch to fill the front seat.

I lit a fire and we drank. This was one of our all-time houses... tri-level, with huge bedrooms off the living room and a picture window that featured a view of Los Angeles all the way to the beach on a good day.

Cars were coming and going, and I wasn't sure who was where. Everyone partied until 5 or 5:30, when couples started tripping off to one bedroom or another. As it was getting light everyone went home. Manny thanked me for being a good hostess and handed me a thousand dollars on top of the carfare.

He called me the next day, and I got to be a fixture at his parties. Manny always gave me $600 or $800 for my trouble. He liked to ball two girls at once - one short and another tall and both blonde and busty. I never did know what he was doing in California, but it looked like a permanent move. He even had a private phone installed at the Luau, which was so exclusive some people couldn't even get drinks there.

I didn't know it at the time, but the government was hot to get Manny before a Senate committee and they were going over him like he just came back from the moon. One day I was in my dining room looking out the window, and noticed a car slow up a little too much on the curve outside. It just didn't look right. Then the car went up the hill, came back down, and parked a little ways away by Jack LaLanne's house. Two men got out and walked across from my house, looking sideways. I smelled cops all over the place. This was about a month after we had the party.

About then my phone started acting weird. I'd hear strange clicks in it. And later some really freaky calls came in. Like: "Hi, my name is Bill Paley and Henry Schmelch told me to give you a call. Why don't you come over?"

I mean, Jesus. I should just come over, right? Police must be really stupid to think a girl in my position would bite on that one. And then guys would call and start trying to talk about money. That was even more absurd. After about four of those calls, I started getting nervous.

One evening a little later my dog started barking in the house. Richard happened to be home so he picked up the baseball bat we kept by the door. He went into the garage and, sure enough, there was some clown in there. He had a flashlight, and he was studying the steering column. I guess he wanted to check the registration, but all he would have had to do was to run a make on the license number.

Anyway Richard came up from behind and thundered: "What the fuck are you doing?" The guy almost had a heart attack and mumbled something about the wrong house, and he split fast. Richard saw a second guy out front, so he went out and told them to get their asses off our property and stay the fuck away.

Well, it seemed a fairly safe assumption that something funny was going on, so I called Manny to tell him about it. He gave me a pretty good account of the situation and apologized for causing me so much trouble. I decided to move.

Making a move like that, under the best of circumstances, costs a hell of a lot of money. First you've got your phones and the rent money, besides all the calls you have to make telling people where you are. When you add the lost business, you can lose $20,000, so you just don't go hippity-hop from place to place.

But this was one case where we couldn't be greedy. We had to forget about the money and go. Kim, Sherry and Laura were living there at the time, so we had a lot of stuff. All the furniture and antiques were ours, too. Richard knew, of course, we just couldn't ring up Bekins and tell them to move us. That's much too easily traced, even if the cops don't see 6,000 moving men trooping in and out to a giant moving van outside.

We found a great new house, even better than the one we were leaving, and we got a rental truck. Now picture this: Here are four girls and one man in the dead of night loading an entire house, twenty-foot couch, king-sized beds, dogs and all, into an orange moving van.

We just got the last vibrators tucked away in the back when Richard noticed the heat across the street. The cops had moved into the place facing us, and were peering through the window, watching every move. We drove down the hill, and they started off right after us.

It was a real movie scene. We wanted them to know we knew and they wanted us to know they knew we knew. But it was like we were going to let them realize how hip they weren't. Richard drove onto the freeway and, in this huge rent-a-truck, lost them.

After we got settled, I called Manny and told him where we were. He met me and handed me an envelope, saying, "Here, kid, this is for your trouble." It had $3,000 in it.

I saw Manny a few times after that, but you can be sure I never took him home again. He was a good guy, a really nice generous gangster. After the incident with Manny, I took it a little easy. It was like giving the police the finger. You can only do that for so long, and then they're going to end up fingering you.

Manny and I lost touch after a while. Then in 1965 I picked up a newspaper and read that two days before Manny was to appear before a Senate investigating committee, a car whizzed by him at his house in Chicago and someone machine-gunned him to death.

* * *

One guy I met through Big Jim was a bookie from Vegas who I'm told was considered one of the world's biggest and best. He was a real Damon Runyon type, rough-speaking and hard. He used women like some guys used a vibrator... he didn't like them much.

He was real cloak-and-dagger. I went up to his room at the Beverly Hills Hotel. The bed and tables were covered with little bits of paper with numbers on them, and he scurried around to pick them up and hide them as soon as I walked in. The phones were ringing like crazy.

He was one of the few types I didn't get good vibes from. I somehow knew that this guy could be mean. I only stayed about an hour... very quick. I saw him a few times around the hotel later, but that was all.

* * *

One very gentlemanly hood I knew well was Allen Smiley. He was sitting on the same couch with Bugsy Siegel years ago when somebody stuck a gun through a window and blew Bugsy's head off.

When I was released from Corona Prison in 1968 (which I discuss in greater detail in Chapter 15), after a meteoric drop from riches to rags, I was living in a horribly morbid halfway house on Crenshaw run by Quakers who tried hard, but had nothing to work with. I hated it, but

I had no place else to go. After a week I decided to go out and see what was happening in the world, for a change, so I put on what good clothes I had left and went to a place on the Strip. I went up to the bar and found my old pal, Allen Smiley.

Allen almost didn't recognize me and I half didn't want him to. He was a great guy, lots of class, but he hung around with all sorts of mafia types and I was just out of prison for a non-sufficient funds check and on parole. But we started talking and I gave him a fill-in of what I'd been doing. He introduced me to this fantastic looking white-haired guy he was with, very well dressed, named Johnny Roselli. It happened that Roselli had just been indicted in the Friar's Club scandal where some very big names had been fleeced in rigged card games with electronic devices in the ceiling.

As everyone was getting drunker, I noticed a couple of straight-looking guys sitting at the other end of the bar. I didn't pay much attention. But then Roselli stood up and said to them, "Okay, boys, you can go home now. We're just going to take the lady home." Allen cracked up and said, "Don't worry, it's just the FBI." Oh, Jesus, I thought, a parole violation already. Associating with known felons.

They drove me to the halfway house in this super ratty area of Crenshaw and Washington, and Johnny asked, "What the fuck are you doing living in a dump like that?"

As we pulled up to the place, some butch from inside was making out with another girl in a Thunderbird, and I was really embarrassed. I told him I didn't have much choice, and he begged me to let him fly me back east and at least rent me an apartment somewhere with no strings attached.

I didn't take him up on it, but he certainly would have come through. It was typical of the system. Here was this man I barely knew, who had enough problems of his own, really wanting to help me. You have to respect that. All I got from the "good guys" was the crummy halfway house, full of druggies and dykes and all that shit.

* * *

In 1965 I met Ed the burglar, who I mentioned briefly near the beginning of this chapter. He was cooking pizzas in a little restaurant on

Santa Monica near Western. He looked something like a blond Clint Eastwood in a puffy white chef's hat. I was working there as a waitress and just cleaning up to close when I could tell Ed was screwing up his courage to come over. He asked if he could help, and we started talking. Within forty-eight hours he had asked me to marry him.

Ed went to jail when he was eighteen. He was thirty-two when I met him, and he'd been out for five months. Later I discovered he'd only had about two girlfriends in his life. The first time he balled anyone was when he was very young. The second and last time before meeting me was with a nurse at work camp. I never did figure out how he managed the second one, but he got the girl pregnant.

For pretty obvious reasons, he was tremendously shy. It was really difficult talking to him. I mean, what is a guy who's been in jail most of his life going to say if you start discussing things that happened two years ago? Usually he just listened.

The first night he walked me over to the apartment where I was staying with another girl who worked at the restaurant. We talked for a while and then suddenly he leaned over and kissed me. It was a nice kiss, like a little boy.

He tried to talk me into moving into his building, almost subtly. Then he said flatly that the girl I was living with was dating a guy just out of San Quentin, and my probation officers wouldn't be too happy about it. Naturally I didn't think about any danger in associating with him. What the hell, he was a nice guy and I liked him. I found a cute little $128 a week apartment near his, and he paid for it.

I still had my blue book and a couple of phone calls would have set me up again in great shape, but I just wasn't into it then. I wanted some time to get my head together, and Ed was sort of comfortable.

He was terribly lonely. Like a lot of guys who spent time in jail, he had been deprived of warmth and feeling for so long that he was like a puppy. He almost seemed to be sitting on his haunches hoping for a pat on the head.

It was especially bad for Ed. He told me his father hated him, for some reason, and threw him over a cliff when he was a young child. His mother screamed and panicked, and his father took off and left them. He was like a permanent downer with a grudge against the world. Ed's strongest childhood memories were of his drunken father beating up on his mother. As a young man, all he had to think about was prison.

Two days after that first night, Ed and I were having a drink before work, and he asked me if I would marry him.

At first I thought he had run out of topics of conversation. But he really meant it. It was flattering, I told him, but impossible. He hadn't the faintest idea of my then defunct Screw System with Richard. For all he knew, I liked working in a pizza dump.

Actually when Ed learned more about me, he simply whipped up a lot more money around him and pushed marriage all the harder. It was a pretty bad scene for Ed. My tastes still ran a little expensive, and he couldn't stand not flooding me with stuff.

We kept going out, but he started disappearing mysteriously about seven at night and coming back at ten. I knew it wasn't another woman, but I was curious. Then one night he came back grinning like a kid and said, "Come here, I've got something I want to show you."

He had about $3,000, and he gave me $1,000. I told him, "Listen, please don't get yourself into trouble." He told me it was card money. He had won it at poker. I wanted to believe him so badly that I think I really did. I took the money and got myself a nice apartment.

Ed and I only balled about half a dozen times in three months. He made fantastic love, but he was a little unsure of himself because he hadn't had much practice. I figured that a little cultivation could turn him into something incredible. But I had a few other hang-ups going then, and we didn't spend much time in bed. Ed was a little disturbed and kept accusing me of punishing him or Richard.

He kept producing piles of "poker money" and I suddenly found myself in the reverse position I had been in with Richard when I first got to California. Now I was playing Pygmalion. I helped Ed to speak better English. He had no sense at all about clothes, so I took his measurements and went to Sy Devore custom tailors in Hollywood for complete outfits. I bought him jewelry and took him to good places. He bought himself a cute little Sprite sports car because I liked it.

Ed kept up his crummy $80-a-week job to keep the heat off from his parole officer, but he was making so much on the side he was having trouble hiding signs of it. I would always insist that he not tell me anything about what he was doing, but I guess I knew it.

He was the most beautiful burglar I had ever seen. He was a second-story man, and a real pro. He'd break into empty houses and stores and rip off everything inside. He always carried a radio tuned to the police to keep a step ahead. He carried a gun when he had to, but didn't use it as far as I know.

His specialty was picking a huge store with lots of flashing signs and activity. He would slip in before closing and stash himself inside. When the place locked up he would clean it out.

One day he came to my place and said, "Here, hold this for me, will you?" It was a box with $32,000 in it. That was December, and Ed had gotten in on the Christmas business. I remember that well because another burglar almost got it all. I kept the money for Ed for a while, but then I decided to be funny and wrap it up for a Christmas gift.

A few nights before Christmas someone broke into my apartment and got away with just about everything of value. But he didn't touch the presents under the tree and missed the $32,000.

Ed always wore a green outfit with a green hat, and I called him the Jolly Green Giant because he was so tall. My mother and stepfather loved him because I had broken my pattern of bringing home Latins. Also, Ed would give my mother a mink or a diamond if he had a particularly good night, so she was thrilled to death. I'm not sure if she thought about where it was coming from, but at least Ed was blond and he wasn't an Italian or a Mexican.

He hated being a thief, but he really had no choice. That's what the system usually does, of course. A man is locked up with no chance at all to improve his education and background. And then when he comes out, no one wants to touch him. Ed loved to work, and he would have kept at a job twenty hours a day if it made any sense. But he was getting nowhere as a pizza cook, and he knew it.

Later I felt terrible about Ed because it was really due to me that he got back into crime. He might have done it anyway, but I was used to good things and he knew it. No matter what I said, he insisted on giving me things. If I happened to mention perfume in a conversation, there would be enough Ma Griffe to fill a bathroom sink waiting for me when I got home. Of course, I was the one who taught him about Ma Griffe and Joy.

After a while he started getting really persistent about marriage, and he got a little impatient with me. By then he was super-cool, with magnificent clothes and classy manners. He loved Vegas and women and gambling, so he would occasionally slip away for a weekend there. Eventually Ed came over and laid it out flat. Once and for all, he wanted to know, was I going to marry him or not? He gave me a thousand dollars and asked me to go to Palm Springs to think it over.

I went and took a girlfriend along, but it was a drag. We swam and messed around, but I was really up against it. On one hand I really liked Ed, and I saw a future with him. He was smart and with some money he had stashed away we could probably organize something that would keep us out of trouble.

On the other hand, there was a guy who had helped me and who I continued to see as a very close friend. He loved me, and he was up for murder and fighting a death sentence. I just couldn't drop out on him. There were a lot of other things messing up my mind, and it wasn't an easy choice.

But then while in Palm Springs I fell off a horse and fractured my back, so the decision was made for me.

I spent a long time in the hospital. Ed came rushing over at first and visited me often, but gradually he got involved with a chorus girl in Vegas. I had a big fight with him over that, and I told him to stay the hell away from me and he did.

Sadly, that wasn't the last I heard of Ed. He needed a lot of money to sustain his new lifestyle - the one I'd introduced him to - and in his position the only way he was going to get it was by using his gun. Eventually the police picked him up. Someone he worked with squealed on him, and he answered the description of a guy who'd been knocking off supermarkets for lots of money.

He was acquitted for lack of evidence. While the jury thought he was innocent, the Parole Board was sure he was back into crime. They caught him going to Las Vegas without his parole officer's permission.

I got to know a lot more outlaws during my time in prison. But like the hoods I first met when I was nineteen, and dozens of big-time bad guys I knew over the years, they were mostly men with a strict code of personal ethics who just wanted to fuck the system.

I never really lost my respect for them, as a group, from Mickey Cohen on down... even if some of them were cheap.

Chapter Thirteen

I would always jump at the chance to go to a party. Parties were where you met company directors who also needed classy women for entertaining - or bribing - people. And you never knew who else would turn up.

At one party I just happened to hit, for example, I met a famous bullfighter. We liked each other right away and I was his date for the evening. He was a perfect gentleman and, later, a tremendous lover.

He had miles of scars from being gored, but they were kind of sexy. We made love with his son sleeping in the next room. I felt a little weird about that. After that we were good friends. I could always count on at least $500 from him, and he introduced me to a lot of his rich friends.

Apart from the money, it was fun being out with someone like him. He got applause every place he went, and my stock went up just by being around him.

My work days were pretty relaxed when Richard wasn't giving me a hard time. I never woke up before 9:30 and almost always ate breakfast out. We swam a lot and played tennis.

My one rule was Never on Sunday - I think I only broke it a few times in all my career. That was strictly a rest day and even Richard was lucky to get any on the Sabbath.

I've got to admit, there is an awfully thin line between screwing a guy because it's worth something and just balling him because you like him. If it's for pay, there are rules. If it's for play, anything goes, and the hell with it.

It's not so bad for hard-headed business women in brothels and on the streets. But for someone like me, who never promised anything and never set a price, decisions were sometimes pretty hard.

And then there were special cases. For example, I once heard about a guy I'll call Melvin who bought a very famous property from Howard Hughes for millions and millions of dollars.

He had a terrible impotency problem. He simply couldn't get it up, no matter how much he wanted to. This guy, I figured, had to be a gold mine for the girl who finally made it. And I decided I would be the one.

Arranging a meeting was no problem, and Melvin asked me to dinner. We went out a few times and eventually wound up in his bedroom.

I worked over him like I was researching a textbook on conquering impotency. I used every trick I had ever heard about - talking about sex in case he couldn't get his mind off business, using vibrators and soapsuds, stripping and dancing and posing nude - you name it.

We relaxed with some good wine, and I tried again, building up slowly with music and incense and endless fondling, tickling and kissing.

Melvin was tremendously charming and a warm and considerate lover, but his joint was as limp as a garden hose and there was no way I could attract its attention. Then it got to be an obsession, the only thing I thought about for days. I tried again another night with the same results.

He was totally crushed and embarrassed to the point of tears. He handed me a thick stack of hundreds, I don't even know how many, but I refused. I wouldn't even take cab fare.

Other times I would ball guys for free just because they turned me on, and I needed a break. That used to infuriate Richard. Mainly I think he was afraid I was wasting the merchandise and risking a bad reputation, but I also suspect he was jealous.

After all, he was my husband and if I went to bed with another guy purely because I liked him, it meant I was being unfaithful. And Richard didn't like me to be unfaithful.

The guys who got it free from me were physically good looking men who showed signs of being able to satisfy me as well as themselves. It wasn't always easy to tell, since so many gorgeous guys are freaked out on their own bodies and just consider women as an occasional alternative to masturbation.

Often they were glamorous, handsome types like the young actor, Bob, who I mentioned earlier, who was balling me when Richard came storming into the motel room.

* * *

When I first saw my football hero - that backfield star of an Eastern pro-team - for instance, thoughts of money were - believe it or not - not even in my head.

I had gone back to Philadelphia to visit my sons around late 1961 and was staying in a hotel. My father was coming over to meet me, and I was in the dining room looking very sharp in furs and carefully done hair.

The football hero walked into the room, and I did an authentic cartoon-style double take. He was enormous, a fantastic Italian with dark eyes and curly hair and a hoody-looking trench coat. I was sure he was an authentic gangster, and I was panting all over the table. He sat down three tables away and kept checking me out. All of a sudden he stood up, walked over and said, "Hi!" and sat down - at my table.

He really came on heavy, telling me he played professional football for the Philadelphia Eagles and gave me some entertaining background. I told him I was a model from California and my name was Romney Ames.

I also told him I was waiting for my father. He was deciding whether or not to believe me when my father walked in. The three of us talked for a while, with my dad seizing the chance for some free tickets and a great new name to drop, and my new friend suggested we meet for a drink later.

We really clicked, laughing and going from club to club. He was incredibly egotistical, but he had a lot behind it. He even sent my boys an autographed picture and a football. We got thoroughly plastered together and went back to his hotel and balled. We were both too drunk to enjoy it much, but I remember his body was breathtaking, exactly like a marble sculpture.

I saw him a couple of times before I had to go back to California. A few years later I went out with him again in Philadelphia. That was when we balled while he talked to his girlfriend in New York over the phone.

He never gave me anything, but then some guys don't have to.

There were a few others I slept with for free - some who offered money I refused, and others who understood that I didn't want anything from them. But Richard had always come down so hard on free-asses, and I had such a hard approach toward giving it away for nothing, that it wasn't easy for me to do.

Once when I was being kept by Walter the Roach in that penthouse on Wilshire Boulevard, I met a fabulous looking young Greek actor named Nico. The first or second day after I moved in, I was down by the pool and he came over and introduced himself.

He was tremendously good looking, tall and dark and smooth. He had come over recently from Greece and his accent was still pretty thick, but he was witty and interesting. Nico never could figure out what was going on with me, since I wasn't really living in the building but pretending to for Walter's sake.

At that time, Nico was just getting big in films and he threw cocktail parties all the time. He always invited me, and a couple of times I went. At one he gave me my first - and last - martini, a triple that was powerful enough to pickle the olive.

It clobbered me almost immediately, and I excused myself to go upstairs. He went along to make sure I was all right, and he came inside. We sat down on the couch and started kissing and hugging.

I really wanted to ball Nico then. He was magnificent. But I had this thing about being added to someone's list, and about being a free-ass. I was already home so there was no reason for him to give me cab fare. He tried to date me a few times after that, but I simply couldn't get past my inhibitions.

Years later I ran into Nico again. He had done extremely well and was into producing and directing. He had a beautiful home, and he invited Kim and me over there with some other guy. Nico was lying on a bed reading a script when we got there, and I went in to talk to him. He took me in his arms, and I was a lot more open than I had been previously.

We lay there for a half hour necking like a couple of teenagers in the back of a car. But in the intervening years nothing had changed - I just didn't feel like giving it away, and Nico didn't push.

* * *

The one time I really did let go, when I just decided money and ego simply didn't matter, I brought the whole operation down around me in one momentous landslide.

It started in the spring of 1964 when Kim and I had that chance to go to New York with two very, very rich and attractive young men from Phoenix. As I said, Richard didn't want us to go because he was afraid - as he always was when I went near Philadelphia - that I wouldn't come back. As it turned out, I did stay.

We first met Phil and Eric, who set Kim and me up in this fantastic Jenkintown place. Phil was anything but for free. But while he was in Pittsburgh, leaving me to entertain myself, I met Dr. Herschel Kaplan.

Just looking at Dr. Kaplan made my panties wet. The chemistry was simply explosive. The second I saw him I knew something had to be arranged fast and it was going to be on the house.

I met him by the pool at our apartment building a few weeks after we moved in. He came over and introduced himself without any silly excuses or lines. Within twenty minutes, he had invited Kim and me both out to dinner. I liked that because he made no attempt to separate us and make a play only for one. As it turned out, Kim was feeling lousy and she stayed home.

Herschel was a nice Jewish boy from a good family with a classic upbringing. He was a gynecologist-pediatrician who, I soon found out, enjoyed looking at female equipment from a personal viewpoint as well as a professional one. He had just gone into practice in Philadelphia with a well-known specialist, and he looked enormously successful. He drove a little white Jaguar and dressed elegantly. His manners were excellent, and his conversation fascinating.

It didn't take long to get into bed, and when we did, I couldn't believe it. He was such a good lover that I would get goose bumps for hours afterwards. I had always played cute little games with men - I had to be chased, followed, worried over. But with Herschel, it was completely different. He was so affectionate that I knew he sincerely cared about me from the very beginning, and I treated him like I would a man I loved even before I realized I loved him.

We had such a great time balling that I used to look forward to getting home and into bed all through dinner. No matter how much I had liked men in the past, and how hot I was for them, I could always switch off long enough to enjoy a long leisurely meal and an evening on the town.

But with Herschel I was reaching under the table for his thigh before the steaks arrived. He knew his profession well, and there's a lot of technical stuff about turning people on that you don't get from practical experience. Herschel knew his way around down there like nothing I had ever seen. He prescribed himself amyl nitrate and we would scream and moan and pound the bed in unbelievable ecstasy when we came together - which was most of the time.

Over the weeks I knew Herschel, I developed a deep, warm respect for him that went far beyond the fun we had in bed. He was tremendously dedicated to medicine. No matter where we were or what was happening, he never hesitated a moment if he was asked to go on a call. I would go to the hospital with him and wait in the little room where doctors' wives stay when their husbands are busy. And then he would come back all relaxed, and would think about how he had just brought a new life into the world.

Herschel lived in the same building where Phil had his office-apartment. Even when Phil was in town from Pittsburgh and I was with him in his office, I would sometimes excuse myself and run up three floors to see Herschel. After a while I was so hot for him that the thought of making it with anyone else actually made me sick to my stomach. Every time Phil made a pass at me - which wasn't unreasonable considering I was costing him at least $5,000 a month - it almost made me retch. Oops, I figured, trouble.

Not only was Phil laying out all this bread and getting a little nervous, but I had a greedy husband in California who was getting wildly anxious to bring me back home to look after our rapidly disintegrating Hollywood Screw System. A few girls were still with us then, but the phone calls for Kim and me were starting to slow down a bit, and Richard was worried we would lose too many regulars if we didn't get home soon.

All these things were flying around my head when I went out for a magnificent evening with Herschel. It was one of those nights straight out of an Arpege ad. I was dancing on clouds and all that sort of drivel. Really, I was happy as hell and comfortable and so was Herschel. He looked at me seriously and told me he loved me. I had heard that more times than I could count in a week, but Herschel meant it.

That night I went home and wrote a "Dear Richard" letter. I didn't mention Herschel to Richard, but I said we were drifting off in two different directions, and it was time to call off the whole thing. We had had a pretty good life I told him, but I just couldn't handle any more of the hassles and the pressures. I liked him, I said, but there was just too much bullshit. From the way I worded the letter it was final.

At the time we lived in one of our nouveau-loaded Hollywood palaces. We had fabulously expensive furnishings, antiques, art pieces - one marble statue was worth more than $15,000. We owned a Cadillac, a Lincoln and a station wagon, and closets and closets of furs and clothing. I told Richard he could have the whole thing, everything. I just wanted freedom.

I had figured that giving him all our stuff would take the edge off his anger. But of course, that's not how Richard's mind worked. Apart from the car payments, he immediately thought of the thousands of dollars that wouldn't come in every week and the work he would have to do with someone else if he wanted to get going again.

Above all, I had kicked him in the balls, and his Spanish macho ego was howling to beat hell. I had said to him in effect, "Okay, you prick, you've always said I was nothing without you - now let's see how it works." Frankly, all Richard was doing in the last few years was answering a few phones, shopping for groceries occasionally and bitching. I was beginning to consider him overpaid.

Once I had written Richard, my bridges were burned. But everything was beautiful with Herschel, I thought, so what the hell. Of course he hadn't asked, but I could see myself as his wife, and it was an attractive picture. I knew I could make a good wife for someone like him, and I could be satisfied with his kind of life. There was my own past that could present a problem, I knew, but I didn't think that would stop things.

I had told Herschel a little about Richard. I said he was an actor, and we were separated. After all, there were 3,000 miles between us. And I think he had an inkling that something was going on with Phil, but he didn't seem particularly upset.

After breaking it off with Richard, I planned to lay it all out for Herschel. You can't have these little surprises for people that keep springing out at awkward times. If you're going to have an honest, strong relationship, things have got to be on the table.

I had no doubts at all in my mind. He was a guy, for example, who I could give presents to without the slightest thought of scheming. When I gave him things like gold tipped matches with his initials on the box, or a red silk robe, he was so obviously pleased that it gave me enormous satisfaction, and it ended at that.

I was sure we could make it. Every minute we spent together was fun for both of us - we laughed, balled, talked and just generally grooved on each other's company. It wouldn't be easy once Herschel learned more about me, I knew, because he had his life laid out on a master plan.

He was thirty-three then and, by the time he was thirty-eight, he would be a professor of medicine at a good school doing research. He would marry between ages thirty-eight and forty and retire before he was forty-five. (And he's kept to it, by the way. He is married and into really important research, but I guess he's still easy. I told him I was writing a book and he asked what I'd say about him. I replied I would say he was a good lay, and he roared with laughter.)

So there we were. I had cut myself loose and was selecting the moment to lay things out to Herschel. The key would be the right words and the right moment, and I was searching carefully for both. What I didn't know was that I was too late.

Good old Kim beat me to it.

During the time I was first dating Herschel, Kim was staying around as Phil's secretary and collecting great chunks of money from Eric. She was getting edgy because Eric started seriously falling in love with her, and she wanted to go back to California. Just to keep her happy, I used to take her out with Herschel and me.

After a while, she decided she loved Herschel and had to have him.

I was flying all over the place with Phil, leaving Kim a clear field. Several times Herschel told me she came over to his place when I was gone, and he asked me to get her to stop it. I didn't realize how heavy she was with him, and I figured she was just lonely.

Kim had started acting a little strange around me, and it was hard to pinpoint. We had been best friends for years. We'd made a lot of money - and a lot of people - together, and we knew each other well. But I just couldn't figure it out. I was so preoccupied with my relationships with Phil and Herschel that I wasn't paying much attention.

And then, when things got the most strained on all fronts and I was still deciding how to tell about my past, I started getting abdominal pains and checked into a hospital. I needed a chance to think. But those few days were all Kim needed.

Herschel came to see me in the hospital, and he sat down at the edge of the bed. His eyes were moist and he said, "I know, Rom. I know everything. I understand." That's all he said. Jesus, I thought, I hadn't even told him my real name. And suddenly I figured out why Kim had been acting so weird lately. The next day I was still feeling sick, but I checked out of the hospital and went to my apartment.

I couldn't find Kim and that was unusual since there weren't many places to go around there, and we were generally home about that time. A few hours later, I went down to the drugstore to get a sandwich, and this waitress, a groovy black girl who I had given things to from time to time, pulled me aside and said, "You know, your girlfriend... she's out with Herschel."

Shit, I thought, it's all over.

It was almost funny, like a Peanuts routine. Here's the world-famous super-swift sex queen, mover of men and women, master of the meek, torrid yet tender, shot down by her trusty sidekick who she'd always considered dumber than her. Kim had really done it this time, wiping me out on all fronts before I realized what was happening. When Herschel told me at the hospital that he knew everything I realized Kim was involved, but I wasn't sure what it meant. I thought I could gather up the old forces and talk my way out of it.

But suddenly it was clear as hell. This time I had really been royally fucked. Raped would be a better word.

As I sat there stunned, Kim came bouncing into the drugstore, all smiles and friendly. "Hi," I said, "where've you been?"

"Oh, out." Then she and I went up to the apartment and started talking.

It took about forty-five seconds for things to break out into the open. Kim blew up and started shouting:

"Goddamn it, you've always had every fucking thing you wanted. You wanted Richard and you got him. He didn't want me, he couldn't stand me, it was always you. Well, this time it's going to be different. I've been seeing Herschel and he's mine now, not yours. I stopped you cold, baby. I not only told him everything, I told him things that never

ever happened. And not only that, I'm gonna tell Phil everything, too. I'm gonna bust the shit out of your bubble and let's see you get out of this one..."

I threw a vase at her and yelled, "Motherfucker, you're not going to destroy me. You're not smart enough."

Kim was a hysterical chick anyway, and she shrieked, "I will, I will..."

My mind was really messed up. How could she do it, I had shared every single thing I had, even Richard and Herschel. If I got a pair of shoes, she got a pair of shoes. Down to the smallest detail, I was so careful to make sure she was never slighted. She was the only girl I really trusted, and she was about my only true friend.

Looking back, I forgive her. I can see all the years of jealousy building up over Richard. I had been the top girl, always, and it must have been smoldering inside her for years. But right then, I wasn't hearing any of it from that rotten, motherfucking, disgusting little ungrateful piss-ant bitch.

I heard her screaming, "I will..." and I grabbed a butcher knife out of the sink and dived for her. Then she really screamed and tore out of the apartment so fast the wall is probably still cracked where the door slammed.

I chased her down the stairs, flight after flight, swiping at her back with the knife every time I was close enough. Once I almost got her, damn near ripping the back of the blouse she had gotten with money I had helped her earn.

We were panting and gasping and slipping and falling. She was never more than a few steps ahead of me, and both of us were bouncing off the walls and slamming through the doors at each landing. Our apartment was seven stories up, and I chased her all the way down to the bottom. When we got to the patio, she ran past the pool, and I suddenly caught myself. I stopped dead, looked at the knife and started crying.

I wasn't upset about Kim. I was still sorry she outran me. But it was now fully sinking in, what had been obvious in the drugstore. I had lost Herschel and, not that it mattered so much, also Richard. Now it was even worse. Phil would be finished, too. And I had no breathing time at all. In a few weeks' time I had gone from a tremendously profitable and enjoyable life to absolutely nothing. My time with Herschel had convinced me that I couldn't go back to the kind of life I had before, but I didn't know where else to go.

The first thing I had to do was talk to Herschel, but I knew it was futile. I had a few drinks to steady myself, and then I went over to see him. The minute I walked in, I knew there was no point in saying anything. Kim had really done a job. She had glossed over her own part of everything and made it look as though I had forced her into a life of white slavery at gunpoint. She told him I was mixed up in drugs. She even said that I hated Jews and would never leave Richard.

Herschel was polite and warm, but I just said I had to go. I went out and got so stinking drunk I gave away my mink stole.

Finally I staggered home. When I went in I found the closet doors open and everything gone. Kim had taken all her clothes, and also nearly all of mine. She took every bit of jewelry and all the luggage. There had been about $18,000 worth of clothes and furs in there, and all that was left was a couple of lousy dresses that didn't fit me.

I was so shattered I had to go back and spend the night at Herschel's. There was still nothing to say, but I was lost and empty.

In the meantime, Kim called Phil and told him I was going out with a doctor who lived in his building. That was why I was never there when the phone rang, she said. She told him I was only taking his money and sending it to my husband in California and making a fool of him.

The next day a friend of Phil's called to say that if I felt like going back to California he would send me a ticket and some money for expenses.

I sat down and cried and cried for hours. Later I forced myself to think analytically and try to respond with a little strength. My financial position was zero. Whatever Phil sent over the next day would be my cash resources. What I hadn't given Richard, Kim had stolen. I hadn't made any investments and didn't keep money in the bank. Richard took care of minor details like that.

I called Ronnie Howard, a friend in Los Angeles, and told her I was in trouble. I gave her a little of the background, and she was a great help. "What the hell," she said, "come and stay with me."

Herschel came over the next day as I was packing the few things I had left. He put his arm around me and said, "I want you to know that I've always cared for you." That's all. If he had said anything about staying, I would have done it. But we both knew what our relationship would do to him, especially with Kim on the loose, so he didn't ask.

I flew to Los Angeles from Philadelphia with just about as much money as I had the time I was nineteen, twelve years earlier, to make my fortune.

Chapter Fourteen

Ronnie met me at the airport and drove me to her apartment on Sunset Strip. She had all sorts of surprises. First, um, uh, she had been dating Richard, see? "Well, actually, you know, Virginia, we're pretty good friends. Er, what I mean is…"

By the end of the conversation I got the picture: she wanted me to move back into the house Richard and I owned and resume things like before - except that she would be me, and I would be Kim and Sherry and Vicky…

Well, screw it. I was so hung up on Herschel and down on Richard, it didn't really make much difference. I wasn't going to put out and pass fortunes to Richard anymore. But living in the house wouldn't be a problem. After all, it was mine.

As Ronnie and I were talking it over, who walks in the door but the old foxy fucker himself. First he looked as if someone had kicked him in the balls, and then he whipped out one of his super-cool expressions. "Oh, hello, Virginia." He was cordial but it was like we were strangers. And I could tell he was getting upset and flustered.

Actually, it wasn't that much of a shock for me. I had introduced Ronnie to Richard a while before I went to Philadelphia. I'd known her for years after we had met at a Hilton party. She was always a lady, very soft spoken with absolutely no vulgarity. But she had a violent side that slipped out sometimes and a larceny streak a mile long.

She ran away from home at fifteen because her cop father was so strict, and she married a black musician a year or two later when that just wasn't done. She had a number of arrests behind her for various things, but we were always pretty close.

I hadn't seen her for years when I suddenly got a call from a friend of mine not long before I went to Philadelphia. Ronnie was looking for me and could she have my number? "Sure," I said, and soon afterward she phoned me. She was broke and needed help badly. She told me she was on parole and I couldn't believe all the rules and prohibitions.

Ronnie was scared to leave the county. She wanted me to pass over any calls from men in case I was too busy. I felt sorry for her and promised to do everything I could.

When I went to Philadelphia, she asked if she could buy my little blue book. I told her to take it. "You're a friend," I said. "You're welcome to it." This surprised Ronnie, I remember, because she was extremely businesslike. She wouldn't turn down a $25 date because four of those make a hundred. I never saw it that way, so I gave her the book, introduced her to Richard and took off.

Later, in Philadelphia, Phil was looking for girls for a party and I told him about Ronnie. He sent her some money and a ticket. She was nervous about traveling because of her parole, and she was on a program where they pulled surprise urine tests to see if you're on drugs. But she went anyway, and she latched on to a big-deal New York bank president.

This was after I'd written Richard that it was all over. She had obviously been seeing him a lot. She asked me three different times if I was really through with him, and there was no chance of getting it together again. "Ronnie," I said, "we've been through for seven years, but I just never did anything about it. If you want him, help yourself."

She did. And, of course, Richard wasn't going to mess around without a source of income. He had payments to make and a way-of-life to maintain, and he sure as hell wasn't going to work. By the time I got back to California, Richard and Ronnie were living together in the house, running the Screw System.

I wasn't bitter at all, if secretly a little hurt, because I really did worry about Richard in spite of it all. With Ronnie I knew he was in good hands. And she had been totally honorable about it all.

It was pretty funny for the next few months. I kept forgetting what bedroom to use, and I had a little trouble adjusting to being a tenant in my own house.

One night we all sat down to talk and decided that Richard and I should get a divorce. We piled into one of the cars, God knows whose name it was registered in by then, and drove down to Tijuana for a family divorce, Richard, Ronnie and me.

Richard and I ended our ten year marriage on November 1st, 1964. The three of us celebrated by roaring around Tijuana for a while, then we all went home on whatever the opposite of a honeymoon is.

I continued to live with Richard and Ronnie, but I had lost any desire to make money. I helped and did things around the house, but the atmosphere was getting a little tense.

Richard and I were standing out by the pool one day having an argument, and as usual, when his temper started to get hot he just couldn't keep his hands off me. He shoved me and I slipped and took a bad fall on the concrete.

I felt all right for a while, but the next day I was screaming. The pain in my back was agonizing and since I was home alone I called a doctor who put me in a hospital immediately.

By this time I was so pissed off at Richard that I didn't tell him where I was. Ordinarily he would look and find me but this time, after a few days, when he didn't come looking I thought, screw him!

At the hospital they operated and removed a spinal disc and by the time they got my back into shape so that I could walk again, two months had passed. When they handed me the bill which ran to $13,000, I decided it was time to call Richard and Ronnie.

When the operator told me that their phone was disconnected, I got a little nervous. I called Ronnie's answering service and got nowhere. By then the hospital's credit department was beginning to wonder why I wasn't in a hurry to finally go home.

I did have about $6,000 in cash and was barely able to walk and not knowing when I'd be working again, I figured I'd be stupid to give them my last dollar, so I lied and told them I didn't have enough money in my checking account at the moment. But the hospital told me simply to postdate the check.

Well, I was still in pain and I was loaded with Demerol, and also, I had another problem. To throw Richard off the trail I had checked in under a phony name. So, I wrote a postdated check for $13,000 under a phony name, and committed my first and only felony.

As soon as I left the hospital I went shooting over to the house. It was empty. Richard and Ronnie had cleaned out the place - right down to the four walls. Oh shit, I thought, this is getting monotonous. First Kim had cleaned me out in Philadelphia. Then, after nearly a year of building myself up again to a reasonable level, I was totally screwed over again.

I managed to make it through the next few months with some help from my friends, and once my mother phoned me to say that the police were looking for me because of that hospital check. Then, on top of everything else, my back started hurting so much, I had to check into a hospital again.

This time I checked into a different one and when they insisted upon seeing my hospital insurance card or getting a deposit, I wrote another bad check for $150 and they admitted me. Whatever had been wrong with my back was taken care of quickly and I was sent home.

I'd been in my apartment for only a few days when I answered a loud knocking on the door to find five burly guys flashing badges saying they wanted to talk to me about my ex-husband, Richard Lopez.

I let them in and they started questioning me about Richard's activities. What was he involved in? Where was his money coming from? Who were his friends? Where was he working from? And when I told them I didn't have any of the answers they didn't believe me. I tried to tell them that his business was as much of a mystery to me as it was to them but that didn't cut the mustard.

They wanted me to introduce one of their agents to Richard and help them set him up, with the bottom line being that if I didn't cooperate with them, they would make sure that the hospital pressed the phony check charges against me, which meant prison. They didn't care how I set Richard up. All I had to do was do it or end up in the can.

I agreed to help them just to get them out of the house and as soon as they left I walked two miles - and every step was a painful one - to my mother's place. I was certain that they had my phone tapped. I had the phone number of Richard's answering service and as soon as I got to my mom's I put a call through to him and he returned the call within thirty minutes.

I hadn't spoken to him in well over a year and I told him what I had just gone through with the police and what they wanted me to do. He seemed surprised and denied any wrong doing. He told me that all of his close associates were childhood friends. It was all buddy-buddy stuff, nothing more.

Whether he was telling me the truth I had no way of knowing, but he ended the conversation by saying that he would shortly come to my mom's place and pick me up for some further talk. Very late that night he showed up and we spent three hours together going over his situation and mine. He finally said that he realized what a terrible position I was in and knew of a small house in Malibu that was available, that I could hide there until things blew over.

I hid in Malibu for about three months. Richard would drive down and drop some money off so that I could survive. My mother had told me that the police had been by her place several times looking for me and I was in a constant state of panic. There was no doubt that the police had gotten the hospitals to file bad check charges against me by then.

I had never been in any trouble in my life. My troubles began when I married the wrong man, one who had been totally secretive about the source of his income. Now here I was, hiding out from an arrest warrant that I could have avoided if I'd been willing to turn "snitch" on him.

Any love I might have felt for Richard had long been a thing of the past. There had been too many beatings, punches, and slaps, with resultant bruises, aches and pains, that wiped out anything even resembling love.

I'd been divorced from Richard for over a year now and my decision to dissolve our marriage was helped along by the fact that I had met and fallen in love with Doctor Herschel Kaplan, a handsome MD from Philadelphia.

Unfortunately, Herschel and I didn't work out but our brief relationship turned out to be the best thing that could have happened to me. He opened my eyes and made me see Richard for what he really was, an unfeeling, uncaring, self-centered brute, while Herschel was a kind and loving man, a decent man who I loved and respected. We could have had a good life together, and when it was all over between us we still remained good friends. When Richard hid me in Malibu it was only to make sure that the police didn't get to me and make me tell them what little I knew about him - which was actually nothing.

I came to realize that I couldn't stay holed up in Malibu forever, and besides I didn't want the strain of dealing with Richard who was still involved with Veronica Hughes, or Ronnie Howard, as I knew her.

I made the decision to move in with a school teacher friend of mine who lived in Los Angeles and made the mistake of telling my mom my new address. She inadvertently told my stepfather who in turn told the police.

When they arrested me in front of my friend's house they were fairly kind to me. They didn't put any handcuffs on me when they took me to Sybil Brand Institute for women and booked me. The place looked like a huge hospital with bars, and they threw me into a holding tank with about fifteen girls who had just been busted, too.

Being behind bars was a shocking experience but I had resolved that under no circumstances would I cooperate despite the fact that they approached me several times to tell me that all I had to do was talk and the charges would be dropped. They made it clear that the other alternative was that they would press the District Attorney to ask for jail time. I was between a rock and a hard place. What little I did know about Richard would have meant nothing to them, so what was the point? They wouldn't believe me, anyway.

The tank was a horrible place for everyone ranging from women arrested for traffic violations to murderers. I recoiled at the sight of some poor druggie lying on the floor in her own waste and the matrons saying to her, "You shoved the stuff into your arm, now shit it out!"

There was another girl undergoing horrible withdrawal symptoms. She was throwing up and moaning and one tough broad was giving her a bad time until a few others jumped on her saying: "She's suffering, man; if you don't like it, don't look."

One little old lady kept giving the matrons trouble until they just jacked her arm up behind her and broke it. They all had foul mouths and treated the girls like garbage.

There was a long line of girls waiting to use the one payphone and when my turn came I called my mom. It's a tough thing to have to say to your mother, "Hi, I'm in prison." She was sympathetic but there was no way she could come up with the bail. I gave her Ronnie's phone number and told her to keep calling until she got a response. I also called Ronnie's and Richard's answering service time after time with no luck. At the very least they owed me bail.

After making some ten fruitless calls, the message suddenly came to me loud and clear. Richard was letting me twist in the wind. I was in and he was out and that was my hard luck. He was a traitorous skunk, pure and simple.

How many times over the years he would spout his line of B.S., "Whatever happens, you take care of your own. If one is in trouble, the rest help. Old beefs and brawls don't count when someone is in trouble with the heat." And on and on and on. Pure B.S. I didn't see him again until a year later when I ran into him accidentally. And Ronnie I didn't see each other until four years later when we met in jail.

The most degrading experience took place when I was stripped, showered and sprayed for lice and crabs when I came out of the holding tank. What followed made me feel as though I'd machine-gunned a class full of kindergarten kids. Very stern matrons who looked like they'd come out of a rock quarry instead of a woman's womb, had me fingerprinted and took my mug shot. I filled out nine or ten cards, mostly so that the FBI had handwriting samples. Then they put me into another holding cell and then upstairs in a cellblock.

I found myself in a small cell within a cell and when I heard those doors slam shut, the solid reality of where I was hit me like a ton of bricks and I cried. The futility and loneliness and absolute stupidity of getting locked into a prison cell is something that has to be felt to be imagined. And it's not worth the trouble, believe me.

I spent seventy-two of the longest days of my life in that cell before I was bailed out.

By then I had been really desperate. I wrote to my friend, the race-track king, and another friend, after some others who I thought I could count on wanted no part of the situation, and they both wired money to my mother. But the bail was $1,650, lowered from the original $5,000, and I was still short. A bail bondsman would have had to put up the bond with the deposit my friends had sent, but my mother wouldn't sign the guarantee. She was afraid if the bondsman called her boss to verify that she was working, she would lose her job. I couldn't blame her.

My break finally came, indirectly, through Richard. During our marriage I'd often heard Richard talk about a guy named Ernie Lopez. Now Richard badmouthed everybody but to him Ernie was a god, a big-time hijack specialist who never touched jobs under $100,000. Richard said Ernie was being railroaded to the gas chamber because of his record.

Ernie had been convicted of taking part in a robbery in which five people were shot and one died. His alleged partner admitted to the murder and swore that Ernie was not the man involved with him. But he wouldn't tell them who the man was.

I learned later that Richard and Ernie had a firm business connection I won't discuss. Also, Ernie's girlfriend was a good friend of Richard's.

I was in the bathroom area one morning when I heard some girls talking about a fantastic guy who had just been brought in from San Quentin for a court appearance. He had studied law in prison and was defending himself.

Although he had been convicted of murder, the girls said he had found a flaw in the trial and was awarded a penalty hearing. That meant that he was going before a judge and there was a chance his death penalty could be changed to either life or a long fixed term. The girls spoke of him as though he was some holy man, and I had been listening only half-heartedly until I found out that they were talking about Ernie.

Ernie had been in San Quentin with the husband of a girl named Bobbie who was in my cellblock. Ernie had a message for her from her husband, so he had her summoned. According to law, he was entitled to call in people by a court order as possible witnesses in his penalty hearing. If he wanted to talk to someone, he got an order and the police had to comply.

The minute Bobbie came back, I rushed over to talk to her. She said that Ernie was desperately lonely, since he hadn't seen a woman in five years, and he had asked if she knew any interesting girls he could call over just to talk. I almost choked. "Listen Bobbie," I said, "tell him that my former husband is Richard Lopez, and I would love to meet him." A few mornings later at nine o'clock the matrons came to my cell and got me.

Ernie was in the old county prison, and I couldn't believe all the B.S. involved in getting me out of where I was and into where he was. We finally went up to the thirteenth floor in a little area where lawyers see their clients.

You sit on wooden benches with a divider between you, but you can see who you're talking to. I had no idea what Ernie looked like, and my mind was working furiously when two guards brought him in.

He was about 5'8", stocky with huge, bulging muscles. He wasn't really handsome, but he had a gentle, magnetic look that commanded instant respect. I liked him immediately and loved him after a few minutes.

Of all the men I describe in superlatives, Ernie had to be one of the most amazing men alive. His father had forced him onto the streets when he was three-and-a-half years old to sell newspapers. When he didn't bring home enough money, his father would give him a beating, tie a rope around him and throw him into a closet. The older man would lash him to a highchair and shove food down him through a funnel. Ernie grew up tough.

He got into crime young, and had spent most of his life in jail. His time out of jail came about mainly because of some incredible escapes. Early in his career, he was one of the few to break out of McNeil Island and swim three miles through the icy cold water to freedom. After a year on the streets he returned to his apartment one day and found the police waiting. Some snitch had turned him in.

One cop, he told me, came up from behind and, without a word, fired five shots pointblank into his back. Ernie turned around, hit the guy and ran. Bleeding like crazy, he managed to get a mile away and hide under a house. The police had followed him, cordoned off the area and were shooting at him. He said he heard a strange hissing sound. He looked down and found it was coming from his own chest wounds and realized if he didn't surrender, he would bleed to death.

He crawled out and gave himself up, but the police kicked and beat him badly, breaking a few ribs. They only stopped, he said, when an old lady came up and raised so much hell they had to back down.

Ernie was shackled to a bed in the prison ward at County hospital. On the thirteenth day, after doctors had just removed the last bullet, he got hold of a paperclip and picked the locks on his legs. He made it to the street, but they caught him.

In prison, the guards broke his jaw and tortured him. He spent seven months straight in the hole, coming out every twenty-ninth day because the law demanded it.

In spite of this, Ernie was incredibly kind, generous and gentle. He had the saddest, most beautiful eyes I had ever seen.

Our first meeting lasted only five or ten minutes, but we really dug each other and I knew I would be back. During the next month, he called me two or three times a week, sometimes stretching the visits to an hour and a half by insisting I was a prospective witness.

During that time, I developed a deep feeling of admiration for Ernie. He told me why he was convicted. He wasn't with Red, the guy in the robbery, at all. But a few months later at 4:00 am, the police picked up Red and Ernie when they ran a red light in the same car. They were on their way to check out a bank. The fact that there were all sorts of guns in the trunk didn't help.

Red testified over and over that Ernie had nothing to do with the robbery and the killing, but he would never tell them who his partner really was. Red died of cancer in prison without ever revealing the name of his real partner. Ernie's past, apparently, was evidence enough.

Once he mentioned needing certain books because of a point of law that he hoped might help his defense. When I was arrested I had $100 on me which was credited to me and I could spend it. I arranged for someone to get the books that Ernie needed. I don't know why I thought he didn't have any money, but I just wanted to do it for him.

He was completely overcome and had tears in his eyes when he thanked me. No one had ever shown him that much kindness, he said, and that touched me deeply. Still, what's a lousy $100 when it might save a life - especially his?

On one visit he told me he couldn't believe I had been locked up for a lousy hospital bill and had to get me out of jail. To help him prepare his case he had his own phone in his cellblock and he called a bail bondsman.

Now there are two reputations you can get in prison: you're a fuck-off artist or you're a righteous dude. Ernie was tops and his word was enough. He guaranteed my bail over the phone and on Friday, the thirteenth of August 1965, during the time the Watts riots were going on, I was free again.

That, more than anything else, really saved my sanity. Here was this guy about to die for something he didn't do, who had spent most of his life in jail, and he took the trouble to help me. He never once moaned or lost hope where his own future was concerned. He was just concerned about me. I felt like a horse's ass to be worrying over such silly things like losing Herschel and Richard and being locked up for something small.

If a guy stands up to help you when even your own people won't, he's got to be a good man.

After Ernie arranged my bail, as I was leaving him and about to be released, he stood up and said, "I love you."

I knew I had to do something to help him, and I promised I would. At first I became his legal runner, filing documents, calling on people and investigating things for him. He gave me full power of attorney. It was fun at first, but after a while I felt so much involved that it became the most important thing I had ever done in my life. I know how Angela Davis must have felt, and how important it is to help someone who is trapped and needs you.

Over the following few weeks and months, I discovered a totally new side to Ernie. He was a tremendously sensitive writer. He sent me the most beautiful letters, full of love and great depth of feeling. He phoned me every day, and I saw him as often as I could.

It was about that time I met Ed the Burglar in the pizzeria. Things were hard for Ed because he knew I was seeing Ernie and doing all I could for him. Ed never objected because, like Ernie he'd been in prison most of his life, too, and he knew how much it meant to have visitors. But Ed wanted very much to marry me, and Ernie was one of the main reasons why I couldn't commit myself.

I was out on bail, but of course, I still had to stand trial for the NSF check. My case came up two months after I got out. The seventy-two days I spent inside was just dead time awaiting trial. I got a public defender because I had no money, and Ernie told me how to work it.

"Get the head guy," he said, "and be sure to be dressed up and looking good. Point out to the man that you didn't get any money, it was only a hospital bill for Christ's sake, and you don't have any record."

They assigned me a junior lawyer, but I went to see the top man, and he agreed to take my case. I did everything he told me to do and it worked. The public defender talked to the judge and I got a three year suspended sentence. That meant I was free, but if I violated probation, I could go back into the can again. Which I did, fifteen months later.

I continued helping Ernie, seeing him often, when one day he told me he was planning an escape. He had broken out of every prison he'd been in so far, and he was convinced he could slip out of county jail with no trouble at all.

His plan was to lift himself up through a transom in a holding tank and inch along to a trap door that dropped down just by the exit. I owed him so much and wanted to help him so badly that I rented an apartment for him and did what I could on the outside.

Ernie said the break would come in a few days. Then one day I went to see him, and a matron took me aside and shook me down. I asked her what was wrong. "I'm sure he will tell you," she said.

When Ernie came in with three guards he was looking really dejected. It was the first time I'd seen him that way. It seems that he and Red had been in a holding cell off the courtroom and the judge had gone to lunch. Then, when the guards took off for a few minutes, that was when Ernie decided it was their chance. A transom in the ceiling was their way to freedom.

They loosened some screws with a spoon, and he had hoisted Red up through the transom when the whole thing suddenly came loose and crashed onto the floor. That was the end of his escape plan.

Ernie eventually won his case and his sentence was commuted to life. He was transferred to Folsom State Prison, and it was very hard on him. He had told me that if he didn't get away he knew he would be finished. He had already spent twenty-three years behind bars, and the future didn't look too promising for the next twenty-three.

Even in Folsom, Ernie was still Ernie. At Christmas a strange man showed up with $500 in an envelope - a little present for me from Ernie.

I had a friend who was a writer and I tried to get him to do a book on Ernie. The material was unbelievable after all he had been through. He knew Machine Gun Kelly and was a friend of Alvin Karpis. Ernie was there for the Alcatraz riots when the guards stripped down the prisoners and poured water on them in the cold wind.

Unfortunately I ended up back in jail later partly because of our friendship. One day the following year, 1966, when I was locked up again, I got a message from Ernie saying he was planning another escape and he was going to get me out too. "Oh, Jesus," I replied in a message back, "don't do it."

Not long after that a lawyer who knew Ernie told me what had happened. The cops were taking him from Folsom to a court appearance because of another error in his trial. The Sheriff stopped in Salinas for some reason and took the cuffs off him for a minute.

Ernie slugged the guy and ran. He got about four blocks away, but he ran right in front of a police station without realizing it. The police shot him in the shoulder, wounding him seriously. After surviving the first five bullets years ago, he also managed to live through his sixth. But he was shut up so tightly in Folsom he hardly saw daylight.

Ernie, like Ed the Burglar, to a lesser degree, had so much depth and spirit, he made supposedly straight people look hollow. These guys may be locked up and voted out of society, but men like Ernie and Ed had more class in their little fingers than any of the big-shit millionaires and actors and artists I ever knew.

While I was helping Ernie, just after I was freed on probation for the hospital NSF check, I started having problems with Ed. He had been supporting me in fine style, but he kept getting more and more insistent on marriage. Ed finally gave me an ultimatum, and I went to Palm Springs with a girlfriend to think it over.

That's when I fell off a goddamn horse and ended up right back in the hospital.

Doctors had to fuse my back and play around from late January until April. When I went in, I took along $2,000 with the comfortable certainty that Ed would pick up the bill. But while I was there we had a fight and I told him to piss off. I had given the hospital a $1,000 deposit upon entrance, so I was left with about $1,000.

After a few months I still couldn't walk, but I could sort of hobble around and was getting restless. I owed the hospital around $6,000 I guess. They really didn't know who I was, since I never did get in the habit of using my real name. But I was going to be smart and not do the same stupid thing I did before. Instead of writing a bad check, I slipped out the side door.

I just called a friend and asked her to come get me. I had every intention of paying the hospital. I just wanted to see if I could walk again first. And I knew they had lots of money and could wait a little while for me to give it to them in installments.

I'll say this for the cops in California - they can put things together in a hurry. About five minutes after I went home - okay, maybe three weeks - five narcs came to my apartment.

It was like seeing a cheaply made Grade B movie for the second time or maybe more like a nightmare that you can't awaken from. It was a bad scene.

They hit me with it immediately. I had committed a felony they said, and they could hang me. Until then I had no idea I was in so deep. It seems that if you use an assumed name in California and then split, they get the idea you're trying to defraud them. Grand theft.

But, said the cops, if I would cooperate and help them nail Richard and some other guy, they would make sure the bad check thing would remain a civil matter between me and the hospital.

I gave them the same answer I'd given them before - that I couldn't have told them anything if I wanted to. Richard never told me about his activities even when we were married and I hadn't seen him in months. Apparently he had been hanging around with a heavy dude named Vic who spent $30,000 a year on lawyers to keep himself on the streets. He even had a cop-proof iron door and television cameras around his place.

The cops kept saying that unless I helped them nail Richard and this guy named Vic, they would have the hospital press criminal charges.

While three guys were interrogating me in my living room, two others systematically tore the whole place to shreds. They went through every drawer in the apartment, spilling out the garbage onto the floor and sifting the sugar bowl looking for drugs. I never saw a search warrant, and I was too scared to ask.

Those sons of bitches worked me over exactly like in a bad movie. Really, I think one of those turds thought he was Dirty Harry. Richard had warned me about the baddie and goodie routine, but I thought he was being overly dramatic. But here it was in all of its ridiculous glory. One would thumb through a phone book, then suddenly slam it shut in my face and shout, "Look baby, you're gonna march… you're gonna do three years…" Then his partner, my hero, would calm him down and tell him I was upset. "Aw, don't worry, honey… we just need a few answers…" That crap.

While they were there a millionaire I knew called me up to go out on his yacht, and I had to talk to him while they strained to listen. I told him to call back in an hour. He did and they were still there. "Who was that? What did he want?" they asked. The bastards were there for four or five hours, going through everything.

The first things they found were my letters from Ernie. "Nice friends you got, lady," said one, reading them all from start to finish. "You're telling us you don't know anything, with friends like this. You're insulting us." Then they questioned me about Ed. They inferred that I was some high class moll for every gangster in California. And all of it went into my probation report.

Finally they left, after giving me two weeks to arrange a meeting between Richard and Vic and some of their undercover agents. As soon as they took off, I went to a payphone and called Richard. The ungrateful prick just chewed me out for worrying about nothing, but I could tell he was a little nervous. And he did send me a few hundred dollars.

Richard had been acting funny lately anyway. The few times I talked to him over the phone he would excuse himself, and I was sure I heard him vomiting. Anyway, I refused to snitch, so I was running again.

I hid out in a beach apartment in Malibu for five months, but I couldn't get a job. Eventually I moved back to L.A. where Richard was supposed to send me money to live on. I got some the first month, but then nothing else came. I tried his answering service and got a zero. He had left me flat again. Then someone in my family - I won't say who - turned me in.

I was just getting out of a taxi at a friend's house when the fuzz arrived.

"Are you Virginia Graham?"

"Why, no."

This time they handcuffed me. I really must have embarrassed my poor respectable school teacher friend.

And it did nothing for me.

Chapter Fifteen

This time they had me cold, no bail or screwing around, I went right through Sybil Brand to Corona. I had gotten out on probation but went straight back in for another stupid slip-up. But then, you meet some interesting people in prison... like Susan Atkins, for example, who confessed to me how she and her screwed-up friends butchered Sharon Tate in the house I almost rented.

However I didn't meet Susan until the second time around in Sybil Brand. By then, I had gotten to know the California prison system pretty well.

When the cops picked me up in Los Angeles - after I refused to help finger Richard - I was locked up for five months dead time before my trial. Since I was a probation violator, there was no bail.

Sybil Brand was a real animal cage. You could either stay in a cellblock and hear broads bitching all day and talking about drugs, or you could get into a working dorm. I signed up for the laundry and ironed shirts. And I was glad for the diversion.

One of the gals in with me was a baby-killer. She had four or five children, and the last one was illegitimate. She hated the baby and always mistreated him. One day she flipped out and nearly killed him. She was arrested and put on probation. But she went wild again and hit him with something that opened his side. She poured lye on the wound and tried to sew it up, but she wasn't as lucky as the first time and he died.

She was arrested quickly and was in jail the day the infant was buried. Some girls saw her dancing to music over the loudspeaker and asked her how she could be so cheerful on the day her son was being buried. "Listen," she said, "if it wasn't for that fucking kid, I wouldn't be here."

She did eighteen or twenty months altogether and was released. I was in twenty-one months for walking out on a hospital bill. I mean, Jesus, talk about values.

Life in Sybil Brand was pretty grim. It was cold and all you heard was clanging iron doors and bitching. The matrons kept a lookout for bull dykes, the really obvious homosexuals, and they would throw them separately into the "daddy tank." But almost all the real homosexual action went on in the bathrooms and work areas between supposedly straight girls. I don't know why they picked on the daddies - they were never the ones to push it. The pursuers were always the covert lesbians who showed no signs of being on the make.

Food was miserable - three starchy meals a day eaten with a spoon in total silence. We ate four to a table in the dining room and were forbidden to even smile at each other. A meal might include meatloaf, a scoop of potatoes and some corn. And it's a real pain in the ass trying to cut tough meat with a spoon.

One thing I will say for prison, the damn place was immaculately clean. That's fine if you like clean concrete. At least it's better than dirty, littered concrete.

We were allowed some individual latitude at Corona, where I was sent due to my violation. You could have a throw rug in your cell and you were permitted to fix the cell up with a few pictures and the like. But there was nothing you could do to get away from that dismal expanse of iron bars and concrete, iron bars and concrete.

The cell doors are really something. They're heavy steel with a little peephole so that guards can look in on you any time they want. Under the peephole is something they call a "wicket." This is just big enough to shove your towel through.

Why would you want to do that? Well, if you're desperately ill you're supposed to push your towel halfway through the wicket and let it hang out. Then the guard notices it and calls a nurse.

The only catch is that it could take hours for a guard to notice the towel and more hours for the nurse to arrive. By that time you could be dead. And don't think it hasn't happened.

They have some kind of electronic device for locking all the cell doors simultaneously in an entire tier at 10 pm. When those damn bolts shoot into place it sounds like a hundred machine guns going off. The first time I heard it I jumped twelve feet, or I would have except that the cell wasn't that big.

There was no actual physical brutality to speak of. But as far as I'm concerned, I'd rather get belted in the mouth a couple of times than suffer the humiliation and the mental brutality of the "group therapy" sessions. And nobody really raped anyone. There was plenty of lesbianism going on, but it was more likely the result of the young chicks approaching the butches than the other way around.

If anything, the girls were their own worst enemies. They stole from each other like mad. When somebody "got her drawers boosted," that meant her panties got swiped off a clothesline. Nothing was too trivial to steal - a scarf, a cigarette, whatever. Little things had a lot of value in their eyes.

There were constant shakedowns since the matrons were always on the alert for drugs. Not that there was any place to hide them.

Court appearances at Sybil Brand were regular nightmares. They woke you up at 4 am to let you brush your teeth and comb your hair. That was it. Someone handed you the clothes you were wearing when you were busted, and that was what you wore to court.

After a few times before the judge, with clothes stuffed in a paper bag and locked up in between, a girl really looked and smelled like she belonged in jail. And psychologically, it had that effect. I honestly felt like a criminal every time I went through the degrading process of going to court.

All girls headed for court are rounded up and dispatched to different locked buses at 5 am. Naturally the first case isn't before 9, but we weren't going to be late. You've got to go a number of times for arraignments and pleas and sentencing and everything. I was sent to Santa Monica court and locked there in a cold cell with a concrete bench and a smelly toilet. I sat there from 9 am until 2 pm, pacing back and forth every so often to keep my head straight. At lunchtime I was passed a piece of cheese, two dry slices of bread and an orange.

Before this, the police had questioned me five or six times about Richard and, as always, offered to get the hospital to drop charges if I would cooperate. Christ knows why I was protecting that creep, but I just couldn't bring myself to do it.

The judge in L.A. offered me a 90-day Z program. That meant that I would have to go into controlled group therapy sessions for three months. At the end, the counselor would see me for an hour and determine whether or not to recommend probation.

But I knew all about therapy sessions - snitch sessions - and I wasn't about to let them use phony analysis to get out of me what the cops couldn't. That's all it is, a bunch of girls putting pressure on each other to say things they wouldn't think of saying at any other time. And there's Big Sister counselor in the middle, taking it all down. Bullshit.

The judge said, "Young lady, you leave me no choice," and he sentenced me to Corona for an indeterminate sentence. Oh well, I figured, at least they'll leave me alone.

But - what's new? - I had out-foxed myself again. I still had group therapy sessions, only without much hope of getting out for many months. He put me in the joint on what they call an 11-68. After two months, the institution was to send him a recommendation, and from that, he would decide whether or not to pull me back and grant probation. I had known from the beginning I wasn't about to qualify for any favorable reports because I knew what cooperation meant to the police.

It wasn't me they were after, and that's what ticked me off so much. Every time I told someone inside why I was there, they would crack up laughing. "A hospital bill?... ha-ha-ha..." That was the reaction from everyone - prisoners, guards, lawyers. What a system.

At Corona I went through fifteen months of group therapy, every day for the first two months, and then three times weekly. After my unfavorable report went to the judge, I put in a request to be transferred to a unit run by Dr. Vera Dreiser, a niece of Theodore Dreiser, the famous novelist.

She was one of the few good people connected with the entire California prison system. She was about 5'7" and weighed almost 250 pounds, a real big momma but a sharp dresser and a great woman. She was the only staff psychologist for the 900 women in Corona. After nine years she left the prison because she couldn't help the girls the way she thought they needed to be helped.

I had to go before a panel to say why I wanted to be in her special unit. Since I'm in prison I obviously have a problem, I said, and I think she can help me so it doesn't happen again. That must have made sense even to them. It worked.

Part of Dr. Dreiser's program involved group sessions, three times a week for two hours each. But it was worth it with her. The groups were small, and she conducted them personally. If any girl seemed like she was close to snitching about anyone or anything, Dr. Dreiser cut her off dead. She kept me there the rest of the time I was in Corona, and it made life bearable.

Even though group sessions with Dr. Dreiser were an improvement, they still got incredibly mean and destructive. And the sixty I went through before transferring were torture.

In most sessions - unlike Dr. Dreiser's - there is a counselor who might as well be a matron. Many of them encourage the girls to snitch on each other and bring out information which I'm sure goes straight upstairs as soon as the session is over.

Some girls try to score points by passing along information about others. It is their only contact with the authorities, and they feel if the counselor gives them a good write-up they might get out faster.

A lot of women just don't give a damn, and they channel all their flaming anger at the matrons, the system, society and at the weaker girls in their sessions. They come on like starved jackals, pouncing first on one girl and then on another in packs, tearing her apart until she breaks down and sobs with tears.

For the tough chicks, it's simply entertainment, like watching television but being able to take part. Maybe it was therapy, but from what I saw it did more to seriously confuse girls than anything else in prison.

Those downbeat scenes might start with a counselor asking a nervous little chick to say why she was in prison.

She'd reply, "Well, I stole money because my kids didn't have anything to eat, and I was desperate."

That would signal the wolf pack attack from all around the circle:

"What about your husband, bitch - he ain't worried about the kids?"

"You mean you never took none of it for yourself, motherfucker? Everything for your precious little bastards, right? You never did nothing else?"

"Bullshit!"

"Don't hide behind your children, you selfish little bitch. If you're ripping off people, admit it…"

They would systematically convince her that her husband hated her and had already split. I always took the side of the underdog, and the girls hated me because of it. They hammered at me constantly, trying everything they could to make me crack. It was just sport, amusement, and the farthest thing from anyone's mind was to help the girl they were yelling at.

My mouth was always a strong point, and I could give back better than I got from most of those vampires. But once they really got to me over my kids. During my time in Corona, I had horrible guilt feelings about my sons. I couldn't even watch *Lassie* on television because Jon Provost looked so much like my little Joe Jr. that tears would fill my eyes. Later, I would think of my boys and cry for hours in my cell.

One of the girls picked up on this during a marathon group session. I shot back a snide retort, but the rest of them caught the slight quaver in my voice, and they went to work on me.

They told me what a shitty mother I was and how I was a selfish, hypocritical bitch who only thought of herself while her kids were growing up all fucked up. That wasn't true but it was close enough so that I couldn't control the tears, and I broke down.

That intensified the attack, and it went on until I managed to grab hold. I out-shouted them and took the offensive on something else. But it was a screaming hell, and it left me shattered for days afterward.

Those sessions could be murder for personal relationships. My best friend in jail was Big Terry, an incredible woman, Italian, I think, whose father was executed during prohibition. Her mother had died during childbirth, so she was brought up by two loony aunts. These two aging aunts hadn't talked to each other in ten years, and Terry, seriously, used to have to carry notes back and forth between them when it was important that they communicate.

Finally, the aunts agreed to let a couple take Terry into their home. But the wife, an ex-nurse, was a raving lunatic. She used to tell Terry she was going to operate on her and chase her with a knife all over the apartment, screaming.

Terry left as soon as she could, and she married a black guy named Caesar who was a radical and a dyed-in-the-wool revolutionary. They must have been a wild pair - she was nearly six feet tall and he was about 5'6". Terry said he would go berserk over some racial thing and yell, "Kill the whites...!" She'd let him go on a while and then say, "Hey, jerk, I'm white. You gonna kill me too?" She had spent twenty years in and out of jail, mostly for drugs.

In one group, for reasons I don't even remember, I brought up something really damaging to Terry about her husband, and she threw an ashtray at me. It missed by a few inches - a big heavy thing that would have wiped me out on the spot.

But we survived that and stayed friends. The group makes you do some pretty strange things that you wouldn't think of doing under normal circumstances.

I worked in the clothing section, and all the girls who came into Corona went through me for their stuff. Each girl got three striped dresses, five pairs of cotton panties, a couple of cotton bras, a coat and some shoes. No lacy underwear or any interesting nightgowns were allowed. When you had your period, you went to a special control desk for Kotex - nothing fancy like Tampax.

At 6:30 every morning they popped the doors, and we lined up for breakfast. Afterwards we had five minutes to get to work, by 8 am, where we stayed until lunch. We worked again in the afternoon and had some free time to watch television, read or walk around and talk. There was a record player and a small library, which I ran for a while.

It had thrilling stuff like *Black Beauty*...for grown women. Nothing the least bit racy or political was allowed.

We were locked up at 10 pm, and that was our day. There was a lot of queer action going down at Corona. If you walked down the hall and saw some girl pretending to be ironing or something outside a cell, you knew a couple of girls were inside making it under a bed. The girl outside was the lookout. Kite-carriers were girls who relayed love notes - kites - in their bras. It was a disaster for anyone who got caught with a kite.

Most of the hustling was done, believe it or not, by meek little girls who got lonely after a few months in jail. They made the advances to the big dykey-looking broads. It was seldom the other way around. Some women really pulled a complete turnaround - short hair, heavy walk, stooped shoulders. There were times I thought I had stumbled into a men's prison.

One time a girl was knocked up by one of the few male guards and he was fired on the spot. It must have been a real quickie, and I still don't know how he managed it. Most of them wouldn't risk their jobs that way even if they had the chance.

Conversation in prison was like some dull women's club except there was a lot of talk about drugs. And girls moaned a lot. I never saw a druggie find any smack in jail, but occasionally a Milltown would get in. It would be worth four packs of cigarettes from the prison commissary, which we could visit once a month for limited purchases.

Some horrible hassles developed over what TV program to watch, especially among groups of black girls and white girls. Each girl had her name on a list and we took turns selecting the programs. But if a girl didn't want to watch on her night, screaming fights would break out over who filled in for her. The toughest, loudest and meanest broad always won.

That was when it was the worst for me, watching television. Someone I used to know very well would flash on the screen, and it would rip me up inside... especially when the girls made some stupid crack about him or her. I came so close to shouting, "Shut your damn mouth, you stupid bitch, you have no idea what you're talking about...!"

But, of course you don't open your mouth in the slams. That's the first rule. Only girls of the lowest, hardest and poorest backgrounds command any respect. If the others even suspect you're a stuck-up bitch, your life is hell.

I lived in a cell about ten feet by four and a half feet. We were allowed a tiny throw rug and curtains, for God's sake, and once in a while the guards would close their eyes to a few pictures on the wall. We weren't supposed to have anything, but I pasted up pictures of gorgeous looking men to remind me what they looked like.

The food was actually pretty good in Corona, like in some second class restaurant. Breakfast was cereal, sometimes milk, with eggs and once in a while even a Danish pastry or sausage.

The thing that used to send us up the walls was visits by college groups or other prissy shits like that. We had to sit there on our bunks, with knees together and all ladylike, while those snotty little boobs would troop through staring and trying to look relaxed. It was worse than being in a zoo - we didn't even get peanuts.

Some of the girls would try to gross-out unwelcome visitors, sneering and insulting and threatening as best they could from behind bars. It was amazing how much damage they could do with just a stare or a well-placed filthy remark. But the guards were always there, and you got slapped up the side of the head pretty badly if you caused any trouble during the zoo trips.

I tried to be as pleasant as I could, unless the girls were obviously looking superior or haughty, and I had some interesting chats with college girls coming through. A lot of them were as uncomfortable as we were, sort of like white liberals in a black slum.

But that was just an annoyance. The real tragedy of the system was how they trained girls for a productive life after their release. You could learn two trades at Corona - practical nursing and hairdressing. If you had a minimum tenth grade education and passed a test, then you could get training for eleven months. They gave you the state test, and you applied for your license.

But many girls went through the whole program only to have a license refused by the cosmetology board because they had a drug charge - even a lousy bust for a single joint. How's that for a typical state system? Remember, more than half the people in California jails have some drug thing behind them.

Everyone knows that if there's one thing that really stinks in this country, it's our prison system. And nobody knows it better than an ex-con. Yet, surprisingly, I have some kind words to say for the potential value of the system.

I suppose I'm practically unique, in that prison saved my life, or at least threw me off a sure collision course with some kind of disaster, whether with drugs or whatever. Yes, I'm a living, breathing example of what prison could accomplish for most of the inmates instead of one in ten thousand, granted an ounce of sense and a few dollars' worth of therapy.

I'm lucky on two counts. First, I was not only ready for help but I was eager for it. That could be said, however, for many inmates. More importantly, I not only was ready for help, but I received it - as a result of coming into contact with that rarest of individuals, a truly understanding and conscientious prison psychiatrist, Dr. Dreiser. She not only made me face up to what I had done, but made me figure out why I had done it.

Once you understand why you're acting in an antisocial way, you can stop acting that way, with a lot of effort and a little luck. The proof is that I later became active in a wonderful career, one that enabled me to enrich other people's lives, but at the same time earn an excellent income. There's absolutely no way I would ever return to my old way of life. And you can bet 1,000 to 1 that none of this would have happened if I hadn't been sent to prison and compelled to undergo therapy.

But, my God, how often does that happen under our penal system? And why can't it be made to happen more often? It would be so easy to practice intelligent therapy on a systematic basis instead of by chance.

All right, we may not be able to help more than half the inmates. But even if we helped one out of ten, instead of one out of ten thousand, it would be something. And honestly, all it would take would be humane treatment, psychiatric guidance, and the teaching of a trade. I sincerely believe that under that system even Manson, if helped early on, would have come out of prison a decent citizen instead of the monster that years of brutal, mindless incarceration made of him.

When I was finally released on parole from Corona in April 1968, after more than a year and a half in prison, mainly for refusing to help nail Richard, I was still a pretty whacked up dame. But at least I had a good idea of what was wrong with me. And wait until you hear what I did about it.

Since they won't let you out unless you have a place to go, I was sent to a halfway house run by a hardworking and well-meaning Quaker couple. You have complete freedom in a halfway house, but it is horrible. It's just like prison but without guards - girls sneaking in sex with each other and talking endlessly about drugs. There's even group therapy once a week which was mandatory, and which to this day I vehemently oppose on the grounds that they only confuse most people and do more harm than good.

It was during one of those meetings, attended by a mixed group of men and women, that I noticed this great big, attractive, well-dressed man who resembled Cesar Romero, enter and take a seat.

The session was underway about thirty minutes when some of the men began hitting on me, and believe me, I wasn't the least bit interested and made it known, but to no avail.

I was having trouble getting that point across when my unknown Sir Galahad came to my rescue and those would-be Romeos quickly disappeared.

My gallant rescuer's name was Arnie Castro. He was 6'1", an extremely handsome Latin who came into my life when it was at an all-time low.

Eventually I got away from the halfway house with the help of some friends and a bit of luck, and with permission from my parole officer I married Arnie Castro.

Our relationship lasted for six years - from 1968 to 1973 - and covered the period when I was a fugitive in 1971, through my part as a star witness in the Manson trial, to my life in Hawaii where through hard work I turned everything around and made good.

When I met Arnie at the halfway house he had just been released from jail for narcotic possession. It seems that he'd been a drug addict since he was sixteen. He came from a very respectable family but managed to screw up his life at a very early age.

It didn't take me too long to find out that he was a loser. He was a nice person but not very bright, and when I met him, it wasn't during the best time of my life.

I'd just served time in prison, I'd lost everything and in Arnie I found a kindred spirit - someone else - who like myself, had suffered a great deal because of his stupidity.

And too, like myself, he wanted to straighten out his life. So, we kinda gravitated toward each other and we did help one another in a way. I was the brainy one of the two and knew how to make money. He was working as a hairstylist.

Not too long after we were married Arnie got back on drugs and got a parole violation which sent him to C.R.C., a facility for drug users. And so we were separated for a while. That's when I met a guy named Fred and tried LSD. After Fred went to San Francisco I started looking for a job and found that no one wanted to employ a criminal. I was an ex-con and nobody wanted to have anything to do with me.

After thirteen months of so-called freedom, I felt a tremendous need to talk with Dr. Dreiser. I was so screwed up at the time I was even willing to go back in the joint for a short while if that was the only way I could reach her.

I told my parole officer to come and get me. She was a great girl named Verdine Jones, young and black and as lenient as she could be without losing control of her girls.

She had a tremendous case load, like all parole officers, and was responsible for overseeing some 80 to 100 girls. Even though she was carrying her second child, she would often go out in the middle of the night to help one of her parolees who was in trouble.

According to the rules, the parole officer made monthly house visits to each of her girls. If a parolee wanted to buy a car or get a license to marry or get a divorce or move or leave the county she had to request permission. Although Verdine was constantly overloaded with work, she always did everything she could for me, and I liked her.

When I told Verdine what I wanted she took me to Sybil Brand on an open booking. I didn't have any violations; I had just come in at my own request. She was supposed to come back the next day to take me to see Dr. Dreiser.

But once again, Graham screwed up. The acid had put me on a truth kick, and I told my mother about the LSD. She, in turn, told my stepfather who told Verdine about it and, I think, that delayed Verdine in coming back. She was taking a long, hard look at my situation. When she finally came back and asked me about the acid, I told her everything. I said, "After all, a lot of psychiatrists recommend it and use it, what the hell."

But it was a violation, and she said she'd have to think it over. Eventually she decided she had to tell the Parole Board but recommended only sixty days in the county jail. She said sending me to Corona would do no good at all. But the board didn't see it that way, and they sent me straight back to Corona again.

That was the last time I ever trusted the system. I mean, Jesus, I went in of my own accord with no violations, simply to talk to the only qualified and concerned doctor in the whole goddamned structure, then voluntarily admitted taking acid, and they put me back in prison.

The Parole Board was notorious for that. It's made up mostly of political appointees. There wasn't a single doctor in the bunch when I went before them, so you get an idea of their qualifications. Wow!

But here's that 'fate' thing again. If the acid violation hadn't taken place and had Verdine not whisked me over to see Dr. Dreiser, I would never have fallen into the middle of the Manson case.

Lucky me.

Chapter Sixteen

Susan Atkins walked into my dormitory at Sybil Brand Institute, the Women's House of Detention in Los Angeles, and into my life on the fifth day I was there. She was twenty-one at the time.

She was staggering under a load of sheets, blankets, clothes and a pillow. She dumped them on a bed, looked around and just stood there looking innocent and cute. She was smiling just like a little puppy that was happy about its new home.

I liked her at first sight. She was fresh and pretty with long dark hair. And she was happy, all smiles - that's what really hit me. I'd seen everything in prison: frustration, fear, anger, homosexual love, hate, desperation, but never happiness.

We talked a while and as we did I came to realize her smile was the perpetual grin of an acid head. But it was still friendly and warm and that's all that mattered to me at the moment.

We were in dormitory 8000, a big room like a hospital ward with beds lined up against the walls separated only by short lockers. It held about eighty girls, all either on their way to another facility or serving short sentences. I was there waiting for the Parole Board to meet and consider Verdine's report on my taking acid.

I had just gone back into jail after thirteen months of parole, and at that point I didn't think I'd be staying long.

Susan told me her name was Sadie Mae Glutz, and she didn't say why she was there, but she was so cheerful and upbeat that after a while I suggested that I speak to the guards about letting her work with me as a runner. My job was to deliver messages all over the prison.

It was a good job, not as confining as some of the work being done there. The girl who had worked with me was being deported to England and so Susan - Sadie - got the job. It meant we were in close contact all day long, sometimes sitting together for hours waiting for things to deliver.

I was struck by her continual happy-go-lucky demeanor and youth-

177

ful innocence. At the most unexpected times she would suddenly laugh and sing and start go-go dancing. Everybody else began calling her "crazy Sadie" but I thought of her as just a kid - a "little lost girl" putting on a big act to hide the fear she really felt.

She seemed more out of place in Sybil Brand than anyone else there which finally led me to ask her, "Look Sadie, what the hell are you doing in this dump anyway?" I was a mother scolding a wayward youngster - and I figured she was probably in for smoking grass or something.

And when she said, "First degree murder," I almost fell off my stool. She explained that she and Bobby Beausoleil were charged with the Gary Hinman murder. All that information coming out of her sweet, innocent face just didn't make sense to me. I couldn't believe it.

But gradually it came out. She started talking about her family and how they lived on a ranch and were extremely happy. I thought she meant a regular family - a mother, father - the regular bit because she told me about a little son she really loved.

But when she revealed that some girl had told the police that she, Sadie, had been with Beausoleil when Hinman was murdered, she became pretty upset. And then her mood suddenly changed and she cracked up laughing and asked, "Isn't it funny? The police think Beausoleil killed the guy. How could I hold a big man's arms pinned behind him while someone else stabbed him? It was the other way around. It was me who stabbed him."

I told her, "For Christ's sake, keep quiet! When you're in the can don't tell stuff like that to anyone!" But she just shrugged her shoulders and kept talking. What really bugged me was that she described killing Hinman just like it was a normal, everyday thing to do.

I was pretty shaken up but I put it all out of my head. I'd heard stuff like that before, and I had no intention of remembering any of it. That's something you don't pass on to anyone else.

She asked about me, and I told her what I had done and a little about the people I knew. "I've never known a lot of celebrities, but I will someday," Susan said, sort of grinning to herself.

She told me about Dennis Wilson of the Beach Boys and some of the other people who had hung around with her and her friends. That's when I finally realized that by family she meant some sort of commune with a lot of girls and a few guys and a leader that everyone held in awe.

For the next few days, Susan kept referring to the leader as Him and finally she told me that his name was Charlie. She said that Charlie had given her the name "Sadie Glutz" and that he was a beautiful person with God-like qualities, and she spoke of him as Jesus Christ. She talked about life at the ranch and how at night around a campfire Charlie would preach to them about the plans he had to lead them to better lives.

She said that he had been in several prisons and that those experiences had only made him stronger. Everyone at the ranch lived under Charlie's orders - nobody ever questioned his authority. He was their leader - their father.

Then she told me how he would often put himself on a cross and "We would all kneel before him," and then very quietly she added, "Charlie is our love. He is Jesus Christ!"

At that moment I remember saying to myself, "You are crazy, Sadie!"

Then in the late afternoon on November 6 - this was 1969 - little Sadie came flipping down the walkway like a tail-wagging Cocker Spaniel, sat down next to me on my bed and started talking. She told me again about the Hinman murder and LSD, and I tried to cut her off.

"Sadie," I said, "someday you're gonna say the wrong thing to the wrong person."

"But I know I can trust you," she said. "I can see it in your eyes. You have kind eyes. They're the windows to your soul."

I guess those words will haunt me for the rest of my life. She trusted me because we were friends and because our separate acid trips formed some sort of bond for her. Later that trust tore me up inside when I tried to decide what to do.

I told her how Ed the Burglar had been screwed by an informant. "I know you're right," she said, "but I'm not too worried. The police are so far off in so many of these things..."

She paused for a moment and then what she revealed... I would spend many troubled, sleepless nights for years to come wishing that she had chosen someone else to share her confidence with. I would have given anything for it not to have been me.

"You know those murders up in Benedict Canyon?" Susan asked.

"Benedict Canyon?" I echoed.

"Yeah, the Tate murders. Well, you know who did it, don't you?"

I said I had no idea.

"Well, you're looking at her."

I really didn't believe her, and I remembered that Richard and I had almost rented that house on Cielo Drive. I had known Jay Sebring, the hairstylist who was one of the victims. I had admired Sharon Tate's work in *Valley of the Dolls*.

When Richard and I started up our party girl operation we contacted a real estate agent and began looking at some classy houses to lease. My feeling had always been - the bigger the front - the bigger the paycheck. You had to look like money if you wanted to make money.

That's how we came to the house at 10050 Cielo Drive. The way the agent described it made it appear to be exactly what we were looking for. We drove up and gave it a careful going over.

However, there was another place on Cherokee Lane that was off Coldwater Canyon that we wanted to see before making up our minds, and that was the house we finally decided to take. But we were impressed by the Cielo house.

But for some reason, I always remembered that house on Cielo Drive even though I'd seen it back in 1964 and the murders didn't take place there until a few years later.

But I never forgot it and when Susan Atkins opened up about the terrible things that she had participated in and described the place to me, it suddenly hit me that she could be talking about a house I'd been in. The one on Cielo Drive where Sharon Tate had been murdered.

I asked her some questions about the house and her replies erased any doubts I might have had. I suddenly felt icy cold all over when I realized we were talking about the same place.

The five still unsolved murders that were committed on those premises with weird ritual overtones ranked as the bloodiest and most gruesome in California. Now Sadie was telling me she had done it.

I swallowed hard and said, "You gotta be kidding." And in reply she just smiled and said, "Uh-huh."

I asked her a few questions and she related the entire grisly scenario, detail by detail.

She said they'd picked the house because it was isolated. It had been rented by Terry Melcher, Doris Day's son, and Charlie was mad at him because he had told them that he was going to get rid of all his worldly goods and join the Family, and then backed out. But that really had nothing to do with it, she said. It just happened to be a good place for a murder.

Susan and the girls and one guy... It was later learned that they were Susan Atkins, Charles "Tex" Watson, Patricia Krenwinkel and Linda Kasabian... didn't know anyone in the house and whether there were one or ten it didn't matter because they were all going to die.

She said that it was her belief that by killing the people inside she would be doing them a favor, releasing them to another world. Murdering them, she said, was murdering a part of herself, because they were her and she was them.

This is how she described the scene to me and what had taken place.

Everyone was dressed in black, and they walked up the hill to the house, leaving their car parked below. There was a gate at the entrance to the driveway and fearing that it might be electrified they decided to go over the fence, but first Tex Watson climbed a utility pole and cut the telephone wires.

At that moment a car with its headlights on came down the road from the house. Warning the girls to be quiet, Tex had them hide in the shrubbery and when the car approached him he walked up to it, thrust his pistol through the open window and shot 18-year-old Steven Parent four times. No one else was in the car.

Everyone was afraid the people inside the house might have heard the shots, and they waited a while and when nobody came out to investigate, they broke into the house.

Once inside they split up. Susan said she saw a girl sitting up in bed reading a book and a man asleep on a couch. In another room Sharon Tate was sitting up in bed and talking to Jay Sebring who was seated on the bed's edge.

She took Tate and Sebring by surprise and waved a huge buck knife, forcing them into the living room. They didn't resist because "They were fearful," said Susan.

Susan then described how they tied the end of a rope around Tate's neck, threw it over a beam and then tied the other end around Sebring's neck. That way, if they struggled, they would choke each other.

As Susan was telling me all this, my stomach was tightening and turning and I kept wondering if it was really true. I was stunned but I kept my face as straight as possible. She was talking rapidly, clearly enjoying telling it all to me. Her story had some holes in it, simply because of information she skipped over and because I was too stunned to ask any questions.

But the more she revealed to me, the more I became convinced she was telling the truth. Susan described the man who was asleep on the couch - Wojciech Frykowski. She struggled with him, but he got past her and ran until she caught up with him and stabbed him four times in the back with her buck knife that she called her "friend."

When he got to the patio door he was staggering. At this point Susan stood up and put her hand on her hip, stiffening her face in mock solemnity. "And would you believe that he was screaming, 'Help! Help!' and nobody came?" she said to me seriously, then she just doubled over with laughter.

She said that somebody finished the guy off on the lawn, and another Family girl chased the second female victim - Abigail Folger - out into the yard and killed her.

According to Susan, Sharon Tate, who was pregnant, was the last one to die. She seemed totally delighted in telling me how Sharon Tate begged for her and her baby's life.

She told me how she looked Tate in the eye as Sharon sobbed and pleaded and said, "Please, please don't kill me, I don't want to die. I just want to have my baby. Don't kill me!"

Susan was looking at her face-to-face when she replied, "Bitch, I have no feelings for you. You might as well face it, you're gonna die... And then I killed her."

By this time my knees were trembling, and I kept trying to put this sweet looking little hippie together with the horror she was relating to me. But Susan was still caught up in her grisly story, chatting amiably and hurrying on as if she were some high school girl telling another girl about the first time a guy put his hand under her dress. She also kept watching me for a reaction.

After stabbing Tate, Susan said she licked the blood on her hands and thought, "To taste death but yet to give life... wow, what a trip!"

The group had planned to make it really grisly, according to Susan. They wanted to smash the victims' eyeballs against the walls and cut their fingers off. But she said they didn't have time, for some reason, so she just smeared her hand in blood and left a palm print on a desk. She broke out laughing and said she knew the cops would never find the print or trace it to her because "The vibes were right." She was in tune with the Universe and the killings were meant to be.

Tired, but at peace with the world, Susan told how the group drove off and got rid of their bloody weapons and clothes. They spotted a water hose on the front lawn of somebody's house and got out to wash the blood off their hands.

Susan remembered how some old guy came out of the house and tried to give them a hard time for using his hose. He walked around to the driver's side and said he was some kind of Sheriff.

Susan said she was rolling around laughing because the dumb shit was acting so all important and tough, and they had just stopped to wash off the blood from killing five people. When the man stuck his hand in the car to grab the keys, they just roared away, almost taking off his arm. But he damn near lost a helluva lot more than that.

That ended the afternoon's conversation. We, mostly Susan, had talked for an hour and a half. It was almost time for body count at 6 pm, so I excused myself to take a shower. I just had to get away, I couldn't take another word. The macabre tableaux had finally sunk in and I couldn't bear holding my cool anymore.

I think that's why she talked to me, because I kept my face immobile, showing nothing, just taking it in. She had a big thing about fixing eye contact with people, and she thought that if a person lowered his eyes, it showed a weak character. But it just got to be too much for me - I was completely shattered.

I was heading for the shower, with my mind racing way ahead of me, when I saw Ronnie Howard.

Ronnie, the same Ronnie who had taken my place with Richard, had been picked up for forging drug prescriptions, and was also in dormitory 8000. I was still mad at her over the check business, but when you find a friend in jail, you forget a lot of things.

She had a job as a messenger, delivering messages from attorneys and others, and giving them to runners - like Susan and me - to relay around the prison, so we had a lot of time to talk to each other.

When I saw her, I was frantic and I burst out, "Ronnie, goddamnit, come here. I have to talk to you... this dizzy bitch over here just told me she killed Sharon Tate and Jay Sebring, and I can't believe it. Oh, God, why did she have to tell me? I can't handle this. Man, that's too heavy for anybody to carry!"

Ronnie saw how deeply shaken I was, but we couldn't talk then. She told me to see her after count.

The responsibility was crushing. I had always disliked snitches, and for the past two years I had developed a pathological hatred for them. I saw more people get their asses hung - including myself - because of some shit with a big mouth, and I despised it.

Hell, that was really why I went to prison, because I refused to snitch on Richard, even though I was pissed off at him and under heavy pressure to do it. But what Susan had told me was just too much to take. I had no idea if I was going to tell anyone else, but I had to tell Ronnie.

Later, when Susan went to take a shower, Ronnie and I met in the TV room. Ronnie's first question was whether Susan was telling the truth or was just plain crazy. I ran down the whole story for her and her eyes got wide. "Wow!" she said. "What are you going to do?"

I said I didn't know, but my husband was coming to visit in a few days. He'd just been released, and I would discuss it with him. Ronnie suggested that I keep talking to Susan to find out what else she had to say and to see if she was really telling the truth. I realized that I did remember that house well, and I could ask questions about it to see if she had really been there.

I let a day go by and then hit Susan with a few careful questions as casually as I could. She didn't say much more, so I dropped it. The next day, by coincidence a bunk opened next to Ronnie and they put Susan in it. They did this a lot - switching girls around. But Ronnie seized the opportunity, and though she had never paid much attention to Susan before, this time she came on like the Welcome Wagon.

I walked up to their beds because there was something I wanted to tell Ronnie, and Susan swung her legs over the side of her bunk. "Hey, dig this," Susan said to me. "You know that beautiful cat I was telling you about the other day? Well, dig on this, listen carefully now. His last name is Manson. Think about it. M-A-N-S-O-N. Man's son, isn't that fantastic? He's so..." and she made a worshipful hand gesture.

That was the first time she mentioned Manson's name. Before she had called him Charlie and then Jesus. She had told me how he was going to take the Family to a hole in the center of Death Valley that only he could find. A civilization was living there, solely in wait for the Manson Family to come and lead it. There would be a world revolution, she said, and only their underground people would be safe. She said Manson had been paroled from San Quentin and was now in Inyo.

Then, of course, I had it all. If I wanted, I could go to the authorities and have the entire Family put away. She had described not only the Tate murders but some others as well, and she had said there would be many more. It was a tremendous burden.

But even if I wanted to snitch, it wasn't that easy. One important factor was that I would probably be killed. In prison women will take anything - baby killers, child molesters, mass murderers - but not snitches. Many of the girls had been sent up because of informers, and they hated them. I had seen girls have the shit kicked out of them simply for passing information to the guards about their cellmates that wouldn't amount to more than a bad report. The information I had would mean execution for Atkins and those with her.

I sweated with the dilemma all night long. I had a chance to put away some dangerous people and prevent other murders. But I would be going against everything in me that hated snitches, and I might be marking myself for death. Ronnie and I kept talking about it, and I kept to my plan of discussing it with my husband when he came to visit.

A few days later, before my husband came, Susan came back over to my bed with a movie magazine in her hand. It had a cover picture of Elizabeth Taylor and Richard Burton, and she began flipping through it and talking about how she hated all the stars in it.

They represented wealth and the Establishment that the Family opposed. Their beauty and talent were evil, she said. Then she told me about the Family's plans to turn the beauty - the evil - into something good.

With Elizabeth Taylor, she said, the Family would take a knife with a red hot blade and burn the ugliness on her face to bring out the true beauty. Susan wanted to take her eyes out because they were the symbol of her ugliness.

They planned on castrating Burton and nailing his balls to Eddie Fisher, pickled in a little bottle of alcohol. She said they had the plans worked out to the last detail.

Steve McQueen was on their list because he was involved in political issues that they opposed, but Susan didn't say much about what they planned to do with him.

She went wild about Tom Jones, whose talent she said was a sham and who still succeeded. On the other hand, Charlie Manson's music was real and beautiful, but he wasn't making it. She wanted to make love to Tom Jones and, just as he was climaxing, cut out his vocal chords with a knife. She said she wasn't interested in killing him, just slashing his throat.

Susan named a few other stars, but when she described what they had in store for Frank Sinatra, I quailed. I still felt close to Sinatra, and I respected him tremendously.

She said they knew where his house was in Palm Springs, where they planned to have a few girls go to his front door and knock. They felt he wouldn't hesitate opening it, whereupon they would overpower him, tie him up, put a meat hook into the ceiling, hang him up by his heels and while playing his music they would skin him alive. They were planning on making wallets and lamp shades out of the skin which they would then sell, "So that everybody would have a little piece of Frank."

Throughout this horrendous recitation I could only manage to keep my face straight by biting a deep cut into my lower lip - and for obvious reasons. The most horrible thing was that I knew how easy it would be to get to him.

I had been in his Palm Springs home, where they planned to get him, and I knew how relaxed he was with unannounced visitors. I could see him opening the door and seeing the chick who was now behind bars, talking to me.

By the time my husband showed up, my head was screwed up so bad I didn't know what to think. We were in the prison visiting room, looking at each other through a pane of glass but talking over closed circuit phones.

I was afraid to say anything for fear the phones were tapped and taped, but I was so hyped up that in the middle of the conversation I blurted: "Listen, there's a girl upstairs that told me she murdered Sharon Tate and Jay and all the others and I don't know what to do!"

"Listen, Honey," he replied, "in a place like this you hear a lot of things like that. Ignore it. Pretend you didn't hear it." I said I couldn't because it was so horrible, and he cut me off saying that we had more important things to talk about than what some ding-a-ling said upstairs.

I told Ronnie that I was going to try to forget the whole thing as he had suggested. My Parole Board was meeting the next day. I knew I would be sent to Corona, so I told her to do what she thought best. I said that if she wanted to befriend Susan and find out more about it, it was up to her. If she needed a witness, she could call me but I really wanted to stay the hell out of it.

Six days after Susan told me about the murders, on November 12, they took me to Corona where I had trouble sleeping. The minute I got to Corona I put in a request to see Dr. Dreiser. Wanting to see her was how I ended back in jail anyway, but now it was doubly important. I knew she could be trusted, and I had to get her advice. I got a note back saying that I should apply to see someone else, Dr. Dreiser wasn't available. Oh shit, I thought to myself, what do I do now?

There was nothing to do but wait, and I made it through a few more days. Then one night I had a dream: There were some figures off in the distance, and they came closer and closer until I could see they were Sharon Tate and Jay Sebring. Sharon had on a long, flowing white gown, and she was floating toward me with her arms outstretched.

Jay was walking next to her and he was looking straight ahead and he was saying over and over again, "You know what you have to do." Just then the cell doors popped open, and I woke up. I knew what I had to do.

A few days earlier I had put in a request to see Mary Ann Domm, who had been my counselor at Corona before. There had been no answer. After breakfast that morning, when I had awakened from that dream, I hurried through my work and went out to watch the main gate where she would come in. This was the girls' only real chance to catch a counselor without an appointment and there was always a crowd lying in wait. That morning ten or twelve hit her with the usual crap: "My husband came and I couldn't see him." "I've got bedbugs." And there I was joining the crowd.

We were halfway across the yard when I moved in close enough to her and said, "Miss Domm, I've got to talk with you."

She gave me an irritated look, like, 'Oh no, not another one,' and said, "What is it, Virginia?"

I said, "Someone in Sybil Brand told me she murdered Sharon Tate. I don't know if it's true, but I have to talk to you."

I said it as softly and as quickly as I could, and she said, "What?"

"Yes," I told her, "you heard me right."

I was in her office within thirty minutes and I spilled the whole thing, and for the first time in weeks I felt immeasurably relieved. It was as though a huge, cancerous abscess that I'd been carrying within had been lanced and now all the terrible poison it had contained was draining out.

I later learned that Miss Domm had checked with the head of Corona to see if I was some kind of mental case prone to illusions. Then she phoned Los Angeles homicide.

I was involved in an afternoon group session when the guards pulled me away and took me to an administration office, where only a few top people knew what was going on. A detective sergeant ushered me in and closed the door. He also - although I didn't know it - turned on a tape recorder.

For two hours he questioned me, going over everything very, very carefully. When he asked me if I knew anyone else who knew about Susan's confession, I decided to tell him about Ronnie. I didn't know that on the morning of that same day, she had given the police a complete rundown of what Susan had also told her.

Twelve days had passed since I'd left Sybil Brand.

The sergeant asked me if I knew there was a $25,000 reward leading to the conviction of the Tate murderers. Until that moment, I wasn't aware that there was a thin dime at stake. I never was able to figure out the sequence of events that had placed me in this position. Why did Susan Atkins choose me?

Vincent Bugliosi, the District Attorney who prosecuted the killers said to me, "It's amazing - this whole case. Your chance of being where you were was a million to one." He said the more he investigated the more bizarre it became.

I only know that my life was totally changed.

I know I wanted to save lives, but I don't suppose I'll ever know what brought about that strange dream that finally made me talk.

But why me?

It certainly wasn't money. For years people have accused me of snitching for the reward and I point out that I wished I'd known about the reward from the very start. With my mercenary tendencies it would have probably sent me to the cops immediately and saved me two weeks of absolute hell trying to make up my mind - what to do.

And I guess I'll always ask the question: Why me?

I do know that I was chosen to testify at length first, inasmuch that Ronnie's memory of the events and her conversations with Susan Atkins weren't as clear as mine.

Chapter Seventeen

My snitching on Susan Atkins certainly made the state prosecutors happy but it didn't have any effect on my Parole Board. I spent another six months in Corona after my first interview with the police and a few times I thought I was one dead lady.

I had to wait a year before I was called to testify and I was as nervous as hell that the Manson Family might find a way to keep me from appearing - dead or alive - in court. But nothing was as scary as waiting until the word got around that I was the one who'd snitched.

Most prisoners despise the thought of anyone cooperating with the law, and women can be insane about it. I had thought all that over before making my decision. And once it was done - I was one scared woman.

Five days after I told the police about my talks with Susan Atkins, I was watching television with about 120 girls in my unit at Corona. Suddenly there was a break in the program with a news flash: "The Sharon Tate murder case is believed solved because of an informant. Stay tuned for details."

My blood ran cold and my backbone started slithering like a snake. I stood there quivering with my heart banging away in my chest. Slowly I started edging away from where I'd been seated, keeping my back to the wall. I inched toward the control area, where the guards kept watch for any trouble, although I knew if it came they would never get to me in time.

I had no idea whether they would give my name or any hints about my identity. But my curiosity was just too strong for me to leave the room.

The news program started and I stared at the screen, watching the girls out of the corners of my eyes. The broadcaster announced that a girl in prison told police that Susan Atkins confessed to killing Sharon Tate and the others. He gave a few more details, and I was close to passing out from fright. Then, suddenly, they flashed Ronnie's picture on the screen.

God, I almost drowned out the guy with my loud sigh of relief. I remember feeling bad for Ronnie because I knew all the shit that would come down on her because of it, but I was enormously relieved to have had my part in the case kept a secret.

I don't know why the police released her name and not mine - but with a roomful of girls cursing and flipping fingers at the television screen, I wasn't arguing.

I couldn't believe the reaction of the girls. Although I knew the prisoner's code, I had half thought that this would be different. Here was a savage, freaky murder of a pregnant woman and some innocent people who just happened to be there.

Even these animals had to understand how important it is to stop maniacal killings like this, I thought. But not a single girl said she felt Ronnie had done the right thing.

Later I heard that Ronnie, for her own safety, was put in an isolation cell at Sybil Brand, but it didn't help much. Girls walked past her and drew their fingers across their throats to indicate she was as good as dead. They bad-mouthed the shit out of her. One girl even tossed a note in her cell saying someone was going to get her. That was introduced as evidence at the trial against Atkins.

The girls who watched the news report with me at Corona were bad enough. One said, "That motherfucking snitch... if she comes up here somebody ought to stick a shiv in her." They decided that Ronnie was a "...filthy, rotten, low-life bitch," and her life wasn't worth a damn.

Every time they mentioned Ronnie's name, I substituted my own. I panicked and went directly to the control area to ask to speak to the woman in charge of my section. At that point, only about five women in Corona knew about my statement. But evidently the guards had been told that if I wanted to talk to someone, they'd better hustle. They sent me right to Miss Hamilton, head of the receiving center.

I told her about the television report, and said I was scared. Miss Hamilton was super-cool. She advised me to go back and take it easy. If anyone made a move, she said, I should go to the guards. It sounded like pretty lousy security to me, and anyone who wanted to do a number on me with a shiv could do it without any problems.

But good old Dr. Dreiser heard about it, and she yanked me into her unit for protection. She was tremendously concerned about me. Later, when I left Corona on parole she begged me to be careful. "Please, Virginia," she said with tears in her eyes, "don't let them bring you back in a pine box."

Susan Atkins' lawyer had to be told the identity of the witnesses, so eventually word about me got around Sybil Brand. The case was the biggest thing that ever hit there, and the girls sat glued to the television watching film of Susan going to court. Then one day I met a girl from Sybil Brand who I had known before being transferred to Corona. I was friendly when I saw her, but she was as cold as ice.

I finally asked her what was wrong and she cut loose: "I thought you were good people, but I heard you were really the one who blew the whistle on Susan Atkins, and I think it's pretty fucking shitty."

Oh, Christ.

I told her how I knew Jay Sebring and what had been planned for Sinatra and then I said, "You know I'm not a rat... and listen, baby, you would have done the same goddamned thing. And if you didn't, you're as sick as they are!"

"I don't care how you clean it up," she replied. "You broke the rules!"

During the next day or two I started getting funny looks, and I decided to do something about it.

At the next group therapy session, I laid it all out. The girls in the group were strangely protective of each other and all were sworn to secrecy about anything that came out in the sessions. There were thirteen in the group, and only sixty in the whole unit, so I thought I would be safe.

Since I told them in front of Dr. Dreiser, they wouldn't come down too hard. If any one of them passed the word to someone out of the group, Dr. Dreiser would throw her out of the unit.

It did me a lot of good psychologically, but I was furious at having to defend my reasons. Girls accused me of doing it for the money or attention - they just wouldn't believe I snitched without some other motive. A few of my friends told me I did the right thing, but the word got around Corona and it was a tough six months.

The prison had a main campus, and I stayed clear of that. I'm sure that if anyone made a move for me the girls in my unit would have protected me, but it was an unnerving experience.

When I was finally released on parole, I was amazed by the support Manson had outside. The immediate murderers were locked up, but other Family members were hot for revenge. It blew my mind how Manson became a cult hero for the youth, persecuted by the Establishment because of his long hair. People wore T-shirts with his picture and with big lettering saying, "Sadie Glutz is a snitch."

I began to wonder if I wasn't better off back in Corona.

When I got out, I quietly moved to a crummy little place in El Sereno to lay low and wait to be called to testify. I couldn't really work because I didn't know what was going to happen, and I wasn't too keen to walk around L.A. with so many of the Manson Family on the loose.

Finally I decided this whole thing might at least be worth some money - which I desperately needed - and I figured the best deal would be to get a good lawyer. It had to be the right guy. I mean, there are lawyers and then there are lawyers. First I tried a friend of Big Jim, but he didn't see much in it for him and wasn't very excited.

In prison I had met Lucille Miller, the famous murderess, and she told me about Robert K. Steinberg. He was a cousin of F. Lee Bailey, and a big deal in Los Angeles, so I called him. Bob was interested in the case. He sent an investigator over for me in his Rolls, and he loaned me money from the beginning.

I had to get my Parole Board's permission to hire a lawyer. They couldn't see the need and it was a sweat. But my parole officer was a great chick named Iris Knapp, and she was impressed with Bob Steinberg. He had a little-boy charm, with twinkling, honest eyes. Bob was also a county commissioner and an associate of Sam Yorty, then mayor of Los Angeles, so he got the board's seal of approval.

I badly needed a job at that time, and Bob needed a receptionist-clerk, so I went to work for him. He was always a good friend, when friends were definitely in short supply.

I can't remember how many times we went down to the District Attorney's office to go over my statement with Vincent Bugliosi. I have to say this about Bugliosi. Although I've never had much love for authority of any kind, he was absolutely fair, straight and honest. I had nothing but respect for him. He never once even hinted that I might alter my testimony a little bit to help the state's case. He was careful to the other extreme, in fact.

Bugliosi apparently decided I would be a better witness because Ronnie couldn't stick to the subject, so I was scheduled to testify first.

Before the trial, Bob lined up a few interviews. I was nervous because I was under court order not to say anything, but the interviews weren't to be used until I testified and Bob worked it out okay. I taped a personal interview with Channel 4. My parole officer sat in to make sure I didn't say anything I wasn't supposed to, and Bob warned them about what they couldn't ask me. They held it until the night I testified.

Meanwhile things were coming down all over the place. Ronnie and I were obviously going to be heavy witnesses, and the defense attorneys tried everything they could think of to keep us off the stands. Finally the judge ruled that we could testify, but our statements had to be edited to make certain we only mentioned things that Susan Atkins said she did herself. Anything she said about others in the group would be hearsay.

This meant I had to give a new statement. The first time I talked to the police, a lawyer I won't name had advised me not to mention Atkins' stuff about the other planned murders - Sinatra, Taylor, Burton and all. Bob said I had better give the state everything, and he told Bugliosi that I had a lot of added testimony to go into my new statement.

The defense had copies of my original statement, but they had no idea about all the new material on the celebrity murder plans. It worked this way: I made my new statement to the police, who took it to the judge the night before I was to testify. He distributed photocopies of the admissible statement to each of the defense attorneys.

They must have fainted on the spot.

Then, in some mysterious manner, a copy of my transcript just happened to fall into the hands of Bill Farr, a reporter for the Los Angeles Herald-Examiner. It was splashed across the front page on the morning I was to testify. The front page of the October 9, 1970 edition of the Los Angeles Herald-Examiner had a headline in bold lettering that read:

LIZ, SINATRA ON DEATH LIST - TATE WITNESS
Ghastly Tortures Planned for Stars

The article was accompanied by a photo of myself and my attorney, Bob, with the cutline "Virginia Graham, A Key Witness in the Tate Trial - Susan Atkins' former cellmate is accompanied by attorney Robert Steinberg."

Wow, did the shit hit the fan! Atkins' lawyer, Daye Shinn, jumped up and said, "I want to find out how the press got her transcripts," trying to imply that Bob or I leaked it, for Christ's sake, when neither of us did.

Naturally there was a motion for a mistrial, but the judge rejected it. He asked me point blank: "Miss Graham, do you know how your transcript was given to reporter Bill Farr?" I replied, "No, Sir, I don't."

Bob was bounding up and down because they were trying to accuse me of it, and I was scared of a possible contempt charge. The defense attorneys wanted to keep me from testifying, saying that my statement was already public.

The poor guy who got caught in the maneuver was the reporter, Bill Farr. He didn't know whether the opposition paper - the L.A. Times - had the statement as well, so the story had to be used. So poor Bill went to jail simply because he refused to break a confidence and say who gave the transcript to him.

What a screwed up system we have. The guy was just trying to do his job, and he got nailed for it. All I know for sure is that I didn't give out the transcript.

The defense was having a hell of a time, anyway, at this point, because of Atkins' various confessions. I heard the police had made a deal with her that if she pleaded guilty, they would try to keep her out of the gas chamber.

Whether that's true or not, she was advised by her lawyer at the time to plead guilty and try for life imprisonment and to write a book. She laid it all out in a manuscript that was published before the trial - *The Killing of Sharon Tate* - which had everything in it but a flat admission of actually murdering Tate.

On top of that, after copping to the police, she testified before a grand jury for two hours, which resulted in the indictments of the others.

After all of the confessions, she saw Charles Manson once on permission from the authorities and repudiated everything.

Although the state no longer had her confession, the defense attorneys were up a tree. The prosecutors went on a desperate search for strong witnesses. They apparently worked on each of the Manson Family separately until they turned up Linda Kasabian, who decided to turn state's evidence in exchange for immunity.

Those weren't the only behind-the-scenes dramas. From the start there was a tremendous competition between Ronnie and me over who really brought out the Atkins confession. She wanted badly to testify first. I have to admit I fought her pretty hard, but it was only because of Richard.

I knew he was trying to manipulate her to cut me out of any reward money and it pissed me off. That was one reason I wanted Steinberg as a lawyer. She had gotten a good lawyer, and more than fighting fire with fire, I figured I needed an atom bomb.

Ronnie got in touch with me a few times after I got out of Corona and before I testified, but I made sure Bob heard every conversation. She had gone to Minnesota for safety, with her family, and she somehow found out where I was working. She phoned long distance, and I put her on hold while I got Bob on the line.

I asked her point blank why she didn't tell the police about me when she first talked to them. She was evasive. I put a few more questions to her just so Bob would know who was telling the truth.

She wanted to know if we could get together when she returned to L.A., but Bob shook his head no. I wanted to get together with Ronnie because I was sure we could make some good deals with the foreign press and all, and I wanted her to use Bob as her lawyer too.

One night after she came back I tried to call her at Richard's sister's house, and I talked to the sister's husband, Tom Hicks. I told him to ask Ronnie to call me because I wanted my attorney to represent her as well. He came on very cagey, saying, "After all, she was the one Atkins talked to." I started laughing and suggested he get his facts straight.

Later, it turned out that Tom had taped our entire conversation and one day when I was talking to the D.A. he came bounding in with the tape and told them to listen to it. He was trying to discredit my story that I was the first one that Atkins had approached. The D.A.'s staff just laughed and asked what he had against me. One of them wondered if I wanted to press charges, since recording from a telephone without prior consent of both parties was illegal, and that ended that.

In the midst of hassles from every side, I took the stand in October 1970.

Chapter Eighteen

I was sitting in the witness box when they brought Susan Atkins in for me to identify. I hadn't seen her since I left Sybil Brand, and I felt guilty about facing her. She had trusted me, but after much hellish agonizing I was absolutely convinced there was no other choice left for me but to spill everything to the police.

She came slouching in with a gait known as the jailhouse bounce. It was a sort of draggy, jerky walk that some of the guys and chicks in the joint pick up to show defiance and unity with each other.

Susan wore neither bra nor panties - she never wore either - and had on only a little blue uniform with a white stripe and rubber thongs. She had let the hair grow under her arms and on her legs and looked deathly pale from being indoors all the time.

When she walked by, she didn't recognize me. I had been much thinner in jail and had short dark hair. Now, on the stand my hair was red and I was looking jazzy with lots of make-up and sharp clothes.

The D.A. asked me to identify the girl who spoke to me in Sybil Brand. I pointed to Susan and said, "Yes, that's her there."

She fixed me with her whammy-stare and glared directly into my eyes. I remembered that this had been a thing with her. Eye contact was the key to the soul and whoever broke first was the weaker.

We stood facing each other for more than a minute, just staring eye-to-eye, then she suddenly dropped her gaze and screamed: "Take off the wig, and show your face so that the world can see... You're not even a good actress!"

I was really pissed off. I replied, "You should know. You're doing the act of your life."

This was just one incident of many that took place in a trial that often had the air of a carnival about it. At one point the defendants scratched deep X marks on their foreheads to signify that they had X'd themselves out of society. The girls had used bobby pins to do it. Toward the end of the trial they also shaved their heads, though I never could figure out how the hell they had access to razors at Sybil Brand.

And then President Nixon carelessly revealed to someone his feelings about Manson and the trial, with the result that an L.A. newspaper, among others, carried the headline MANSON GUILTY, NIXON DECLARES. The judge banned the paper from the courtroom, but someone had accidentally left a copy near Manson who grabbed it and displayed its front page contents to the jury.

After rejecting hundreds of attorneys, Manson chose Irving Kanarek to represent him, and all through the trial Kanarek kept jumping up with objections and motions that obviously needled the judge and cracked up the courtroom.

Manson kept trying to defend himself and put down Kanarek several times, and at one point made a lunge at the judge.

Ronnie and I weren't supposed to be too friendly because the prosecution didn't want anyone to charge that we had collaborated on our statements, which never happened. She was sitting on one side of the court and I was on the other. We kept waving and making hand signals while the cops were having fits. I'd call, "Hey, how are you?" and she'd grin and wave.

In spite of it all, the state went far out of its way to ensure the Manson Family a fair trial. I wish I had had one-half as good a chance at justice as they had. The defense grasped at every straw possible and I was amazed at how cool the judge and everyone else stayed throughout the whole thing.

I testified during three days of trial, mostly answering questions from Atkins' attorney, Daye Shinn. I wasn't a bit nervous because I was telling the truth. Actually, the only guy who worried me on the defense team - the three girls and Manson were all tried together - was Paul Fitzgerald.

I was telling the truth, so I wasn't afraid of being rattled. But Fitzgerald was a brilliant young attorney who gave up a public defender's job to take the case for personal reasons, and I expected him to really work me over. Bob had prepared me for heavy tactics, but he couldn't coach me, so I was a bit leery. As it turned out my worries had all been for naught. Fitzgerald never even questioned me.

The other attorneys included one man named Ronald Hughes - who was trying his first case and who died in a landslide during the trial -

and he tried everything to unnerve me. One morning I was getting out of Rob's Rolls and about to enter the courthouse when Hughes, who was standing nearby with some of Manson's un-jailed girls yelled, "Hey, Virginia, turn around so the girls can see you!" Bob was furious.

I spent my first day on the stand from 9 in the morning until 4 in the afternoon. I was really worn out, but I tried not to show it. Daye Shinn kept asking what I thought were the most ridiculous questions. Once he suggested that I had made a pass at Atkins in jail, and I cracked up laughing. Then the defense tried to say that Ronnie and I were police plants which was even funnier.

At one point Shinn asked me if it was true that I got $100 a night. That was as far as he got before Bob and the D.A. leaped out of their seats to object.

Bugliosi questioned me about Atkins' confession, and he asked me if Susan had told me anything that she had said to Sharon Tate.

I repeated Atkins' words as she told them to me a year earlier in dormitory 8000: "Look bitch… you're gonna die." I told him how Susan said she looked Tate in the eyes and killed her. The whole thing came out.

I recounted Susan's description of her Family and their approach to life. I testified how she told me she heard only strong words, so that if a victim said, "Please don't kill me," all that came through was "Kill me."

After it was all over, Shinn passed Bob and me out in the hall, and said loudly to me, "I hope you enjoy spending the money." I answered, "Don't worry, Sweetie, I will." Then he said to Bob, "Your client just got my client the gas chamber."

Ronnie testified for about a quarter of an hour a few days after me, backing up my testimony.

The police decided to give me protection for a couple of days, but Bob and I were getting nervous. I had been required to say on the stand how I made my living. When I said I was a clerk in a law office, everyone knew I was working for him.

Anyone could have breezed through the front door of Bob's office and knocked off the entire staff. I was worried for the others as well as myself. By then my face was well known. I had been all over the front pages, and I was hardly Miss Incognito.

Then I saw that everyone else was making a bundle off the trial, so I decided it was time to join in. I was a little tired of the press and their free interviews. My Parole Board still had to give me permission to say anything. They were hoping I would just stop making waves.

With each passing day I became more and more nervous that the Manson Family would track me down and exact their revenge. So Parole Board or not, I quietly disappeared.

Chapter Nineteen

It was in June of 1970 that I jumped parole in California and went to Tucson, Arizona where I lived with Arnie Castro's sister, Alice. On August 13, 1971 I went to Hawaii with my husband Arnie and took the name Kathleen Castro. That was four months after the end of the Manson trial and proved to be the smartest thing I ever did.

The $12,500 that I received as my share of the reward money enabled me to make the move with ease. Ronnie was awarded the same amount and the boy who found the gun was given $2,500. That money helped me to start a new and productive life.

There was no doubt in my mind that leaving California without permission would result in a warrant being issued for my immediate arrest. I well knew the risk I was taking. Being caught meant going back into the slammer but there was no other way. I was bound and determined to make a new life for myself.

I vowed that I would never ever become involved with anything even remotely illegal, and I am proud to say that during my twenty-two years in Hawaii, I remained steadfast and faithful to that concept.

I was instrumental in conceiving and bringing into being one of the most magnificent health spas on the islands. I also directed one of the most prestigious modeling schools and successfully managed many of the most respected art galleries there.

It was during my early years in Honolulu that I met a wonderful lady, Elsa Ritchie, who became my friend. She helped me to acquire a lease on what had been a 6,500 square foot gymnasium which I set about converting into a magnificent spa in the Hawaiian Hilton Hotel, calling it The Sun Palace.

It was an unusual idea and a great challenge. I arranged for the financing, did all the planning and paperwork, got it over the legal hurdles and succeeded in bringing it to fruition. I even worked out an arrangement with the hotel to set aside a block of fifty rooms for a live-in spa package which would cost a client $1,500 a week.

I did have some help and along the way managed to accumulate three female partners: one was a very talented Asian woman, Norma Takashita, who owned a design business and who did a truly magnificent job designing and furnishing the interior most elegantly.

Another was my sister-in-law, Alice, who did a very efficient job handling the office and administrative end of the business, and then there was Allison Grayson.

I first met Allison when she was the manager of a figure reducing salon, and after a short while she became what I thought was a trusted friend - but boy, did I learn.

She had been a singer for a number of years and also did some voice over work for a number of celebrities.

She was pretty, had great charm and a beautiful voice but was financially strapped. She had fallen on hard times after her divorce from her husband, who went on to become a biggie in the music business.

When I was putting the finishing touches to The Sun Palace I came to realize that Allison, the image she projected and her Hollywood entertainment background, would be the perfect front for our enterprise. All she had to do was decorate an office and meet and greet would-be clients.

When I approached her she told me she was flat broke and, being the patron saint of all underdogs, I figured, "What the hell..." and gave her a full partnership without her having to invest a thin dime. If that wasn't friendship - what was? I was fashioning my own noose but didn't even know it at the time.

It was about that time when I heard from my publisher, Bernard Geis, about my book. He wanted me to fly to New York to discuss a publicity tour.

The publicists had come up with a gimmick that they were certain would generate an enormous amount of exposure for the book. The idea was for me to appear on a major television network show and confess to a nationwide audience that I was a fugitive in hiding and that I was turning myself in.

They also felt that by doing so I might possibly generate a certain amount of public sympathy which would move the Parole Board to either reinstate me or release me permanently.

It was a calculated risk, a gamble, but I was assured that lawyers would be engaged to protect my rights.

I was told that I could find myself with a bestseller involving both the book and a possible hit movie, and that big money - big money was in the offing - so I agreed to go along.

Now I wasn't completely blind to the chance that I could also be arrested while on tour, and made the decision to prepare for that contingency and protect The Sun Palace, which is why I confided in Allison.

My feeling was that someone should know all the facts about my background in the event that I was taken into custody, and be prepared to answer any negative publicity that could hurt the spa, so I told Allison about the book - everything.

She appeared to be very sympathetic, and when I told her I wanted her to manage the place while I was away, she readily agreed and only asked that she be allowed to make any necessary decisions that might arise - and I agreed.

We opened The Sun Palace on May 16, 1972, and from all indications we were on our way. In late May of that same year - less than two weeks later - I left for New York. My schedule called for me to be away for only two weeks and I was sure the place could get along without me for such a short period.

Little did I know that while on the mainland I would be forced to back out of the publicity tour and become involved with one of the great loves of my life, which would also cost me my partnership in The Sun Palace.

I stayed away too long and gave Allison the chance to build up her case against me and do a cut-throat number on me.

What about Arnie? He had held a license as a hairdresser in California but since there was no reciprocity law in Hawaii, I sent him back to a hairdressing school. By the time he got his new license I had built a beauty salon for him in the spa - and he was in business.

Here again, I was backing the wrong horse - like so many other so-called intimates - and he would also turn out to be a horse's ass. We were married in 1968. Divorced in 1974.

His affairs with other women in Hawaii had been brought to my attention by a friend, and also affairs he had in Tucson, Arizona before we went to Hawaii, so my decision was not difficult concerning what occurred in my life when I went back east to discuss the publicity tour.

Chapter Twenty

What happens when a good looking blonde with great legs and a magnificent rear meets a dynamite looking, blue-eyed Italian who happens to be one of Philadelphia's finest "boys in blue" - particularly when the blonde happens to be a fugitive with an outstanding warrant for her arrest?

Common sense would indicate that she run the other way - and fast. But I loved to play the longshots - the odds, and that day in June 1973 when Officer Lou Corgliano walked into a diner at South Philadelphia's Broad and Snyder and took the counter stool next to mine - my life underwent a radical change, again.

I was in Philadelphia, en route to New York, to go see my publisher about the public relations tour. I was having lunch when I realized that someone had slipped into the seat next to mine.

I was chatting with Maude, a waitress, and turned to see who it was that was sitting next to me when I looked into the most incredible blue eyes, smiling at me in a way that was saying more than just "hello."

The waitress knew him and his partner who was seated on the other side of him, and as a matter of good manners she said to him, "Lou, this is Virginia. She just got in from Hawaii."

With that opening gambit, we started talking and it took me fifteen minutes to realize as that song says, "That this could be the start of something big."

Lou bore a great resemblance to Fabian Forte, the teenage idol of the 60's. Like Fabian, Lou also had an excellent singing voice, and when he was twenty had been offered a recording contract which he turned down when his fiancée asked him to choose between her and a career in music.

Fortunately or unfortunately he chose his sweetheart and joined the police force when he was twenty-one. He was ambitious and bright and had a smoldering, sensual look about him that he was not aware of.

I watched the reaction of the females around us as we sat there at the counter and it was amazing. There were two women sitting close by who couldn't take their eyes off him. I loved it.

When we finished our meals, I remarked that I was planning to go shopping in the downtown area and he offered to give me a lift. I needed a wardrobe for my upcoming trip which would take me to several cities around the country.

I thought about the risk for someone with my past becoming involved with an officer-of-the-law and immediately realized the total insanity of it.

But then, I was among other things, a believer in "living it up" and it also occurred to me that if playing around with this gorgeous hunk could possibly open the door to my past, at least there would be some real good times along the way. What the hell - life was to be lived!

Then too, I had plans of divorcing Arnie when I got back to Hawaii. My friend's husband had the concessions for the tourist camera girls and flower girls at all the leading hotels. Arnie was working in the photo lab when I discovered that he was having affairs with some of the girls there. That tore it with me.

I didn't realize then that my meeting Lou would result in my divorcing Arnie much sooner than I had planned. But now, here I was, little me, sitting with two cops in a lovely new Cadillac and enjoying every minute of it.

Besides his police work, Lou owned a gift shop which allowed him to enjoy some of the better things that he wouldn't have been able to afford on a cop's salary. The Caddy we were in was one of them.

Throughout my life I have always been very reserved in expressing any interest in the men I have come in contact with - particularly at a first meeting - but with Lou the sparks just flew between us. It was an instant attraction.

Along with that smoldering sensual look, Lou had an aura of innocence, a soft boyish quality and a body women would die for. It was a world class, unbeatable combination that was pushing all my buttons.

When he eventually dropped me off at one of the better stores he asked if I would consider having dinner with him sometime, and I said I would and told him where I was staying.

Later that evening he called and we made arrangements for dinner, when suddenly I began to get cold feet. It hit me that I was playing a dangerous game. After all he was a cop and if somehow he was to find out that I was a parole violator, who knows what he would do.

But I was torn. I knew the smarter thing was to play it safe but somehow I couldn't resist him. I'd had experiences with many men and certainly knew how to handle myself in any given situation, including how to put the brakes on my emotions. But this situation held a strange fascination for me.

I was 6,000 miles from my home in Hawaii and planning on an evening out with someone who could possibly be the one to send me back to prison. Was I nuts? He was someone I could have considered my mortal enemy - a policeman. If he found out the truth about me, how could he not turn me in? To do otherwise was to put his career on the force in jeopardy. His job as a cop would go down the toilet, and me with it.

I wrestled with the problem and when Lou picked me up promptly as arranged, there I was ready, willing and able.

I was dressed all in white and really looked great, and when he greeted me I could sense that he was nervous - as nervous as I was - but the electricity between us was absolutely staggering.

Lou was the perfect gentleman, opening doors, pulling the chair out at the table, doing all the many things that this lady loves coming from a man.

We had a drink at one of the many clubs that Philadelphia is notorious for and then went on to dinner, and through it all we held hands and acted like a couple of teenage kids out on their first date.

As the evening wore on we made small talk and listened to the music. I remember Gladys Knight singing "Midnight Train to Georgia" and when the time came for parting, neither one of us wanted to be the first to say goodbye.

I only knew that just by touching this man's hand, deep feelings that I had been suppressing for so many years came to life within me. I fell in love with Lou, and he with me that first night.

He took me straight home at the end of the evening and we didn't want to let each other go. He told me he was going to be out of town for a week and would call me as soon as he returned. I couldn't wait for his call.

The next day I went to a jeweler's and bought a beautiful twenty dollar gold piece mounted on a heavy chain and had it delivered to him at his precinct station.

I knew that if he opened the box in the presence of his fellow officers he would come in for some ribbing, but I was determined that he'd remember this lady.

I have always been very generous and really enjoy giving to those people I care about. To me, money is a medium of exchange to be enjoyed while we're here and I was going to barrage this Adonis of a man with everything I had, and did.

When he got my gift he was totally floored by it and for me that was just the beginning.

But Lou had a problem which he neglected to share with me at the beginning - he was married. On reflection, if I had known that first night I might have ended it then and there but he kept it from me for a few weeks, and by then I didn't care.

For quite a long time, Lou never made any sexual moves and that was one of the things that sold me on him. We hugged and kissed and sat in his car by the airport watching the planes take off and arrive, with some serious feelings involved. It was then that he told me he was married and also said he was falling in love with me.

If I was certain of anything that I had been certain of in my life it was that this was the man, the mate I had really been looking for, for a long time. Money had always been important to me but now it was totally otherwise.

I saw something in this man, a sincerity, a decency, an honesty that I hadn't seen in a man for a long time, and I was determined he'd be mine.

We were seeing each other quite often. He'd drop by at 8 am when he was off shift and spend a few minutes with me, and those few minutes with him were always exciting.

During that period I was conferring with my publisher on the upcoming publicity tour.

I was having a problem with the title they had chosen for the book on the grounds that it was very misleading and totally untrue. It was entitled *The Joy of Hooking*.

I also came to realize the plans for the tour included my making television appearances as well as interviews with big city newspapers all across the country. And suddenly I began to be bedeviled by old fears - retaliation on the part of the fanatical followers of Charlie Manson. Making so many public appearances to exploit the book would leave me wide open. I would be a sitting target.

It occurred to me that I needed a bodyguard and then a bright idea hit me - who better for the job than Officer Lou Corgliano? He would be perfect - from both a personal and a professional point of view. All I had to do now was convince him.

And, too, I quickly came to realize that sometime in the very near future I would have to level with him and tell him who I really was. And that moment of truth came quicker than I had expected. And in more ways than one.

Meanwhile, several weeks had passed since I'd left Hawaii and I decided it was time to call Allison Grayson and see how things were progressing with the spa.

We'd spent only a few moments going through the "Hello" and "How are things with you" niceties when she came right to the point. It was a haymaker that caught me off guard and knocked me for a loop.

"I've given it a great deal of thought and I've come to the conclusion," she said, "that that book of yours could destroy the business. Publicity like that we don't need."

As soon as I regained my composure I reminded her that I'd been up front with her from the very first day so that in the event there was any kickback from the book, steps could be taken to offset it. And I was about to tell her how that could be done when she cut me off.

"No," she said very firmly, "I don't think so. I've consulted some people in the field - publicity experts - and they tell me that damage control in this situation is not possible. The stink would always be there."

And before I could voice my objections she added in a very ominous tone, "I think it best for everyone concerned that as of this moment you sever your connections with the spa. And if you have any notions of taking any legal action let me remind you that going into a court of law is one thing you want to stay out of - if you get my meaning. I'm sure there are people in Los Angeles who would like to know where they can find Virginia Graham."

Her meaning was loud and clear. All she had to do was make one call to the D.A.'s office in L.A. and I would be back in the slammer, and it would be done without the benefit of a nationwide television audience helping the sale of the book. What a waste that would be.

All I could think of to say was, "You seem to be holding all the cards right now, Allison, but as they say, the game isn't over until the fat lady sings - and in this game - she hasn't even begun to hum. I'll be getting back to you… honey. You can bet your sweet ass on that." And I hung up.

That last remark of mine was all bluff and bravado. I knew that I had to back away from the spa for the time being. If anybody was going to blow the whistle on me - I was going to be the one to do it and at a time of my own choosing, on a major television talk show where it could help the sale of the book and maybe even me - somehow.

They say that if a storm is on the horizon - do your best to ride it out. It seemed apropos at the moment. My name was on the lease for the spa and Allison couldn't sell it or make any major moves without my signature. And too, there was nobody in the top hierarchy of the spa who really had what it took to run it successfully, least of all Allison.

In less than a year they had to close the doors. It had failed as I knew it would. Fortunately, I had friends who ran the Hilton Hawaiian Hotel and they didn't hold me to the lease. I felt sorry to see the spa go under. It was the kind of thing that Hawaii needed - it belonged there.

I'd had my moment of truth with Allison Grayson, and now I had to confront Lou - my beloved Lou - with my past. Even though I knew that he loved me and that he was aware of my very deep feelings for him, I was fearful that when I told him about my past - it might be the end.

Then one evening, shortly after my talk with Allison, Lou and I had a quiet, lovely dinner together and when he drove me back to my apartment that I rented, I asked him to come in and visit, that there was something important I wanted to discuss with him.

We were comfortably seated in my living room when I looked straight into his eyes, took a deep breath and said, "You've probably been wondering why I keep running back to New York so often." He nodded his head. "It did occur to me," he replied.

"Well," I pushed on, "I've written a book…"

His eyes opened wide. "A book…? About what?"

"It's my autobiography, Lou. And when it's published you won't find it in the bookstores under the name of Kathleen Castro because my real name is Virginia Graham..." And with that I told him about injuring my back, my time in the hospital, the bad checks, my time in prison, my meeting Susan Atkins, my part in the Manson trial, my violating my parole by going to Hawaii and hiding there under a different name. I also told him about Arnie.

And I don't remember whether I stopped to breathe all during the telling of it. And when I was through I searched his face for his reaction.

He looked at me and then away and did it two or three times. It had obviously been an awful lot to assimilate so that for a moment he didn't know what to think or say. He was really taken aback and for a few more moments he was quiet. Then he took a deep breath. He looked into my eyes and said quietly, "You sure as hell have been one pretty busy lady."

And having said that he shook his head and grinned, and I knew that my fears had been groundless. He really did love me and he understood me. He knew that basically I was a good, honest human being and that I wouldn't willingly hurt anyone.

At that moment I said a silent prayer, "Thank you God, for sending me Lou."

At this point in time Lou was very seriously thinking about leaving his wife. Their marriage had been in trouble for some time. However, they had a small son and daughter who he dearly loved, and his wife threatened that if he left her she would make sure that he would never see their children again. That's why he stayed there - for the sake of the kids.

Lou, during the months we'd known each other revealed his marital unhappiness to me a little at a time, and after a while I was able to piece together the complete picture. His was a life of dull and quiet complacency. As far as his wife was concerned, she had her children, her little house, her family, television, the church and Lou - in that order.

Any drive he might have had to move up in life, any desire for anything better, she quickly crushed. Her outlook was completely negative and she made it clear that in her estimation he had gone as far as he

211

could with his abilities. For a long time he had given up his hopes and dreams until I came along. Where she had no faith in him - I knew different.

I encouraged him and told him that I truly believed that he could accomplish whatever goals he set for himself. I told him to reach for the sky, if that's what he wanted. And why not? I gave him my philosophy which was to always fly high because the rewards are on the top of the mountains where it's sunny and bright and not down in the valley where it's damp and dark.

And I know that I reached him because he began making plans and important decisions regarding both his career and his personal life.

It was about then that I decided to find a smashing apartment where Lou and I could spend some truly prime time together and really get to know one another. I managed to lease a beautiful place in Longport, New Jersey overlooking the ocean.

At dinner that night we drank Dom Pérignon champagne and ate by candlelight, and what followed was beautiful beyond belief.

He picked me up in his strong arms and carried me into the bedroom. While kissing me and whispering how much he loved me, we could hear the surf crashing on the shore as he carefully removed my clothes. Up to that moment we had never been sexually intimate, despite our very strong feelings. We didn't merely have sex that night, not in the conventional sense of the word. We had much more than that. What we had was a truly thrilling, overwhelming and illuminating experience of total togetherness - a true union of loving hearts that I will always remember. I knew without the slightest whisper of a doubt that I had finally found the man I wanted to spend the rest of my years with.

For some weeks Lou and I had been talking about the possibility of our going to Hawaii and it was in November 1973 when he told his wife that he was going to Honolulu, that he was terribly unhappy with their relationship, and needed to get away to think things over.

She took him completely by surprise when she replied, "Don't give me that 'need to be alone' crap."

Lou didn't say a word. He brushed her hand away before she could say anything else, picked up his bags and walked out the door. He spent the night at a motel near the airport. I met him the next morning and we boarded a flight to Honolulu, where we checked into the Sheraton

Waikiki.

On the afternoon of the second day we were there, the phone rang and when Lou answered it, it was very obvious that his troubles were just beginning; it was his wife who had called every hotel until she tracked him down.

I couldn't hear what she had to say but I heard Lou very quietly and firmly stating that he didn't love her and hadn't for a long time, that he loved someone else who gave him back his pride and his self-esteem and made him feel like a man and not just a paycheck. And before he hung up he almost shouted: "It's over with us! You hear me! It's over! And you and nobody else can change that! Goodbye!" At that moment I almost felt sorry for her.

He had said everything he wanted to say, the truth was out and having released himself of that burden he seemed happy, but I couldn't help but sense within him an underlying feeling of sadness. He was obviously thinking about his children.

It was Lou's first trip to the islands and he loved everything about the place. It was Elsa Ritchie, my friend, who was secretary to the vice-president who set up an interview with the president, Don Matson, who was looking for a Chief of Security for the prestigious Hilton Hawaiian Village.

Lou went for the interview and Don Matson was very impressed with his credentials and offered him the position which included health insurance, pension fund and a considerably larger salary than he was earning with the Philly police force. The job was his for the taking in six weeks, when the present head of security retired.

When Lou came out of Don Matson's office, he was all smiles. He couldn't believe all this was happening to him. He had the job of his dreams, in the land of his dreams and he was with the woman he loved. It all seemed too good to be true, and he knew it.

He was on a two week vacation, at the end of which he knew he would have to return to resign from his position with the force. That offered no problem. But he dreaded the thought of having to face his wife and his mother and his dad. And how would he explain what was happening to the children?

Virginia Graham and Officer Lou Corgliano in Hawaii, 1973

What we didn't know was that when his parents heard that Lou had left his family, they had flipped out. They were old fashioned Italians and very Catholic. With them, when you got married it was forever, and they immediately joined forces with his wife to help her free him from the clutches of that vecchia puttana - "that old whore."

The two weeks passed quickly and we both went back to the mainland: Lou to a motel in Philadelphia and I to New York for further conferences on my book and subsequent publicity tour.

The very first evening that he reported at his precinct to work his shift, to his great embarrassment, his entire family showed up. His wife, his mother and father and his two children all were there, passionately imploring him to come home. It had all been arranged in advance and approved by the Lieutenant who agreed with the consensus that "Lou has to come to his senses."

This went on and on for days without end. His mother would throw her Italian "Mama Mia" fit, his father telling him he should have his head examined and his wife in a constant state of hysteria. And too, his lieutenant saying over and over again, "Lou, why do you wanna throw away ten good years on the force and a beautiful family like that?"

There were periods of tranquility when he was sure that they had given up, but then without warning they would show up again and raise their usual brand of hell. And in the face of it all, he held firm. It would go on like that for four weeks.

With great patience, he tried to explain to his parents that he wanted to go to Hawaii. "I got a once-in-a-lifetime chance at a great job, in a very beautiful place with a beautiful lady who I love and who loves me. For years I've been very unhappy and now I got a chance to be happy. Don't you want me to be happy?"

But it all fell on deaf ears. No one was listening and they kept up their unrelenting pressure.

Lou and I spoke on the phone every day and although I had no idea what was going on and he didn't tell me, I could hear the sadness in his voice. All he wanted was the freedom to live the kind of life he had dreamed about. He wanted to live but "they" wouldn't let him.

With passing time they used the two youngsters more and more, rehearsing them in what to say like: "Daddy, why are you going away? Don't you love us anymore?" or "Daddy, we don't want you to leave us. We want you to stay here with us. Daddy, we love you! Why don't you love us?"

He could handle his wife and his parents, but the tear-stained faces of his beloved son and daughter were the toughest aspects that he had to cope with. Not only didn't he budge, but he requested a one year leave of absence from the force which was granted.

He had his ticket and his flight schedule for Honolulu, and I had rented a fabulous apartment for us at the Hilton Lagoon. And the night before his departure, his police pals threw him a going-away party.

He was at the airport at 7:00 am, an hour before his flight time and he decided to make one more try to make his mother and father understand why he was doing what he was doing. He got on the phone and when he reached his mother she informed him that his father had had a heart attack the night before, and she added, "It was because of you, Lou, because of you!"

Now, there was no way that he could possibly get on that plane. When he reached me in Hawaii he was almost in tears. I tried to comfort him the best I could, but I knew then that "they" had won. And when he hung up I cried.

Not too long after, he went back to his wife and kids. And not too long after that I got a call from a priest, a boyhood friend of his who was very liberal in his dogma. He told me that Lou had loved me but that he couldn't handle all the guilt. And hearing that, I cried again.

But I knew it wasn't over. Lou had been hired by Bernard Geis, my publisher, to be my bodyguard during my tour which was scheduled to start in three months.

Meanwhile, he and I continued to talk on the phone and he was very unhappy. He told me that I had showed him a way of life that he'd always wanted and that he would never stop loving me but he had duties and obligations, and he was going to try one more time, but he'd never forget me.

This time I was the pessimist and told him that I gave their reconciliation six months - no more. My thinking, as I explained it to him, was that she would neither forgive nor forget the time he spent with me.

And when he said he would never forget me - he didn't.

Lou and I saw each other again when he came to New York to be my bodyguard. His wife was having jealous fits back in Philadelphia. He and I were still in love and it was exciting being together again.

Chapter Twenty-one

My itinerary called for print media interviews and personal appearances on radio and television. Then came the night I was doing a radio talk show. Lou and his cousin, Sam, also a private detective, were at the station with me when I received a call from a Manson sympathizer threatening to kill me.

Lou and Sam rushed me out of there, with guns in hand and had me back at my room at The Drake Hotel in fifteen minutes. Lou and I talked for hours and he convinced me that if I continued on with the tour I could be killed. Before the night was over, I made the decision to take his advice. I would forget all about the book and the money that helping to sell it could bring me. Once more I would run and hide. You never knew where one of Manson's nuts might pop up.

And I decided to do the right thing where Lou was concerned. I had to be strong and set him free so that he could get on with his life. It would never work out with us - his family ties were too strong.

So I left New York and flew to stay with friends in Tucson and he went back to Philadelphia and his wife and family. Four months later I went back to the islands, only this time instead of Honolulu I settled down in Maui and tried to forget him. I also got my divorce from Arnie Castro.

Virginia Graham
back in Hawaii, 1974

* * *

It was in mid-1976 that I was able to come out from under that dark cloud that had covered me for so long. I could stop hiding. I found out that Los Angeles no longer had a warrant out for my arrest. I finally had my freedom - freedom from fear.

I had enlisted the aid of an old acquaintance - a newspaper reporter from Los Angeles whose name was Hal Jacques. I told him my problem and asked him to see what he could do. I was tired of hiding - tired of running. I explained that for I had lived an honorable and productive life since getting out of prison, and believed that should count for something.

Hal agreed with my reasoning and in turn enlisted the services of Stuart Goldfarb, an attorney and a good friend who had me collect recommendations from business people, officials and friends on the islands and get them to him, which I did.

Armed with all this material, Stuart met with the appropriate Los Angeles authorities and was surprised to learn that there was no warrant out for me and in fact there hadn't been since 1973.

Despite the fact that I had violated my parole by leaving California without permission, since no new charges had been filed against me - the fact that I had lived an exemplary life for the following three years - the parole violation had been dropped as of 1973!

The irony is that I could have gone back and fought Allison and taken the spa back because her threats to expose me weren't threats at all since I was no longer a fugitive.

* * *

For four years I made no attempt to contact Lou, but I thought about him and dreamed about him, and I still do to this day. Then one day I dialed his precinct in Philadelphia and reached him. He was shocked when he heard my voice.

"My God, where are you? Do you know how much time I spent looking for you? I looked everywhere - everywhere. Where are you?" And then he added, "My wife and I were divorced three years ago. You were right. She couldn't forget you and she wouldn't forgive me. Why didn't you call me?"

And then he went on to say that he had met a young woman named Rita and they were planning on getting married in the not too distant future. "And you know something," he said very quietly, "she reminds me - she's a lot like you."

Frankly, I was happy for him that his life had taken a happy turn. He was a great guy and he deserved the best. We still talked, once in a while I'd call his precinct and leave a message: "Tell Officer Corgliano that his friend from Hawaii called and that I'm coming for him."

I like to think of it as a gag message but deep down inside - who knows?

During one of our last conversations, Lou told me that his ex-wife succeeded in turning his children against him. They wouldn't talk to him and it hurt him, deeply. His mother kept him at arm's length. She didn't have too much to do with him because she didn't approve of his second wife. She was the typical Italian mother - her way or no way.

* * *

It was either in 1977 or 1978 that I returned to California for a visit and one of the first people I made contact with was one of my former parole officers, Iris Knapp, who had been eminently fair in handling my case. I was fond of her, and asked her to come and visit.

We made an appointment and when the time came, there was a knock on the door and when I opened it, there was Iris and I was happy to see her.

I had never known Iris to be an especially religious person, and I was taken aback when I noticed that when she came through the doorway she blessed herself.

We sat down and for a few moments made some small talk, when suddenly our conversation took a surprising turn. She told me that she had become friendly with Susan Atkins who was still behind bars. And I was even more surprised when she began defending and rationalizing Susan's crimes.

She told me that Susan had found Jesus and was now a Christian. When Iris added that she, herself, was going to leave her job as a parole officer and become a full-time ordained Evangelistic minister - I was floored.

I had an apartment at the time and in the living room where we were visiting I had a small Buddha sitting on a table. Around my neck I'd hung a gold chain with a little Tiki god which I'd gotten in Hawaii.

Now, Iris turned to look at the Buddha and very solemnly told me that it was the sign of the devil and that the Tiki gold charm on the chain was evil and that she wanted to pray over me.

I was momentarily stunned. I'd always known Iris to be a level-headed, common-sense person and I didn't know what to think or do, so as not to offend her, I decided to go along with her.

As soon as I'd removed the offending necklace, she placed her hand on my head and began praying rather loudly. And while doing so she seemed to me to be in a trancelike state, saying over and over, "Lord, come into her soul," and then to my utter amazement added, "Let Virginia and Susan talk together and become friends."

When she concluded praying, she sat down and told me that she and Susan Atkins had become close friends and that it was her deep belief that Susan did not take any part in the actual killings in the Tate house, but had merely said so because Charlie told her to and because it made her feel important. And too, she wanted to give my phone number to Susan so that we could "Walk together with God."

I was shocked beyond belief at the realization that Iris had an alliance with Susan Atkins. Somehow Susan had conned Iris and the thought really spooked me. I wanted no part of it and I wanted Iris out of my home and out of my life. Something very ominous and terribly destructive had taken place.

Before Iris left she asked me if I had any objection to receiving calls from Susan. I managed to stammer around and reply, "If she wants to." But I had no intention of ever engaging in any dialogue with that butcher.

Iris hadn't been there when Susan, with great relish, revealed to me how she had in cold blood murdered those poor souls in that house up on Cielo Drive.

I was so shocked and unnerved by Iris' visit that I couldn't get it out of my mind for days afterward. And it was about a week later when I wasn't at home and my roommate, Helen, a friend, answered the phone.

A female voice asked for Virginia Graham, adding, "Is she in?"

Helen replied, "No. Who's calling?" And the voice responded, "It's Susan and she knows what it's about."

I had informed Helen about my meeting with Iris and she became absolutely unglued when she realized that she had been talking with one of the nation's most brutal killers. And by the time I came home she was in a panic over the fact that Susan Atkins had our phone number and shortly thereafter moved out.

I quickly had the number changed and not too long after, I went back to Hawaii.

In thinking back over that incident I can only say that if Susan could convince Iris - a well-educated woman - that she was really innocent of the crimes for which she was serving hard time, then she could fool anyone.

It's a new ploy with prison inmates: "I've found God. I've seen the evil of my ways. I've changed. Thank the Lord for showing me the light! Hallelujah!!!" is their new anthem.

They think it will shorten their prison terms. I pray that the Parole Boards can see them for what they really are.

Chapter Twenty-two

In 1978, Ernie Lopez was paroled from Folsom after twenty years behind bars, much of that time on Death Row. All for a crime he steadfastly claimed he had no part in.

I flew from Hawaii to Los Angeles and went to Newport Beach where I rented an elegantly furnished apartment across from Fashion Island in a complex called The Sandpiper, and when Ernie arrived he was driving a sparkling black, shiny, brand new Cadillac Eldorado.

In a very short while I had a completely new picture of Ernie and it was not the image of a tremendously sensitive man - the one I'd seen behind bars for an hour or two from time-to-time.

I saw the first sign of his ugly side when during our second evening together I suggested that we drive into Los Angeles, have dinner at Perino's, and then drop in at the Ambassador Hotel where Sammy Davis Jr. was headlining the show "That's Sammy Davis." I said, "He's such a great talent. He can do everything, dance, sing - everything."

That's when Ernie revealed the man he'd been hiding inside. In no uncertain terms and at great length he told me off for admiring a black man. And he went on to express his deep hatred and prejudices against black people in general.

I was shocked but then I remembered hearing rumors that in Folsom he had been one of the leaders of the infamous Mexican Mafia. I'd heard about the frequent battles between the Black and Mexican inmates, but I discounted the rumors of Ernie's involvement as just plain bullshit. But in the face of his virulent outbreak of hatred - what was I to think?

I tried to rationalize his behavior by telling myself that doing hard time in prison does ugly things to people and that spending time with me on the outside would change that. I knew it wouldn't happen overnight but I was willing to be patient. After all, I was obligated to do my best for him because he was the only one who had lifted a hand to help me when I was in prison. And too, he did display a warm and affectionate manner to me. That hadn't changed.

But with passing days there was an innate coldness and bitterness toward society, the system and life, and I came to realize how terribly out of touch with life he was.

His attitude was that if you weren't his friend, if you didn't agree with him one hundred percent, you were his enemy.

He had been in prison for twenty years fighting the death sentence for a crime he denied he was involved in and I personally believed he was innocent. And as a result, beneath that calm, cool and collected surface, there boiled and seethed an all-encompassing anger toward the world.

There were other signs that disturbed me; meetings with people who at best could be called "shady"; talk about trips to Mexico which was not in keeping with his parole, and small snatches of talk about enterprises that were illegal. He was very secretive and at times his behavior seemed bizarre.

It didn't take me too long to come to the conclusion that Ernie's world was not my world and we were only together for about a month when I told him I was making plans to go back to Hawaii. I managed to convince him how great it would be if he could come over and join me after I got established. When he finally agreed, I called my friend Angela, who had an apartment on Maui and made arrangements to stay with her.

If the truth be known, I really wanted desperately to get away from Ernie.

Ernie was unable to drive me to the airport, claiming that he had a "business meeting!" He had a twenty-four-year-old Mexican boy pick me up and drive me there. This young man idolized Ernie. All the way to our destination all he did was talk about Ernie's life. He adored Ernie, who it turns out was a legend among his peers. By the time I boarded my flight there was no doubt in my mind that I was doing the right thing by leaving.

For the next two years, Ernie called me every day and it was through him I learned that Ronnie Howard had been murdered on October 3rd, 1979. It was then that Ernie expressed his concern that the Manson Family might have been involved and he warned me to be careful.

When I saw Richard Lopez in 1981 - I hadn't seen him since 1965 - he told me that Ronnie had been beaten about the head by two black men. He explained that he and Ronnie had just returned from Las Vegas and had stopped at a bar to have a drink when they got into an argument which resulted in her getting up and walking out on him.

He said that when he went out to look for her he saw her get into a car in the parking lot with two black men and drive away, and that when she returned home twenty-four hours later she had been savagely beaten.

Richard revealed that he and a friend took her to the Presbyterian Hospital where she died the following day from a swelling of the brain. The police investigated and questioned Richard, but no charges were ever filed and her murder remains unsolved.

I have my own theory about how Ronnie came to her untimely death - however it cannot be proven - but I can attest to the fact that Richard had a terrible temper and during our ten year marriage I received many bad beatings at his hands. Draw your own conclusions. And Richard can no longer be brought before the bar of justice. He has since passed away.

I lost touch with Ernie for a couple of years, but then made contact with him in 1981 which proved to be the last time we would see one another. I was about to fly from Tucson to Hawaii when he met me at the airport and tried hard to convince me to forget Hawaii and go back with him. I refused and he was not very happy with my decision and left.

I did notice that at our last meeting, he was wearing quite a bit of jewelry which included a heavy gold chain with an Italian gold horn and diamond and a very expensive Rolex watch. Also, he seemed to be especially nervous and kept looking around, so much so that it made me nervous, too.

I have never seen or heard from Ernie Lopez since that afternoon and that was in 1981.

Chapter Twenty-three

My one true love, my soul mate, and my deepest regret for letting him get away, was with Leo J. Valez, Jr. - Bill. Even though I had not seen Bill since 1953, I never forgot him and always held a very special place in my heart for him and the love we shared.

In the late seventies, after much agonizing, I came to realize that if I ever hoped to aspire toward living a normal life, made secure by the love of a truly caring husband, it could only be possible with Bill.

And having made that decision I vowed that no matter what it took I would find him. Little did I know that many years would be involved before I would end my search.

I wrote and called everywhere. My postage and phone bills were astronomical but that didn't stop me. I made contact with the top brass at Fort Bragg, North Carolina where Bill had been stationed with the 87th Airborne before being shipped out to Korea. I followed their leads, but to no avail.

I got in touch with a group called "The Rakasans," former paratroopers who'd all been members of Bill's unit, in the hope that one of his former buddies might know his whereabouts. That pursuit was also fruitless. I called everywhere in and out of the continental United States but ran into a brick wall. I even called "Pappy" Boyington of the Black Sheep.

But persistence overcomes resistance. I continued my search and my first break came from a lady friend, Betty, who was married to a retired army Colonel who contacted the Pentagon on my behalf and put me in touch with a Colonel Silva who said he would help me.

After many days of researching thousands of records, Colonel Silva came up with three men named "Leo J. Valez" and dropped two who didn't match Bill's background. He sent me a slip of paper with the address of a man named Leo J. Valez, Jr. who lived in Minneapolis.

Was this my Bill? If he was - was he married? And if he was married I certainly didn't want to create any problems for him. I had to give much thought to what I would say to this "Leo J. Valez, Jr." when communicating with him.

At the time my mother was very ill with polymyositis. She had liked Bill, and always asked if I'd heard from him as did my stepfather. With that in mind I decided to send a telegram stating that Mrs. Naomi B. Graham was terminally ill and had requested that I try and locate him.

In that telegram I left both my telephone number at work and my number at home, asking him to call. I sent the wire off and waited. By the time I reached my place of employment there was a message waiting for me on the answering machine.

With shaking hands I turned it on and despite all the many intervening years I instantly recognized the voice that said, "This is Leo J. Valez..." Now when I dialed his number I was shaking so badly that when he answered the phone I couldn't speak for a moment.

And when I finally found my voice I said, "Bill, is that you - is that really you?" And he replied with great emotion, "Oh my God - it's a miracle! Where have you been all these years?"

And then he added, "Last night I was sitting on the edge of my bed and I prayed that God either let me die or let something good come into my life. I was actually crying, since I am constantly in great pain, and until this moment, had nothing to go on living for.

"Then at 8:00 am a telegram came and it was from you, God did answer my prayer, He sent you to me. Why couldn't it have been a little sooner?"

He couldn't believe that I had tracked him down after 30 years. At first he said he didn't want me to see him in the shape he was in and explained that the doctors had told him that his time was short. We didn't know then but he would be gone in six months.

I was determined to see him. Despite all his protests, I refused to accept no for an answer - not after my long years of searching, and the following day - May 10, 1984 - I was on the first flight out to Minneapolis.

As I climbed the stairs to his modest apartment I could barely contain myself. He told me that the door would be unlocked when I arrived. He explained that he suffered from emphysema and was continually on oxygen which meant that the tubes that went into his nose were attached to an oxygen tank and that made answering the door difficult.

When I reached the door to his apartment, I knocked and that voice that I remembered so well called, "Come in!" When I stepped inside there was my first love, my handsome, strong paratrooper who would always be a part of me.

Despite the gaunt look and the sallow complexion, he was still handsome with those big blue eyes and not a single grey hair, and he was smiling.

He was sitting up in a hospital bed that was in the middle of the room, and on seeing me he tried manfully to get out of bed. I walked quickly to him so that he wouldn't have to struggle, and when I reached him we enveloped ourselves in each other's arms with the same passion that existed when we were kids.

The first thing he did was express his concern that I would be turned off by his condition, by the pallor of his skin, the tubes and the tank.

How wrong he was! With all the love that I could summon up in my heart I told him that despite everything, I only loved him more and that I had never stopped loving him and never would.

With that he relaxed and seemed happy and contented.

We talked for hours until I realized how difficult it was for him to breathe and I tried to do all the talking. When it was time to retire I decided to sleep on the couch in the living room, just so that we could be close.

I stayed with him for three days and didn't want to leave him, but I did have a life in Arizona, a job and other responsibilities.

But the most important thing of all was that I had found him, and on finding him we had rekindled a love that had taken root when I was fourteen and he was nineteen. And of equal importance was the fact that he was now happy.

During the time I was there some of his friends came by and told me that they hadn't seen Bill look so well in two years. My presence was obviously doing him some good.

When the time came for me to leave we decided that we were going to be married, no matter how little time there was.

He said he was going to see if he could transfer to the Veterans Administration in Tucson and when I finally took my leave of him I wouldn't say goodbye, instead only, "Til we meet again." And when I walked out his front door I didn't look back.

When I got back to Arizona Bill would call me every day and I called him sometimes twice a day. We were trying to make arrangements to be married.

I had a very nice home and a good position in Arizona and truly believed that the dry climate might help him, but unfortunately his health worsened and between July and November he ended up in the hospital on three occasions.

I had planned on returning to Minneapolis on November 10th, but on the evening of November 8th I called him and he was only able to speak in a whisper.

"Babe," he said, "always remember that I loved you when you were a little girl and I love you now. Never forget that."

He was having such a difficult time breathing that he was barely able to speak. Those were his last words to me.

I later learned that after he finished his conversation with me, he called his landlady who lived next door. She rushed over, called 911, and they responded and rushed him to the hospital where Bill went into a coma and passed away the following morning.

When I got word that Bill was gone, the first thought that came to my mind was "No more pain." I was grateful for that and I was grateful, too, that his last months were happy ones and that we had shared them in planning happier times, dreaming happier dreams.

He had completed his God given time on earth and our circle which had begun thirty-eight years before was now also complete. Boy meets girl, boy loses girl, boy meets girl. It was that simple. How lucky we were.

While his passing left me with a sense of loss there was also within me a sense of fulfillment.

Two weeks later the mail brought a short note from Bill's landlady. It was in a large white envelope which also contained a smaller envelope. It was addressed to me and was in Bill's handwriting.

The landlady was writing to say how sorry she was about Bill's passing. "He was a good tenant," she wrote, "and was no trouble at all." Then she explained, "When I went into his bedroom after he died - I was getting his things together - I found in a drawer in his night table, this letter he wrote to you which somehow never got mailed. I thought you ought to have it."

It was dated October 25th, 1984. His level of energy was so low that his writing was hard to read. Here's what he wrote:

Dear Love,

I can't even begin to tell you how wonderful I feel about us. Yet, I'm really somewhat afraid. I thank God in prayer for all that has happened which has brought us together again.

At the same time I question His timing. My health, my financial status, leaves much to be desired as far as resuming a cared about relationship. The one time I actually want to be the "altogether Macho Man" I find it quite impossible. Damn!

[The following paragraph was dated a day later:]

Hi! Bet you didn't realize that I stopped writing this last night.

Just finished hearing your voice again. Lucky me! Virginia, please don't ever think you're being too inquisitive, nosy or whatever with me. I appreciate your caring concern. God knows you've put the desire to live again in my mind and heart. I had given up only because I really didn't care. Believe it.

Together maybe we can help each other. I need you. I want you. I do not want to burden you or take advantage of the wonderful love you offer. That's the main worry.

At any rate the 10th will soon be here, I'm happy just thinking about seeing you again. Wonder of wonders! It seems a dream. You will never fully realize the joy you have given my life.

Hon, I can't concentrate on a letter. Forgive me. I'll see you soon. Think of you constantly. Take care my love.

Love you, Bill

As I read each line, I could hear his voice. I could hear Bill speaking these very same words to me and I felt his loss so deeply that I began to cry without restraint. The tears poured from my eyes in a torrent, and I can't remember ever crying so hard before.

It took hours for me to pull myself together. When I did I felt the need to speak to Bill one last time, and so I looked to the heavens and I answered his letter. It was short and simple.

I said, "Rest easy, my beautiful darling. We will meet again."

Chapter Twenty-four

In 1986 I was the director of an art gallery called Collectors Fine Art on the island of Kona. My mother had passed away two months earlier and I thought about her very often, and couldn't get over my continual feeling of sadness.

Down the street from the gallery was an excellent little restaurant where I would have many of my meals. On this particular morning I was having breakfast when I couldn't help but notice a tall, well-built, elegantly dressed man who used his knife and fork the way a surgeon would use his scalpel.

I suddenly realized that this wasn't the first time I'd seen him there having his breakfast. When he saw me looking in his direction, he smiled and nodded his head and we started talking.

The next morning he joined me at my table. He introduced himself as Alexander Tuszewski. He said he was in real estate and had only arrived in Kona a few days earlier to visit his daughter. He had been married to Holly Wade, a very wealthy woman from Kauai and Palm Springs. He had come to Maui in 1961 as the Food and Beverages Director at the Hilton Hotel.

He was 6'1", weighed 220 pounds and had blue eyes and dark brown hair. His charming manners and his accent were a combination that made strong women feel faint. Ask me - I know.

He was quite a package. He was born in Poland, the grandson of a German baron, spoke thirteen languages, lived all over the world, was very well educated, had a brilliant mind, and was the greatest charmer to ever come down the pike.

He was everything that a woman could wish for and I felt that heaven had finally sent me a soul mate. He said he was invested in real estate and other enterprises as well, and was also in the restaurant business. He had once owned the famous Dolphin restaurant in Hanalei.

He had been Dave Chasen's right hand man in the world renowned Chasen's in Beverly Hills, had been affiliated with the Brown Derby in

Hollywood, and from 1959 to 1960 had been one of the managers of New York City's prestigious Four Seasons.

It was an impressive record, recited by a very impressive, elegant gentleman. Looking back at my three previous husbands, I could only come to the conclusion that none of them could hold a candle to this guy. He was world class stuff.

He had it all, and I was sure I was dreaming when we were married on June 28th, 1987. It didn't take too long to discover that my dream man was a bogeyman and my dream was a nightmare.

I think that most men are attracted to me because I'm attractive, competent, confident and a money maker. I've been told that I have that aura of wealth. It's my belief that Alex thought that I had a lot of money, and as a result turned out to be a number one mooch.

His charm wore off when I found myself paying out $5,000 every month for our house, his car, our meals and other living expenses. He turned out to be just plain lazy with all sorts of excuses as to why he couldn't work. I realized that he lived in a world of what used to be and it in no way resembled the reality of here and now.

He managed to get a few jobs with some very prestigious firms but they would only last a few months, and then he'd be back at his old stand hitting me up constantly for pocket money.

At this stage of the game I was beginning to realize that when it came to picking husbands that I had a taste for shit.

* * *

But when it came to lovers - that was a different story. In December 1987 I received the following letter from Lou:

My Dearest Friend Kathie,

I was so happy when I returned from vacation to see that your letter had arrived. Knowing that you still feel the same about me makes me especially happy because I still feel that way about you, and I hope it never ends. Someday I will return!! That will prove it.

You know, I want you to remember that I will always be here if you need me, even though we don't communicate as often as we should. Our letters and phone calls are too far apart and that's not good. If anything ever happens to you, I'll never know.

Let's make a deal and promise to make contact with each other at least once a month. Even a postcard, saying everything's okay.

I love you and you are my dearest friend and probably know more about me than anyone else, so you know I mean what I say. It's not over and never will be over. There's more to come!! Just as you feel it, so do I, and that doesn't sound crazy. There has to be a 'Grand Finale.'

Well my love, I must close this letter. The natives are getting restless. Take care and keep in touch. I'll write again soon.

Love ya, Lou

P.S. I don't have any recent pictures of myself, but when I return from St. Maarten, I'll send you one. By the way, send me a picture of yourself. Lou.

Every woman should be as lucky and have a Lou Corgliano in her life. In a world of ever changing values and principles, it's heartwarming and very reassuring to know that love can prevail in spite of passing time and the lack of physical contact.

And like I always say, "It ain't over til the fat lady sings." And I'll be damned if I don't think I can hear her humming.

It was hard to believe that I'd first set eyes on Lou in June 1973, and here he was in December 1987 - more than thirteen years later - still talking to me of love. How lucky can you get?

* * *

The big blowout that marked the end of marriage number four took place on the evening of August 14, 1989. We'd been married for two years when this so-called recovering alcoholic came home with a fifth of Scotch and informed me that he was going to have a few drinks. And drink he did. It took him four hours to finish that fifth, and by then he was falling down drunk.

Finally, he came to me and standing up as straight as he could he said, "Do you know who I am? I, madam, am a direct descendant of the noble Teutonic Knights. Royal blood runs through my veins. I am a magnificent and superior human being," and then he fell flat on his royal face.

And then I had my say. I, too, stood up, and looking down at him while he was sprawled on the floor I told that so-called magnificent and superior human being, "Do you know what you really are? You're a first class idiot and a worthless piece of humanity who has never grown up! I'm tired of putting up with your phony crap! And I won't - so I'm outta here! Bye-bye, baby!"

Then I called my friend, Donna, to come and pick me up. While I waited for her I packed a couple of bags and went out onto the driveway to wait some more.

Just then, His Royal Nothingness, joined me out on the driveway without a stitch of clothing on. He was buck naked and he cursed me out. I had to fight off the urge to slam him right in the kisser. Fortunately, Donna arrived a moment later and she drove me to her home.

The next day he began calling non-stop, and to discourage him we put the answering machine on.

At that time Alex was working for Dave Del Dotto, a top real estate mogul who gave seminars on how to make millions in real estate. He was on Dave's team and was due to fly to Chicago with Del Dotto at 7:00 am. He made the flight, but only with the help of the company president, Karl Noons. And once I knew that Alex was en route elsewhere I went back to the house.

It had been a bad scene and I came to realize that life was too short to have to put up with such crap. I promised myself that never in my lifetime would I allow a man, or anyone, to abuse me or use me and I've never deviated from that principle.

It made me sad to realize, too, that this once elegant, class act had turned into a dreary, slobbering drunk. I later learned that he was a recovering alcoholic who'd had a very serious problem, and that all of his life he had allowed his love for booze to destroy everything that he tried to build.

When he called me from Chicago he was drunk. I told him, "You either go back to A.A. for help or I'm history," to which he replied, "If I want to drink - I'm going to drink and screw you!" He then slammed the receiver down.

Alex was coming home on August 29th, so I left Hawaii on the 28th. I also left my home and my job. Before doing so, however, I sold half of the furniture and left the rest for him. I then caught a flight to Tucson where we owned a house we'd bought during the first year of our marriage.

We had an arrangement where I would make the $1,500 monthly payment on our house in Hawaii and he would take care of the $720 monthly payment on our Tucson place. When I got off the plane in Tucson I thought I had a home, but when I got out of the cab at the house I discovered that it had gone into foreclosure. Alex had lied. He hadn't made any payments and now I was homeless.

I was utterly exhausted from the long flight and I was really pissed at that Polish asshole I'd married. In one fell swoop I'd lost a home in Hawaii, another home in Tucson, and saw my fourth marriage go down the toilet. This sure as hell wasn't my lucky day. I was so tired that I allowed myself the rare privilege of feeling sorry for myself.

I checked into a lousy motel, had a crummy dinner in a crummy diner where for dessert I had a good case of the blues. I had a very dreary time, and about a month later I went to San Francisco to stay with two dear friends.

Three weeks later, on October 17th, 1989, I drove onto the San Francisco Bay Bridge and came off of it at exactly 5:00 pm. Four minutes later, at 5:04 pm, the city was hit by a massive earthquake that brought the bridge down with great loss of life.

The difference between life and death for me had been a matter of only four minutes - four minutes! The thought of how close I'd been to becoming one of the statistics shocked the living hell out of me and made me think long and hard as to why I had been spared, and I think that maybe I got the message.

As long as I could remember it had been my top priority to possess things. And "things" meant money to buy homes, cars, furs, fine furniture, expensive clothes, perfumes and other "things." In recent weeks I'd been brooding over losing two more houses and other "things," and when I thought about how close I'd come to dying on the bridge I asked myself, "Virginia, are those the last homes you expect to have? And what good would it do having a house and all those other "things" if you weren't alive to enjoy them?"

I remembered many other upheavals and cataclysms that had taken place in my life, and there could still be others to come, so I said to myself, "Virginia, you are a survivor. You've got the most important thing of all - life! You are alive and while you're alive, you've still got a future in which anything and everything is possible."

And I remembered a funny story about a multi-millionaire who had died, and who according to the will was being buried in a gold Cadillac. And as the deceased, sitting up behind the wheel of this incredible vehicle was being lowered into this massive grave, one gravedigger was heard to say to another gravedigger, "Look at that, solid gold wheels, solid gold steering wheel," and the other digger replied, "Yeah man, that's what I call living."

Chapter Twenty-five

As of 1993 I was back in my beloved Hawaii doing the work I loved best - managing a fine art gallery. I'd spent a few months managing a gallery in Las Vegas, and while I find Vegas an exciting and fun town, there's nothing like Aloha Land.

I discovered a long time ago that in my line of work I get the best of all worlds. I am surrounded by beautiful paintings, and quite often I meet the artists themselves. I am always involved with people who love fine art as much as I do and it pays well. What more could a girl ask for?

I was still legally married to Alex, whom I hadn't seen for some time and had no plans of seeing. And someday when I would find the time, I'd go to an attorney and file for a divorce. What was the hurry? That day finally came, and Alex and I were divorced in 1994. He died a year later in 1995.

In recent years I find myself more and more at peace with the world. In looking back, I can find any number of things that I would have done differently - different paths I would have taken. But isn't that true of us all?

But as they say in show business - it's been one helluva run. I can't believe that so many years have passed since I was a little girl growing up in Philadelphia. I can say though that the years between have been exciting, sad, joyous, intriguing, fun and often lonely. One thing is certain - it sure hasn't been dull. You can bet the family jewels on that.

I often think of my mother whom I dearly loved, yet never wanted to be like. She had the misfortune of living at a time when most wives lived lives of quiet desperation, existing in their husband's shadow, letting things happen to them instead of making things happen.

I can remember only one time when she stood up and asserted herself. During World War II, as the wife of a serviceman she applied for an allotment only to learn that my philandering father had another wife who was already getting it.

It was probably her proudest moment when she went to the War Department, filed a complaint, fought it out and finally got what was rightfully hers. But after divorcing my father, she married a man who bent her to his will and she lived in his shadow thereafter.

And I was her only child, a rebellious daughter who she did not understand and whose lifestyle she did not approve of, who rejected authority and who was ambitious and determined enough to make her dreams a reality - no matter the cost.

But despite our many differences, I know that she loved me as I loved her. It all came together when she was seventy-eight years of age and sitting in a wheelchair. She looked deep into my eyes and said, "I want you to know I was wrong all these years. You have courage - the courage I never had. Forgive me. You were right."

To hear those words from my dying mother - they were words that I had waited all my life to hear. She had finally understood the ways and wherefores of my life and she was telling me that if she had suffered any pain, the fault was of her own doing, not mine. With those words she had set me free.

I only wish that she could have had an easier, happier life because I truly believe that in her entire life she never deliberately set out to hurt anyone. She deserved better. She was my beloved, beautiful angel.

I forgave my father many years ago. All children need a father to guide them and counsel them in their early years. From the age of eight I saw less and less of him and then rarely at all. But during the years he was there for me, he instilled within me his credo which was to always reach for the stars, to have lofty goals, to love life and live it to the fullest. And for that I truly thank him.

He worked hard and strived to be successful but somehow he always fell a step short of achieving it. He was a very handsome man and I've always believed that he expended too much of his energy in pursuing the ladies, energy that could have been better by far put toward achieving his goals.

About my husbands: my first husband never really knew how much I loved him. The fact that we married too young and his marrying out of his religion were obstacles too great for us to overcome. His family ruled him and he lacked the courage to fight them. He was a good father to our sons and lived vicariously through them. He was also an adoring grandfather. My only wish was that he instilled in his grand-children the need to set goals for themselves and to have the courage to achieve them, and not be thwarted by the neurotic and antiquated ideas from the old country and the mean-minded people who endorse them. My first husband died in 2008.

Richard Lopez, my second husband, was a strikingly handsome man, who had a quick wit and lots of style and lived life to the fullest. He never reached his full potential and fell in with the wrong people. He reinforced those beliefs instilled in me by my father, that I was a very special lady who could do whatever she set her mind on. He convinced me that I just had to fight hard enough. He had a terrible temper and was a wife beater. I was not a very easy person to get along with, and when you add that to the many frustrations he suffered in his career - it makes for a very quick tempered individual. We had some very productive years together. For all the good things I thank him. He's gone now. May God rest his restless soul.

My third husband, Arnie Castro, was an accident, pure and simple. I was lonely and he was there. I did my very best to help him and in his limited capacity I know he tried hard to be the husband he couldn't be. I feel no anger toward him. It was an unfortunate set of circumstances - it just didn't work out. Arnie died in 1998.

I had a great deal of faith in Alex Tuszewski, my last husband. In Alex, I felt that I had finally the hero, the warrior I had been looking for, but he was my greatest disappointment. He was all lies from start to finish. He was a weak man who lived a life of fantasy and who was not ashamed to let a woman support him and his illusions of grandeur. Sad to say, behind the cultured, slick facade was just a plain old drunk. Too bad - but that's life. You win some - you lose... all the time?

I frankly admit that I'm a four-time loser where marriage is concerned. In the marital arena, I know now that I'm neither as knowledgeable nor as wise as I believed myself to be. I have doubts now where I never had doubts before about the male animal.

Some very wise lady, I don't remember who, once said about men, "Love 'em but don't marry 'em." How right she was.

I've made the decision that I can do without men, that I don't need them in my life to be happy. I've had many lovers and many male friends, and I truly believe that there are some women who should not be married - and that I'm one of them. I'm far too independent for most men and they just can't handle that.

As for my sons, I love them both. I adore both Joe Jr. and Dennis because they are thoughtful, kind, respectful and generous men.

I shouldn't complain. After all, I did all the things I dreamed about and then some. I've been from "rags to riches" and "riches to rags." I've hobnobbed with world famous celebrities, lived in palatial mansions, dined in four-star restaurants and partied on magnificent yachts.

I've also been in prison where I rubbed shoulders with the dregs of society, slept in tiny cells with bunk beds, eaten second rate food in sparse prison dining halls and have worn handcuffs. And I was the confidant of a heartless bloodthirsty murderer who found pleasure in killing.

I've made many mistakes and I've paid for them, but I never let the downside of my life make me hard or cruel. You learn from your mistakes and that's how I learned.

I love people and I love animals, and I have great optimism about the future. I believe that what the mind of man can perceive, his hands can achieve. We've just got to have faith and believe in the goodness of mankind.

I'm glad that I was born at the time when I was. It gave me the chance to see women evolve into something more than just sexual objects, baby factories and housekeepers. Today there are women holding cabinet posts and sitting on the Supreme Court. But the "good ole boy" clubs are still fighting us. But girls, let me tell you, they're running scared.

Do I have any regrets? The word "regret" means to me admitting failure, and in reply I have to say that considering my beginnings that I did very well. I pretty much had it all and pretty much did everything. I had the mansions, the minks, the jewelry and the millionaires.

To young women, and young men, who are so far down that they have no place else to go but up I can only say, live free, reach for the stars, aim high, fight for your beliefs and never, never let anyone intimidate or abuse you.

We only come this way but once. Time is the very essence of life, so make every hour count for something. Strive for something better, read, go to galleries, study, get an education, listen only to truly wise people and then make your own decisions. I make mine, and as long as there is a breath left in my body I will continue to do so.

Yes, as of 1993 I was back home in my Hawaii where I was living at peace with myself and in harmony with its breathtaking, magnificent land; one that is so beautiful, so overwhelmingly beautiful, that you can get teary-eyed just looking.

And I still have my dreams, and believe me, I'll make them come true. I just won't go blindly charging after them as I once would have done. No, for the next leg of the journey, this gal is going to take it slow and easy, and take more time to think. And too, what's the rush? I am in paradise.

By the way, Lou, I'm still coming for you.

And aloha to all!

Afterword

In 1999 I left Hawaii and went to Scottsdale, Arizona to run an art gallery. Unfortunately, I had injured my back and couldn't stand so back surgery was a must. Since my return to the mainland my youngest son Dennis has opened up several beauty salons in New Jersey and is now contemplating moving to Boca Raton, Florida. I'm so proud that Dennis has become so successful in the beauty business in New Jersey and has been in negotiations with a new salon in Boca Raton. The apple doesn't fall far from the tree. We not only share our love for beauty, but I have always felt it so ironic that his favorite singer is Frank Sinatra, who he listens to every Sunday.

* * *

In 2001 a re-make of the original 1976 *Helter Skelter* movie based on Vincent Bugliosi's book of the same name, which was subsequently released in 2004, was being worked on. In connection with that I received the following letter from Vincent Bugliosi, which is transcribed as well:

6-11-01

Dear Virginia,

It was wonderful hearing from you, and seeing that you still have your very special, indomitable spirit.

I am right in the middle of my book promotion for The Betrayal Of America and am extremely busy, so I'll have to be very brief. Indeed, I'm so busy that I only found time today to pick up my mail (about 1½ hour round trip) and just got your letter today.

The script for Helter Skelter is presently being written. I'm pretty sure your character will be in it, but directors always have the last word. As I indicated in my phone message, if you end up being in the script and the director wants your technical assistance I'll be sure to get in touch with you.

I haven't seen Bob in about 5 years. I was so sorry to hear you lost your husband and about the damage to your gallery. But nothing can keep you down.

I was very impressed to learn about your genealogical background, Virginia.

Virginia, I want to tell you once again how much I appreciate your courage and all the help you selflessly gave me in bringing the Manson gang to justice.

Please take good care of yourself.

Your friend,
Vince Bugliosi

Letter from Vincent Bugliosi, dated June 11, 2001

(Transcribed letter)
June-11-2001
Dear Virginia,

It was wonderful hearing from you, and seeing that you still have your very special, indomitable spirit.

I am right in the middle of my book promotion for The Betrayal of America and am extremely busy, so I'll have to be very brief. Indeed, I'm so busy that I only found time today to pick up my mail (about 1 ½ hours round trip) and just got your letter today.

The script for Helter Skelter is presently being written. I'm pretty sure your character will be in it, but directors always have the last word. As I indicated in my phone message, if you end up being in the script and the director wants your technical assistance I'll be sure to get in touch with you.

I haven't seen Bob in about 5 years. I was so sorry to hear you lost your husband and about the damage to your Gallery. But nothing can keep you down.

I was very impressed to learn about your genealogical background, Virginia.

Virginia, I want to tell you once again how much I appreciate your courage and all the help you selflessly gave me in bringing the Manson gang to justice.

Please take good care of yourself.
Your friend,
Vince Bugliosi

* * *

In 2008 it was announced that Susan Atkins had brain cancer, had one of her legs amputated, was paralyzed on one side of her body, had less than six months to live, and she requested a "compassionate re-lease" from prison. There was much controversy about this, and I wrote a letter to the Parole Board registering my opposition to her release. It is my personal belief that none of the convicted murderers should ever get out of prison. Many others also voiced their opinions, some for, and some against. Finally on September 2nd, 2009, for the eighteenth and final time, Susan Atkins was denied parole, and passed away later that month.

* * *

I was contacted by a detective in 2009 who had spoken to a reporter who wanted to do an interview about the Manson case. As an aside, the detective also told me that Charles Manson was still receiving hundreds, sometimes thousands, of letters each month from individuals both young and old. People to this day have a continued fascination with the case.

A reporter from the *Los Angeles Times* contacted me for an interview and to inform me that someone named Maureen Cotter had contacted her to try and get in touch with me. I didn't recognize her name but was curious enough to call her on the phone.

Maureen told me that she was the California Institute for Women's female guard who had been assigned while I was incarcerated, and was instructed to check on me every half hour because of death threats from the Manson Family. She asked if she could come and visit me for an interview. I recalled that we had been friendly while she was a guard protecting me.

Maureen, who did freelance reporting, came to visit with cameras to do an interview for television. She and I became dear friends as she was very close to the Hollywood celebrity group. She had become a very successful business woman in Beverly Hills and was friendly with Elizabeth Taylor's nurse, Shannon Gordon.

Maureen contacted Elizabeth Taylor through Shannon to tell her that she had connected with me, and wanted to do a show honoring me at a theatre in Venice, California since I had saved the lives of many celebrities. Maureen flew me to Venice in August of 2009 to do the show, and while there I stayed in a wonderful historic hotel.

She made all of the arrangements for Elizabeth Taylor to come to the theatre, but Elizabeth Taylor got sick and instead sent Shannon with a letter thanking me. As I walked into the theatre I saw hundreds of people were there to see the show. I took my seat and listened to Maureen address the audience, advising that Elizabeth Taylor had taken ill but had sent her nurse with a letter that she wanted to read to me. Maureen read the letter aloud, and at the end the audience was on their feet clapping, turning toward me as I was standing. I was truly honored and totally taken aback. A copy of Elizabeth Taylor's letter follows:

ELIZABETH TAYLOR

August 6, 2009

Dear Virginia,

Thank you for having the courage to speak out when others chose to remain silent. Many lives were spared and justice was served because of your strength and integrity.

Although your name may not be the most recognized in this tragic event, your heart is celebrated by those who know the power of your selfless act. You placed yourself in harm's way. That is the true definition of the word hero.

Please enjoy your honor tonight and know that we who know the truth, salute you. God bless you....

With my deepest respect,

Letter from Elizabeth Taylor, dated August 6, 2009

(Transcribed letter)
ELIZABETH TAYLOR
August 6, 2009
Dear Virginia,

Thank you for having the courage to speak out when others chose to remain silent. Many lives were spared and justice was served because of your strength and integrity.

Although your name may not be the most recognized in this tragic event, your heart is celebrated by those who know the power of your selfless act. You placed yourself in harm's way. That is the true definition of the word hero.

Please enjoy your honor tonight and know that we who know the truth, salute you. God bless you....

    With my deepest respect,
    Elizabeth Taylor

Elizabeth Taylor and Nurse Shannon Gordon

Maureen has become my dear friend and is writing a screenplay regarding her life in which she references me as the "frosting on the cake."

* * *

Unfortunately, since 2009 I have lost eighty percent of my eyesight due to macular degeneration, but my spirit is still intact. My life has been spectacular and I have no regrets, and I want to tell all the women out there to always go for it, live your dreams, never waver, and get a cat.

* * *

In late 2014 I heard with disbelief that Charles Manson, at age 80, was granted a marriage license to marry his 26-year-old girlfriend, Afton Elaine Burton, who advocates for his innocence. The implications are frightening, and makes me wonder if a new generation of the Manson Family is being born. I hope and pray that it is not the case.

About the Author

Virginia Graham was in the Sybil Brand Institute for Women in California when Susan Atkins was jailed for the murder of Gary Hinman. Susan befriended Virginia and eventually confessed about the Tate/LaBianca murders. In *Manson, Sinatra and Me*, Graham details her own life as a Hollywood party girl during both the good times and the bad, her encounters with Atkins, as well as the Tate/Labianca murder trial as a key witness for the prosecution that was tried and won by District Attorney Vincent Bugliosi.

Made in the USA
Columbia, SC
10 October 2023

24245580R00155